366 SATISFYING, RICH AND CREAMY RECIPES
—ALL COMPLETELY DAIRY-FREE

The word is out: It's time for Americans to cut w
and dairy, and time to drastically increase our int:
grains, and health-packed soy products. Robin Ro
vegetarian cuisine makes it easy. Even the comfort foods we
crave—like macaroni and cheese, fettucine Alfredo, thick
milkshakes—now have a place at a health-conscious table, with
great new :, soft tofu,
and soy ch

- Tips on   ernatives for
  sour cre   ore
- A tempt   e year (plus
  one), to   al ovo-lacto
  to vegar
- Complete descriptions of the new dairy alternatives from nut
  butters to rice milk to soy cheese, with information on buying,
  storing, preparing and making them at home
- Detailed nutritional breakdowns of each recipe

This fabulous guide makes it easy to explore the exciting new
world of healthy cooking.

ROBIN ROBERTSON is the author of *366 Healthful Ways to Cook Tofu
and Other Meat Alternatives* (Plume). A classically trained French
chef, she now teaches creative vegetarian cooking at the individual
and workshop level. She cooks, teaches, and lives in Virginia
Beach, Virginia.

Other Books in Plume's 366 WAYS SERIES include:

366 Healthful Ways to Cook Tofu and Other Meat Alternatives
by Robin Robertson

366

Simply Delicious Dairy-Free Recipes

ROBIN ROBERTSON

A PLUME BOOK

PLUME
Published by the Penguin Group
Penguin Books USA Inc., 375 Hudson Street,
New York, New York 10014, U.S.A.
Penguin Books Ltd, 27 Wrights Lane,
London W8 5TZ, England
Penguin Books Australia Ltd, Ringwood,
Victoria, Australia
Penguin Books Canada Ltd, 10 Alcorn Avenue,
Toronto, Ontario, Canada M4V 3B2
Penguin Books (N.Z.) Ltd, 182-190 Wairau Road,
Auckland 10, New Zealand

Penguin Books Ltd, Registered Offices:
Harmondsworth, Middlesex, England

First published by Plume, an imprint of Dutton Signet, a division of Penguin Books USA Inc.

First Printing, March, 1997
10 9 8 7 6 5 4 3 2 1

Ⓟ REGISTERED TRADEMARK—MARCA REGISTRADA

LIBRARY OF CONGRESS CATALOGING-IN-PUBLICATION DATA

Robertson, Robin (Robin G.)
    366 simply delicious dairy-free recipes / Robin Robertson.
       p.   cm.
    Includes index.
    ISBN 0-452-27623-3
    1. Milk-free diet—Recipes.   I. Title.
    RM234.5.R63   1997
    641.5'63—dc20   96-27542
                                                                   CIP

Printed in the United States of America
Set in Garamond Light
Designed by Leonard Telesca

BOOKS ARE AVAILABLE AT QUANTITY DISCOUNTS WHEN USED TO PROMOTE PRODUCTS OR SERVICES. FOR
INFORMATION PLEASE WRITE TO PREMIUM MARKETING DIVISION, PENGUIN BOOKS USA INC., 375 HUDSON
STREET, NEW YORK, NEW YORK 10014.

This book is dedicated to my best friend—my husband, Jon—with gratitude for his helpful and enthusiastic support, encouragement, and love.

Contents

Introduction

Just about everyone loves dairy products and the creamy, satisfying dishes that can be made with them. Whether it is a psychological preference stemming from childhood (remember how much you loved milk shakes?) or just the desire to indulge in the creamy textures of these delights, dishes made with dairy products often top the list of our favorite comfort foods. They make us feel better.

So Why Seek Alternatives?

We are taught from an early age that dairy is good for us. "Drink your milk," our parents told us. We are persuaded by the dairy industry that if we don't drink milk and eat milk products, we won't get enough calcium. In fact, many vegetarians rely on dairy products as their main source of protein. At the same time, medical studies have begun to caution that dairy products are not actually good for us.

These studies show that dairy products directly contribute to heart disease, many forms of cancer, obesity, respiratory ailments, and other problems. Once thought to aid in the prevention of osteoporosis, it is now reported in medical studies that excessive consumption of milk can *contribute* to osteoporosis. In fact, the protein in milk actually inhibits the body's ability to absorb calcium from dairy products. Man is the only animal that drinks the milk of another species, and the only animal that drinks milk after childhood. When you realize that calcium is found in abundance in tofu, nuts, and many vegetables, flavor and texture begin to look like the only reasons why we continue to use dairy products.

People choose to give up dairy for a variety of medical or ethical reasons. Many people are lactose intolerant, others need to reduce saturated fat and cholesterol, and others are vegetarians trying to give up that last vestige of animal products in their diets. The real problem in eliminating dairy lies in the fact that many of our favorite dishes are prepared with dairy products, and they just taste too good to give up. Many vegetarians, myself among them, were able to give up meat with barely a whimper. But take away our ice cream and macaroni and cheese, and we have a struggle on our hands.

So how can we get healthy and eat right without feeling deprived of our favorite comfort foods? The answer may be found in the plant kingdom. Mother Nature would never be so cruel as to deny us milk— instead, she's provided a host of dairy alternatives. The truth is that there are a surprising number of satisfying dairy alternatives to fill just about any craving.

In this book we'll explore velvety soups and sauces as well as creamy pasta dishes. We'll make tasty side dishes, satisfying main courses, and even delicious "milk" shakes. There's also an entire chapter devoted to delightfully rich desserts, all prepared with these remarkable dairy alternatives.

About Dairy Alternatives

Soy Milk: Nondairy milks made from soybeans are available under various brand names in natural food stores. These "milks" are available in aseptic one-quart containers and may be kept unrefrigerated until opened. They come in plain or "original" flavor, which is best when substituting for milk or cream, and also in vanilla, carob, or chocolate flavors, which are great when making desserts or shakes. There are several brands of soy milk that offer "light" versions with a very low fat content. I enjoy experimenting with the wide variety of flavors and consistencies—there's an alternative to suit every need. Soy milk is also available in a more economical powdered form, which can then be reconstituted with water.

Rice milk: Also available in aseptic containers. I especially like the light flavor of rice milk in certain recipes, and generally keep some on hand to use interchangeably with soy milk.

Nut milks: A delicious milk alternative can also be made from nuts. The best nut for the job is the almond, owing to its delicate flavor, versatility, and nutritional value. Almond milk is available in aseptic containers and can be found on the shelf next to the soy milks in your natural food store. In addition, almond milk can be easily made from scratch at home using your blender. This can be economical if you buy the almonds in bulk. Here's a simple, quick recipe:

Almond Milk

MAKES 1 QUART

1 cup shelled raw almonds   **4 cups water**

Grind almonds in a blender to a fine powder. Add half the water and blend to achieve a smooth puree, about 1 minute. Add remaining water and continue blending 1 to 2 minutes until very smooth and creamy. Place a fine mesh strainer over a bowl, and pour almond milk into strainer, stirring to pass liquid through. For a smoother consistency, pass strained milk through another, finer mesh strainer. Refrigerate almond milk in a covered jar or airtight container.

Cashews are another nut that can easily be made into a milk, but they are so rich that the result actually tends to be more like a cream. You can make it in the same way as almond milk.

Tofu: Tofu is a soft, cheeselike curd made from soybeans. It is an extremely versatile dairy alternative, and is available fresh in tubs, generally referred to as "regular" tofu, or in aseptic packages, which is called "silken" tofu. Both regular and silken tofu are available in soft, medium, and firm textures. Silken tofu varieties can be used to make creamy sauces and desserts. It can also be transformed into a convincing mayonnaise, sour cream, or whipped cream. Soft and medium regular tofu can be used in casseroles and dips, or to replace ricotta cheese and cottage cheese in recipes. Extra-firm regular tofu is the best choice for stir-fries, grilling, or sautéing.

As a general rule, it's important to remove as much liquid as possible from tofu before using it in a recipe. When using firm tofu in a sauté or stir-fry, simply blotting the surface of the tofu will suffice. However, when making sauces and desserts, and especially when using the softer varieties of tofu, it's important to press, squeeze, and/or blot excess liquid from your tofu before using it. I find the best way to remove excess liquid from tofu is to cut the tofu into slabs and place them inside a dish towel or other clean cloth, and then press until as much liquid as possible has been removed.

Other Dairy Alternatives

There are many commercial products available in most natural food stores, ranging from soy yogurt to tofu mayonnaise to soy cheeses—from mozzarella to jalapeño Cheddar. While some of the soy cheeses do contain casein, which is a by-product of dairy, there are some brands available that contain absolutely no dairy. In addition, there are cheese alternatives made from almonds and also from hemp.

Of course, the most common butter alternative is margarine. When choosing a margarine, look for a good quality vegetable margarine that does not contain preservatives. Read the labels: the chemicals listed in many margarines and commercial "nonbutter" spreads are daunting.

Tasty butter alternatives to spread on your morning toast are nut butters and fruit butters, also available in natural food stores. A delicious almond butter or apple butter will provide the same creaminess as regular butter, but with more healthful results. Nut butters have about the same calories as butter, but since their flavor is more concentrated, you may be inclined to use less.

Just because a product is labeled "nondairy" or "fat-free" doesn't necessarily mean it's desirable, particularly nondairy dessert toppings and nondairy creamers. These products are not only loaded with saturated fat, but they also contain many additives. They may be "nondairy," and even "fat-free," but they may also be "nonhealthy," and their lack of nutritional merit makes them what I call "nonfoods."

The dairy alternatives offered in this book offer nutritious options in recipes where we once thought only dairy would do. While there may be nothing low calorie about many of the recipes in this book, they are all cholesterol-free and nutritious, and generally contain significantly fewer calories and saturated fat than their dairy counterparts. Add to that the fact that soybeans do not contain hormones, antibiotics, and other chemicals as most dairy products do, and it should become clear that dairy alternatives, delicious and nutritious in their own right, are infinitely better for your health.

Other Ingredients Used in This Book

Most people interested in giving up dairy products are concerned about their health. As such, they may also want to avoid meat, eggs, and even refined sugar. None of the recipes in this book contain meat, relying instead on meat alternatives such as tofu, tempeh, or seitan. Found in most natural food stores, tempeh is made from soybeans that have been fermented and compressed into meaty slabs. Seitan, or "wheat meat," can be found in a variety of forms. It is available ready-to-eat in the refrigerator cases of natural food stores, and can also be found in the form of a dry mix to which you just add water. Like tofu and tempeh, seitan can also be made from scratch.

In the case of recipes that call for eggs, the ingredient list may read "egg (or equivalent egg replacer)." This refers to commercial egg-replacer products available in natural food stores that work quite well in baking. Often, when an egg in a recipe is used simply for moisture or density, a little soft tofu, nut butter, applesauce, or even water has been used. Generally speaking, two ounces ($1/4$ cup) of soft tofu is the equivalent of one egg. If you do use eggs but still want to lower your cholesterol, you can substitute two egg whites for one whole egg in a recipe.

Where sugar is concerned, recipes may call for "sugar (or a natural sweetener)," allowing for individual preference. In place of refined, granulated sugar, you can add honey, maple syrup, brown rice syrup, or barley malt. Naturally, in the interest of good health, you want to avoid using artificial chemical sweeteners as sugar substitutes.

Several of the desserts in this book call for use of a "nondairy frozen dessert." This refers to several high quality ice cream-like desserts now available in natural food stores, which are made with tofu or rice. While some are sweetened with sugar, others are sweetened with honey, brown rice syrup, and fruit sweeteners. Be sure to check all labels, and do some taste tests to find the ones that are right for you. Please note that these food-based frozen nondairy "ice creams" are much preferred over the chemical-laden, artificially sweetened ice cream substitutes found in the grocery store.

We don't generally think of chocolate as a dairy food, but most chocolate contains milk. There are nondairy chocolate options you may want to explore, such as the wonderful "tofu chocolate" available in natural food stores, which uses tofu instead of milk. Feel free to make your own decision about using regular chocolate. Since this is a book about dairy alternatives, my dessert recipes call for tofu chocolate. However, milk chocolate may be used if you prefer. Other chocolate alternatives can include cocoa and carob.

Some Helpful Hints

When I worked as a professional chef, I got used to starting many recipes with a ladleful or two of melted butter, and most of my best soups and sauces were enriched with butter and heavy cream. Now, in an effort to trim fat from my recipes, I try to keep my use of oils and margarines to a minimum without sacrificing flavor. I use nonstick cooking spray to "grease" my pans. For general cooking, I use safflower oil because it has one of the lowest amounts of saturated fat. If I want to achieve a more buttery flavor, I use corn oil. And of course, there are recipes where only a good quality olive oil or sesame oil will do.

Since time is a luxury for most of us these days, I have found a few shortcuts to help make the time spent in the kitchen "quality" time. When I need to make rice, beans, or vegetable stock, I always make a large quantity and freeze what I don't need immediately in portioned containers. I also keep a variety of canned beans and other "quick fix" ingredients, including vegetable bouillon cubes, miso pastes, and powdered vegetable bases on hand to enrich soups, sauces, and other recipes.

In this book, you will notice many of the recipes call for vegetable stock. I supply a recipe for a basic vegetable stock in Chapter 1, on page 10, which you can use as a guide. However, if making stock just isn't high on your "to do" list, then feel free to use a good quality vegetable bouillon or vegetable base, mixed with water, in equal measure to the amount called for in the recipe.

Another ingredient used in many of the recipes is tofu mayonnaise. While I give a basic tofu mayonnaise recipe on page 258, I suggest that you also keep on hand a jar of commercially prepared tofu mayonnaise. Even though I usually make my own for special recipes, having a jar on hand can be very convenient when you just need a tablespoon or two for a dressing or sandwich spread.

In many of the recipes that call for the use of soy milk, as well as nut and rice milks, you will notice an admonition to avoid boiling them. This is important because boiling may cause these milks to separate, since they are not homogenized. The same rule would apply for microwaving—heat to boiling, but do not boil for any length of time.

1
Soups

When I was a restaurant chef, I was required to prepare three different fresh soups every day. Over time, I developed an extensive repertoire of versatile soup recipes that I've now updated with dairy alternatives.

Soups with tempting names like Oyster Mushroom Bisque or Chilled Cream of Watercress Soup may sound as though they are full of rich cream and butter. However, these delectable soups, and over sixty others in this chapter, are made completely without dairy products. By using soy milk, rice milk, almond milk, and soft tofu as well as pureed vegetables, these soups come out as velvety smooth and rich as the dairy versions, with no cholesterol. Chock full of fresh vegetables, each of these soups can be enjoyed as a wholesome lunch or as a great way to begin dinner. The chilled fruit soups are sweetly refreshing enough to serve as dessert.

Vegetable Stock

This is a basic vegetable stock that can be used to enrich many of the soups, sauces, and other recipes in this book. Feel free to substitute vegetable bouillon cubes or powdered vegetable soup base for a quick and easy alternative to making your own stock. Using bouillon can add saltiness to your stock, so be sure to adjust the seasonings accordingly.

1 tablespoon safflower oil
2 large onions, sliced
2 medium carrots, chopped
2 ribs celery (including leaves), chopped
1 medium potato, diced
1 clove garlic, crushed

½ cup coarsely chopped fresh parsley (including stems), or 2 tablespoons dried
2 bay leaves
½ teaspoon black peppercorns
2 tablespoons low-sodium tamari
8 cups cold water

Heat the oil in a large stock pot over medium heat. Add the onions, carrots, and celery, cover and cook for ten minutes. Add the remaining ingredients, cover, and bring to a boil. Remove the cover, lower the heat and simmer gently for 1½ hours. Strain, pressing the juices out of the vegetables. The stock is now ready to be used in other recipes or portioned and frozen for future use. If a stronger stock is desired, return the stock to a boil and reduce the volume by one quarter.

MAKES 6 CUPS

Calories 117 Kc • Protein 3 Gm • Fat 5 Gm • Percent of calories from fat 36% • Cholesterol 0 mg • Dietary Fiber 3 Gm • Sodium 240 mg • Calcium 48 mg

Vermouth-laced Tomato Soup

When made with garden-fresh tomatoes, this soup is sublime, but substitute canned if fresh are unavailable.

1 tablespoon safflower oil
1 medium onion, minced
1 rib celery, minced
½ cup dry vermouth
4 cups peeled, seeded, and chopped fresh tomatoes
1 clove garlic, minced
2½ cups Vegetable Stock (see page 10)
1 tablespoon tomato paste
Pinch of sugar (or a natural sweetener)

1 tablespoon chopped fresh parsley, or 1 teaspoon dried
1 teaspoon chopped fresh basil, or ¼ teaspoon dried
½ teaspoon chopped fresh thyme, or ⅛ teaspoon dried
½ teaspoon salt
⅛ teaspoon freshly ground pepper
1 cup soy milk

Heat the oil in a large saucepan over medium-low heat. Add the onion and celery and cook, covered, until softened, about 5 minutes. Remove the cover and increase the heat to high. Add the vermouth, tomatoes, and garlic. Stir in the stock, tomato paste, sugar, parsley, basil, and thyme. Season with the salt and pepper and bring to boil. Reduce the heat, cover, and simmer until the vegetables are tender, about 20 minutes. Puree the soup in a blender. Return it to the saucepan, gently stir in the soy milk, adjust the seasonings, and heat through before serving.

4 SERVINGS

Calories 239 Kc • Protein 6 Gm • Fat 8 Gm • Percent of calories from fat 30% • Cholesterol 0 mg • Dietary Fiber 6 Gm • Sodium 504 mg • Calcium 76 mg

Vegetarian Senegalese Soup

Traditionally made with chicken, this vegetarian version is as cool, creamy, and curried as the original.

2 tablespoons safflower oil
2 onions, chopped
1 cup chopped celery
1 Golden Delicious apple, peeled and chopped
1½ tablespoons curry powder
2 tablespoons all-purpose flour

3 cups Vegetable Stock (see page 10)
1 cup soy milk
½ cup golden raisins, plumped in warm water for 10 minutes and drained

Heat the oil in a large saucepan over medium-low heat, add the onions, celery, and apple and cook, covered, for 10 minutes, stirring occasionally, or until the vegetables are softened. Stir in the curry powder and cook the mixture, stirring constantly, for 2 minutes. Stir in the flour and cook, stirring constantly, for 2 more minutes. Add 1 cup of the stock. Bring the liquid to a boil and simmer the mixture, stirring occasionally, for 10 minutes.

Puree the mixture in a food processor, transfer to a bowl, and stir in the remaining 2 cups of stock. Let the mixture cool, stir in the soy milk, and chill for 2 hours, or until cold. Garnish the soup with the raisins.

4 TO 6 SERVINGS

Calories 255 Kc • Protein 5 Gm • Fat 10 Gm • Percent of calories from fat 33% • Cholesterol 0 mg • Dietary Fiber 5 Gm • Sodium 209 mg • Calcium 91 mg

Creamy Onion Soup

A nice change from clear French onion soup.

2 tablespoons corn oil
5 medium onions, thinly sliced
(about 6 cups)
½ teaspoon salt
⅛ teaspoon freshly ground
pepper

2 tablespoons all-purpose flour
3 cups Vegetable Stock (see
page 10)
2 cups almond milk

Heat the oil in a large saucepan over medium-high heat. Add the onions and cook, covered, until softened, about 5 minutes. Remove the cover, season with the salt and pepper, and cook about 5 minutes longer until golden brown. Stir in the flour and mix well. Add the stock and bring the soup to a boil, stirring. Reduce the heat and simmer 30 minutes. Slowly add the almond milk and blend well.

6 SERVINGS

Calories 239 Kc • Protein 6 Gm • Fat 12 Gm • Percent of calories from fat 45% • Cholesterol 0 mg • Dietary Fiber 6 Gm • Sodium 361 mg • Calcium 91 mg

Potato-Watercress Soup

1 bunch watercress, stemmed
and chopped
3 medium potatoes, peeled and
cubed
4 cups Vegetable Stock (see
page 10)

1 cup soy milk
½ teaspoon salt
⅛ teaspoon freshly ground
pepper
Watercress sprigs for garnish

Combine the watercress, potatoes, and stock in a large saucepan, and cook over medium-high heat until the potatoes are tender, about 20 minutes. Working in batches, puree the mixture in a food processor and return it to the saucepan. Stir in the soy milk, salt, and pepper. Cook over low heat until heated through, 2 to 3 minutes. Ladle into bowls, and serve garnished with sprigs of fresh watercress.

6 SERVINGS

Calories 199 Kc • Protein 6 Gm • Fat 4 Gm • Percent of calories from fat 18% • Cholesterol 0 mg • Dietary Fiber 4 Gm • Sodium 385 mg • Calcium 64 mg

Pureed Artichoke Soup with Almonds

½ cup chopped almonds
2 cans artichoke hearts in brine,
   well drained
2 cups Vegetable Stock (see
   page 10)

2 teaspoons fresh lemon juice
1 cup almond milk
Salt and freshly ground white
   pepper

Preheat the oven to 325 degrees. Place the almonds on a baking sheet and bake for 5 to 8 minutes. Reserve. In a medium saucepan, combine the artichoke hearts, stock, and lemon juice, and bring to a boil. Reduce the heat and simmer for 15 minutes. Puree the mixture in a food processor and strain it through a fine sieve, pressing hard on the solids, into the pan. Stir in the almond milk and salt and white pepper to taste, and simmer the soup for 5 minutes. To serve, ladle into soup bowls and sprinkle with the almonds.

4 SERVINGS

Calories 202 Kc • Protein 6 Gm • Fat 15 Gm • Percent of calories from fat 63% • Cholesterol 0 mg • Dietary Fiber 4 Gm • Sodium 144 mg • Calcium 87 mg

Cream of Cauliflower Soup

2 pounds cauliflower, separated
   into florets
2 tablespoons corn oil
2 tablespoons all-purpose flour
2½ cups Vegetable Stock (see
   page 10)
½ teaspoon salt

⅛ teaspoon freshly ground white
   pepper
Pinch nutmeg
1½ cups almond milk
1 tablespoon minced fresh
   parsley for garnish

Place the cauliflower in a steamer basket and steam over boiling water until tender, about 5 minutes. Heat the oil in a medium saucepan over low heat. Add the flour and cook until light beige, about 2 minutes, whisking constantly. Gradually whisk in the stock, increase the heat to medium, and whisk until the mixture thickens and comes to a boil. Stir in the cauliflower, salt, pepper, and nutmeg and return to a boil. Reduce the heat to low, cover and simmer, stirring frequently, until the cauliflower is very tender, about 15 minutes.

Working in batches, puree the cauliflower mixture in a food processor until smooth. Return the pureed soup to the saucepan and bring to a boil over medium-high heat, stirring constantly. Gradually whisk in the almond milk and return to a simmer, stirring constantly. Reduce the heat to very low and simmer for 1 to 2 minutes to blend the flavors, adding more almond milk if the soup is too thick. Adjust the seasonings. Ladle the soup into bowls, and garnish with the minced parsley.

4 TO 6 SERVINGS

Calories 260 Kc • Protein 8 Gm • Fat 15 Gm • Percent of calories from fat 50% • Cholesterol 0 mg • Dietary Fiber 8 Gm • Sodium 478 mg • Calcium 129 mg

Squash Cider Soup

Each year, I find that it's not officially autumn until I've made this soup. Butternut or other winter squashes can be used instead of acorn. In a pinch, you can even substitute canned pumpkin and achieve delicious results.

1 tablespoon safflower oil
1 medium onion, chopped
1 large acorn squash, peeled, seeded, and cut into chunks
3 cups Vegetable Stock (see page 10)

1 cup unsweetened apple cider
1 cup soy milk
Salt and freshly ground pepper
Pinch cinnamon
Minced fresh parsley for garnish

Heat the oil in a large saucepan over medium heat. Add the onion, cover, and cook until softened, stirring occasionally, for about 5 minutes. Add the squash, stock, and apple cider and simmer until the squash is tender, about 20 minutes. In a food processor, puree the squash mixture until smooth. Strain it into another large saucepan, and slowly stir in the soy milk. Place over medium heat and heat through, stirring constantly. Be careful not to let it boil. Season with the salt, pepper, and cinnamon. Ladle the soup into bowls, and garnish with the parsley.

6 SERVINGS

Calories 182 Kc • Protein 4 Gm • Fat 6 Gm • Percent of calories from fat 27% • Cholesterol 0 mg • Dietary Fiber 2 Gm • Sodium 144 mg • Calcium 79 mg

Cream of Corn Soup

The subtle sweetness of fresh corn makes this soup especially delicious, but frozen corn can result in a satisfying soup as well.

1 tablespoon corn oil
1 large onion, chopped
3¼ cups fresh corn kernels (about 7 ears)
1½ cup Vegetable Stock (see page 10)

2½ cups rice milk
½ teaspoon salt
⅛ teaspoon freshly ground white pepper
¼ teaspoon sugar (or a natural sweetener)

Heat the oil in a large saucepan over low heat. Add the onion and cook until softened, stirring occasionally, about 5 minutes. Add 3 cups of the corn kernels and cook 5 minutes, stirring occasionally. Blend in the stock and cook until the vegetables are very soft, stirring occasionally, about 20 minutes. Reduce the heat to low. Stir the rice milk into the soup, and simmer about 5 minutes to let the flavors blend. Remove from the heat. Transfer the soup to a food processor and puree until smooth and well blended. Strain through a fine sieve into a large saucepan. Rewarm over very low heat. Season with the salt, pepper, and sugar. Ladle the soup into bowls and garnish with the ¼ cup reserved corn kernels.

4 TO 6 SERVINGS

Calories 222 Kc • Protein 5 Gm • Fat 5 Gm • Percent of calories from fat 19% • Cholesterol 0 mg • Dietary Fiber 4 Gm • Sodium 351 mg • Calcium 35 mg

Cream of Celery and Apple Soup

The addition of applejack or Calvados adds an elegant touch to this soup, but apple juice also works nicely.

3 Granny Smith apples
1 tablespoon lemon juice
3 tablespoons corn oil
1 cup chopped celery
½ cup chopped onion
½ cup chopped carrot
2 tablespoons all-purpose flour
3 cups Vegetable Stock (see page 10)

2 tablespoons applejack or Calvados
½ teaspoon dried marjoram, crumbled
½ teaspoon salt
⅛ teaspoon freshly ground white pepper
2 cups almond milk
Thin slices of apple for garnish

Peel, core, and chop the apples. Place in a medium bowl, toss with the lemon juice and set aside. Heat 1 tablespoon of the oil in a large saucepan over medium heat. Add the celery, onion, and carrot and cook, covered, stirring occasionally, until the vegetables soften, about 5 to 7 minutes. Reduce the heat to low, add the remaining 2 tablespoons of oil, reserved apples, and flour and stir for 2 minutes. Blend in the stock, applejack, marjoram, salt, and pepper. Increase the heat to medium and cook until the soup thickens. Slowly stir in the almond milk and heat through. Adjust the seasonings, and serve hot, garnished with thin slices of apple.

6 SERVINGS

Calories 282 Kc • Protein 5 Gm • Fat 17 Gm • Percent of calories from fat 51% • Cholesterol 0 mg • Dietary Fiber 6 Gm • Sodium 425 mg • Calcium 92 mg

Oyster Mushroom Bisque

The creamy oyster mushroom tastes slightly like seafood and has a texture similar to oysters, which may keep seafood lovers guessing. I've served it to company who have exclaimed, "But I thought you were vegetarian."

1 tablespoon corn oil
1 small onion, chopped
1 rib celery, chopped
1 medium potato, peeled and diced
2 cups Vegetable Stock (see page 10)
½ teaspoon salt
½ teaspoon minced fresh thyme or ⅛ teaspoon dried

⅛ teaspoon freshly ground white pepper
2 cups almond milk
2 tablespoons low-sodium tamari
1 tablespoon dry sherry (optional)
½ pound oyster mushrooms
1 tablespoon margarine
¼ teaspoon Old Bay seasoning

Heat the oil in a large saucepan over medium-low heat. Add the onion and celery and cook, covered, for about 5 minutes or until softened. Add the potato, stock, salt, thyme, and pepper. Increase the heat and simmer until the potato is very soft, about 15 minutes. Transfer the mixture to a food processor and puree until smooth. Return the mixture to the saucepan, and stir in the almond milk, tamari, and sherry (if desired). Slice or quarter the larger mushrooms, leaving the smaller ones whole or halved. In a medium skillet, sauté the mushrooms in the margarine for 1 to 2 minutes, being careful not to overcook. Sprinkle with Old Bay seasoning and add to the soup. Heat through, being careful not to boil.

4 TO 6 SERVINGS

Calories 225 Kc • Protein 7 Gm • Fat 13 Gm • Percent of calories from fat 49% • Cholesterol 0 mg • Dietary Fiber 4 Gm • Sodium 618 mg • Calcium 67 mg

Cream of Fennel Soup

A splash of Pernod brings out the delicate anise flavor of the fennel, and the peas enhance the pale green color of this elegant soup.

½ cup frozen peas
¼ cup firm silken tofu, drained
¾ teaspoon salt
1 tablespoon safflower oil
1 large bulb fresh fennel,
   trimmed and finely chopped
   (about 1½ cups)
1 leek, white part only, chopped
1 medium onion, chopped
1 large boiling potato, peeled
   and diced

3 cups cold water
2 tablespoons Pernod
1 teaspoon fresh lemon juice
⅛ teaspoon freshly ground
   pepper
¾ cup rice milk
1 tablespoon minced fresh fennel
   leaves, or 1 teaspoon dried

In a small saucepan, cook the peas in lightly salted water for 2 minutes. Drain and puree in a food processor with the tofu and ¼ teaspoon of the salt until the mixture is smooth and creamy. Transfer to a small bowl and reserve.

Heat the oil in a large saucepan over medium heat. Add the fennel, leek, onion, and potato; cook, covered, over medium-low heat until the vegetables begin to soften, about 5 minutes. Add the water and continue cooking another 10 minutes, or until tender.

In a food processor, puree the mixture, in batches if necessary, until smooth. Return the soup to the saucepan; heat over medium-high heat until heated through; add the Pernod, lemon juice, remaining ½ teaspoon salt, and the pepper. Slowly stir in the rice milk and heat to just under boiling. Just before serving, swirl in the reserved pea puree, and sprinkle with the minced fennel leaves.

4 TO 6 SERVINGS

Calories 112 Kc • Protein 4 Gm • Fat 1 Gm • Percent of calories from fat 6% • Cholesterol 0 mg • Dietary Fiber 2 Gm • Sodium 409 mg • Calcium 53 mg

Potato Mushroom Soup

1 tablespoon corn oil
1 small onion, minced
1 rib celery, minced
¾ pound boiling potatoes, peeled and diced (about 2 cups)
¼ cup minced scallion
2 cups sliced mushrooms (about ½ pound)

4 cups Vegetable Stock (see page 10)
½ cup dry white wine
1 teaspoon minced fresh thyme, or ¼ teaspoon dried
½ teaspoon salt
⅛ teaspoon freshly ground pepper
1 cup almond milk

Heat the oil in a large saucepan over medium-high heat. Add the onion, celery, potatoes, and scallion and cook, covered, stirring frequently, until the potatoes are slightly soft, about 10 minutes. Be careful not to brown the vegetables. Add the mushrooms to the saucepan and stir well to combine. Cook, covered, until the mushrooms are soft, about 5 minutes. Add the stock, wine, thyme, salt, and pepper and stir to combine. Reduce the heat to low and simmer, covered, until the potatoes are tender, about 30 minutes. Remove the saucepan from the heat. In a food processor, puree the soup, in batches if necessary. Return the soup to the saucepan and reheat over medium heat until the soup comes to a simmer. Stir in the almond milk. Adjust the seasonings. Heat again to serving temperature.

6 SERVINGS

Calories 259 Kc • Protein 6 Gm • Fat 9 Gm • Percent of calories from fat 32% • Cholesterol 0 mg • Dietary Fiber 5 Gm • Sodium 443 mg • Calcium 76 mg

BLT Soup

This tasty soup was inspired by the classic sandwich of the same name.

1 tablespoon corn oil
1 medium onion, minced
1 medium rib celery, minced
2 tablespoons tomato paste
3 cups Vegetable Stock (see page 10)
1 teaspoon sugar (or a natural sweetener)
1 cup soy milk

Salt and freshly ground white pepper
2 strips tempeh bacon, cooked crisp and chopped (or 2 tablespoons soy bacon bits)
1 romaine lettuce leaf, finely shredded
2 cherry tomatoes, sliced into thin rounds

Heat the oil in a large saucepan over medium-low heat. Add the onion and celery and cook, covered, stirring occasionally, until the vegetables are softened, about 5 minutes. Stir in the tomato paste, stock, and sugar, cover, and simmer until the vegetables are very tender, about 30 minutes.

Transfer the soup mixture to a food processor and puree. Strain through a fine sieve back into the saucepan. Slowly whisk in the soy milk, salt and pepper to taste, and heat slowly over very low heat. When ready to serve, ladle the soup into individual bowls and garnish with a sprinkling of tempeh bacon, some lettuce shreds, and 2 or 3 slices of cherry tomato.

4 SERVINGS

Calories 133 Kc • Protein 3 Gm • Fat 6 Gm • Percent of calories from fat 43% • Cholesterol 0 mg • Dietary Fiber 2 Gm • Sodium 194 mg • Calcium 46 mg

Impromptu Vegetable Soup

There's nothing like a pot of hot soup as a cure for the winter doldrums. But what happens if your vegetable bin only contains a stray onion and a rib or two of limp celery? Not to worry—this recipe relies on frozen vegetables to produce a satisfying soup in no time.

1 tablespoon corn oil
1 large onion, chopped
1 rib celery, chopped
1 clove garlic, minced
3 cups Vegetable Stock (see page 10)
1 cup canned tomato puree
1 teaspoon dried basil

1 bay leaf
Salt and freshly ground pepper
1 10-ounce package frozen mixed vegetables
1 10-ounce package frozen chopped spinach, thawed and drained
1 cup soy milk

Heat the oil in a large saucepan over medium heat, add the onion, celery, and garlic, and cook, covered, about 5 minutes, or until the vegetables begin to soften. Remove the cover, add the stock, tomato puree, basil, bay leaf, and salt and pepper to taste, and bring to a boil. Add the frozen vegetables, return the liquid to a boil, and simmer the soup for 5 to 7 minutes, or until the vegetables are just tender. Discard the bay leaf. In a food processor, puree the soup in batches. Return the soup to the saucepan, stir in the soy milk and slowly bring to serving temperature, being careful not to boil.

6 SERVINGS

Calories 207 Kc • Protein 7 Gm • Fat 7 Gm • Percent of calories from fat 29% • Cholesterol 0 mg • Dietary Fiber 7 Gm • Sodium 409 mg • Calcium 119 mg

Mushroom and Almond Soup

2 tablespoons safflower oil
2 leeks, white part only, minced
1 rib celery, minced
1 large shallot, minced
4 cups thinly sliced mushrooms
  (about 1 pound)
3 tablespoons all-purpose flour
4 cups Vegetable Stock (see
  page 10)
½ teaspoon minced fresh thyme,
  or pinch dried

¼ teaspoon minced fresh basil, or
  pinch dried
1 bay leaf
1 cup almond milk
½ cup almonds, toasted and
  finely ground
Salt and freshly ground white
  pepper

Heat the oil in a large saucepan over medium heat. Add the leeks, celery, and shallot and cook, covered, for 5 minutes. Remove the cover, add 3 cups of the mushrooms, and cook 5 minutes longer, stirring occasionally. Add the flour and cook, stirring, for 3 minutes. Gradually stir in the stock. Add the thyme, basil, and bay leaf and bring to boil. Reduce the heat to low and simmer for 30 minutes. Strain the soup through a fine sieve into a saucepan, pressing on the solids with the back of a spoon. Discard the solids. Add the almond milk, almonds, and the remaining 1 cup of mushrooms to the soup and bring to a simmer. Season with the salt and pepper to taste.

6 SERVINGS

Calories 253 Kc • Protein 7 Gm • Fat 15 Gm • Percent of calories from fat 51% • Cholesterol 0 mg • Dietary Fiber 5 Gm • Sodium 177 mg • Calcium 119 mg

Cream of Escarole Soup

The Yukon Gold potatoes add a buttery richness to this soup.

2 tablespoons corn oil
2 cups chopped onion
2 tablespoons flour
4 cups Vegetable Stock (see page 10)
1 pound Yukon Gold potatoes, peeled and cut into ½-inch cubes

1 teaspoon minced garlic
3 cups chopped escarole
1 tablespoon lemon juice
½ cup soy milk (or more)
½ teaspoon salt
Pinch cayenne

Heat the oil in a large saucepan over medium heat. Add the onion and cook, covered, for 5 minutes, or until softened, stirring occasionally. Add the flour and cook, stirring, for 5 minutes. Slowly stir in the stock and add the potatoes and garlic. Bring to a boil and simmer the mixture, partially covered, for 40 minutes or until the potatoes are very tender. Working in batches, puree the mixture in a food processor and return it to the saucepan. Add the escarole and lemon juice and simmer for 5 minutes. Add enough soy milk to achieve the desired consistency. Add the salt and cayenne and simmer the soup for an additional 5 minutes before serving.

6 SERVINGS

Calories 277 Kc • Protein 7 Gm • Fat 10 Gm • Percent of calories from fat 31% • Cholesterol 0 mg • Dietary Fiber 6 Gm • Sodium 447 mg • Calcium 85 mg

Curried Apple Soup

Pass small bowls of traditional curry accompaniments, such as chopped peanuts or raisins, to garnish this flavorful soup.

2 tablespoons corn oil
1 medium onion, diced
1 rib celery, chopped
1 carrot, chopped
2 medium cooking apples, diced
2 tablespoons all-purpose flour
2 tablespoons curry powder

1 bay leaf
½ teaspoon minced fresh thyme, or pinch dried
Salt and freshly ground pepper
4 cups Vegetable Stock (see page 10)
1 cup rice milk

Heat the oil in large saucepan over medium heat. Add the onion, celery, carrot, and apples. Cover and cook, stirring frequently, until the vegetables are soft, about 10 minutes. Stir in the flour, curry powder, bay leaf, thyme, salt, and pepper to taste and cook 2 minutes. Slowly whisk in the stock. Bring to a boil over medium-high heat. Reduce the heat to low and simmer for 30 minutes, stirring occasionally. Strain the soup into a large bowl, pressing the solids with the back of a spoon to release as much liquid as possible. Discard the solids. Blend in the rice milk and reheat over low heat, if necessary, before serving.

6 TO 8 SERVINGS

Calories 175 Kc • Protein 3 Gm • Fat 7 Gm • Percent of calories from fat 36% • Cholesterol 0 mg • Dietary Fiber 4 Gm • Sodium 159 mg • Calcium 57 mg

Two-Potato Four-Onion Soup

Using a variety of potatoes and onions makes an ordinary soup extra-ordinary. Delicious served hot or cold.

1 tablespoon corn oil
1 medium onion, chopped
1 medium leek, white part only, chopped
1 shallot, chopped
3 cups Vegetable Stock (see page 10)
1 large baking potato, peeled and diced

2 large Yukon Gold potatoes, peeled and diced
1 cup soy milk
Salt and freshly ground pepper
2 teaspoons snipped fresh chives, or ½ teaspoon dried

Heat the oil in a large saucepan over low heat. Add the onion, leek, and shallot and cook, covered, for 5 minutes, stirring occasionally. Add the stock and diced potatoes. Increase the heat to medium-high and bring to a boil. Reduce the heat to low and simmer until the potatoes are tender, about 30 to 45 minutes. Press the mixture through a fine sieve into a large bowl, blend in the soy milk, salt, and pepper to taste, and if desired, refrigerate until cold. Discard the solids. Sprinkle with the chives and serve.

6 SERVINGS

Calories 242 Kc • Protein 6 Gm • Fat 8 Gm • Percent of calories from fat 29% • Cholesterol 0 mg • Dietary Fiber 4 Gm • Sodium 151 mg • Calcium 60 mg

Zucchini Corn Chowder

Two summertime favorites, corn and zucchini, join forces to create this tempting chowder.

4 ears fresh corn (or 2 cups
    frozen corn kernels)
1 tablespoon corn oil
1 large onion, minced
2 cloves garlic, minced
1 cup canned tomato puree
3 cups Vegetable Stock (see
    page 10)

3 cups chopped zucchini
1½ tablespoons minced fresh
    basil, or 1 teaspoon dried
⅛ teaspoon cayenne
Salt
1 cup soy milk

Cook the corn in boiling water until tender, about 5 minutes. Drain and cool. Cut the kernels off the cobs. Heat the oil in a large saucepan over low heat. Add the onion and cook, covered, until tender, about 5 minutes, stirring occasionally. Remove the cover, add the garlic and cook 2 minutes, stirring frequently. Stir in the tomato puree, stock, zucchini, basil, and cayenne and cook until the zucchini is tender, about 10 minutes. Stir in the corn, reserving ½ cup. Taste and season with salt. Puree the soup in a food processor, in batches if necessary, and return to the saucepan. Slowly add the soy milk and reheat to serving temperature. To serve, ladle the soup into bowls and garnish with the reserved ½ cup of corn.

6 SERVINGS

Calories 205 Kc • Protein 6 Gm • Fat 8 Gm • Percent of calories from fat 33% • Cholesterol 0 mg • Dietary Fiber 5 Gm • Sodium 155 mg • Calcium 54 mg

Cabbage Beet Soup

A hearty wintertime soup full of color and flavor.

1 tablespoon corn oil
1 cup chopped onion
1 cup diced carrot
5 cups Vegetable Stock (see page 10)
2 cups chopped cabbage
2 cups peeled, chopped beets
1 teaspoon sugar (or a natural sweetener)
Pinch dried thyme
Pinch ground cloves
Pinch ground nutmeg

Salt and freshly ground pepper
1 cup silken tofu, drained
2 tablespoons fresh lemon juice
2 tablespoons minced fresh dill, or 1 teaspoon dried
½ teaspoon salt
⅛ teaspoon freshly ground pepper
2 tablespoons minced fresh parsley, or 2 teaspoons dried

Heat the oil in a large saucepan over medium-high heat. Add the onion and carrot. Cover and cook, stirring frequently, until the vegetables begin to soften, about 5 minutes. Add the stock, cabbage, beets, sugar, thyme, cloves, and nutmeg. Cover and simmer until the vegetables are tender, about 30 minutes. Season with salt and pepper to taste. Just before serving, reheat the soup, if necessary. In a small bowl, combine the tofu with the lemon juice, dill, salt, and pepper. Ladle the soup into bowls, and swirl a spoonful of the tofu mixture into each bowl, and sprinkle with the parsley. Serve immediately.

6 SERVINGS

Calories 259 Kc • Protein 9 Gm • Fat 9 Gm • Percent of calories from fat 30% • Cholesterol 0 mg • Dietary Fiber 8 Gm • Sodium 598 mg • Calcium 118 mg

Curried Mushroom Soup

2 tablespoons corn oil
¼ cup minced shallot
2 tablespoons all-purpose flour
1 teaspoon curry powder
2½ cups Vegetable Stock (see
    page 10)

1 cup soy milk
½ pound mushrooms, chopped
    (about 3 cups)
Salt and freshly ground pepper
¼ cup silken tofu, drained

Heat the oil in a medium saucepan over low heat. Add the shallot and sauté until tender, about 5 minutes. Increase the heat to medium. Add the flour and curry powder and stir 2 minutes. Remove from the heat. Heat the stock and soy milk in another medium saucepan over medium heat. Blend into the flour mixture whisking constantly. Add the mushrooms, salt and pepper to taste, and simmer 20 minutes, stirring occasionally. In a small bowl, whisk together the tofu with $1/4$ cup of the soup. Gradually pour the mixture back into the soup, whisking constantly. Ladle into bowls and serve immediately.

4 SERVINGS

Calories 196 Kc • Protein 6 Gm • Fat 11 Gm • Percent of calories from fat 50% • Cholesterol 0 mg • Dietary Fiber 2 Gm • Sodium 161 mg • Calcium 54 mg

Cream of Vegetable Soup

1 tablespoon corn oil
1 medium onion, chopped
1 medium potato, peeled and
  diced
1 carrot, chopped
1 cup chopped green beans
1 clove garlic, minced
1 large tomato, peeled, seeded,
  and diced

1 teaspoon sugar (or a natural
  sweetener)
Salt and freshly ground pepper
5 cups Vegetable Stock (see
  page 10)
1 cup soy milk
Chopped parsley for garnish

Heat the oil in a large saucepan over medium heat. Add the onion and cook 5 minutes. Reduce the heat to low and add the potato, carrot, green beans, garlic, tomato, sugar, and salt and pepper to taste. Cover and cook until the vegetables are tender, about 20 minutes. Add the stock and bring to a boil over medium-high heat. Reduce the heat and simmer about 10 minutes. Remove from the heat and let it cool slightly. Puree the soup in a food processor until smooth. Return to the saucepan over medium heat and gradually stir in the soy milk. Heat through but do not boil. Adjust the seasonings. To serve, ladle into bowls and garnish with chopped parsley.

6 TO 8 SERVINGS

Calories 192 Kc • Protein 4 Gm • Fat 8 Gm • Percent of calories from fat 37% • Cholesterol 0 mg • Dietary Fiber 4 Gm • Sodium 196 mg • Calcium 62 mg

Saffron Parsnip Soup

If saffron is not in your budget, substitute a bit of turmeric to achieve a golden hue.

1 tablespoon corn oil
2 medium shallots, minced
1 pound parsnips, peeled and
    chopped
1 small potato, peeled and
    chopped
3 cups Vegetable Stock (see
    page 10)

Pinch crumbled saffron threads
1 teaspoon fresh lemon juice
Salt and white pepper
1 cup rice milk
Snipped chives or minced parsley
    for garnish

Heat the oil in a saucepan over medium heat, add the shallots, and cook, stirring, until softened, about 3 minutes. Add the parsnips, potato, and stock and bring to a boil. Reduce the heat, add the saffron, lemon juice, salt and pepper to taste, and simmer covered for 10 minutes, or until the vegetables are very tender. Remove from the heat and, working in batches if necessary, puree the mixture in a food processor until smooth. Return the puree to the saucepan over low heat and add the rice milk, stirring constantly, until hot. Garnish with snipped chives or minced parsley.

4 SERVINGS

Calories 318 Kc • Protein 5 Gm • Fat 11 Gm • Percent of calories from fat 31% •
Cholesterol 0 mg • Dietary Fiber 8 Gm • Sodium 215 mg • Calcium 87 mg

Asparagus Bisque

1 tablespoon safflower oil
2 medium leeks, white part only, chopped
1 pound fresh asparagus, trimmed and cut into 1-inch lengths

4 cups Vegetable Stock (see page 10)
Salt and freshly ground pepper
1 cup rice milk

Heat the oil in a large saucepan over medium-low heat. Add the leeks and asparagus and cook until the vegetables begin to soften, stirring occasionally, about 5 minutes. Add the stock and simmer until the vegetables are tender, about 10 minutes. With a slotted spoon, remove 6 asparagus tips and reserve for garnish. Transfer the mixture to a food processor and puree until well blended. Strain back into the saucepan through a fine sieve. Season with salt and pepper. Simmer over medium heat for 10 minutes. Slowly blend in the rice milk and simmer 5 minutes. To serve, ladle the soup into bowls and garnish with the reserved asparagus tips.

6 SERVINGS

Calories 161 Kc • Protein 4 Gm • Fat 6 Gm • Percent of calories from fat 34% • Cholesterol 0 mg • Dietary Fiber 3 Gm • Sodium 191 mg • Calcium 69 mg

Spiced Squash Soup

This soup can also be served cold, but I usually serve it warm on chilly autumn nights.

1 medium butternut squash
   (about 1½ pounds), peeled and
   seeded
2 tablespoons corn oil
1 medium onion, chopped
1 rib celery, chopped
1 tablespoon all-purpose flour
¾ teaspoon salt
½ teaspoon sugar (or a natural
   sweetener)

⅛ teaspoon allspice
⅛ teaspoon ground ginger
Pinch nutmeg
Pinch cayenne
3 cups Vegetable Stock (see
   page 10)
1 cup almond milk

Cut the squash into ½-inch slices and set aside. Heat the oil in a large saucepan over medium heat. Add the onion and celery, cover, and cook, stirring occasionally, until the vegetables are softened, about 5 minutes. Stir in the flour, salt, sugar, allspice, ginger, nutmeg, and cayenne and cook 2 minutes. Stir in the stock and squash. Cover and simmer the mixture for 30 minutes, or until the squash is tender. Puree the mixture in a food processor, working in batches if necessary, until smooth. Transfer the soup back to the saucepan, slowly whisk in the almond milk, and adjust the seasonings. Slowly reheat to the desired serving temperature, if necessary, and serve.

4 SERVINGS

Calories 258 Kc • Protein 5 Gm • Fat 14 Gm • Percent of calories from fat 46% • Cholesterol 0 mg • Dietary Fiber 4 Gm • Sodium 632 mg • Calcium 116 mg

Cream of Zucchini Soup

This soup is also wonderful when served chilled. To do so, instead of returning it to the saucepan to reheat, place it in a container and refrigerate, covered, for several hours or overnight.

1 tablespoon corn oil
1 medium onion, chopped
5 cups sliced zucchini
1½ cups Vegetable Stock (see page 10)
1 clove garlic, minced

⅛ teaspoon dried marjoram
Salt and freshly ground pepper
2 cups soy milk
½ cup silken tofu, drained
2 tablespoons minced fresh parsley for garnish

Heat the oil in a large saucepan over medium heat, add the onion, cover, and cook, stirring occasionally, until softened, about 5 minutes. Reduce the heat to low, add the zucchini, stock, garlic, and marjoram, and simmer, covered, until the zucchini is tender, about 15 minutes. Remove from the heat. Season with salt and pepper to taste. Puree the zucchini mixture in a food processor, in batches if necessary, blending until the mixture is very smooth. Transfer the mixture to a large bowl. In a small bowl, combine the soy milk with the tofu and about ⅓ cup of the soup mixture, whisking to blend well. Slowly add the soy milk mixture to the soup. Adjust the seasonings. If a smoother texture is desired, press the mixture through a fine sieve placed over the saucepan. Slowly reheat to the desired serving temperature. Garnish with the parsley.

6 SERVINGS

Calories 210 Kc • Protein 10 Gm • Fat 10 Gm • Percent of calories from fat 42% • Cholesterol 0 mg • Dietary Fiber 3 Gm • Sodium 157 mg • Calcium 91 mg

Creamy Mushroom and Leek Soup

Snipped fresh dill or chives make a nice garnish for this elegant and easy soup.

1 tablespoon corn oil
3 leeks, white part only, chopped
¾ pound mushrooms, sliced (3 cups)
½ cup dry white wine
1 bay leaf

1 teaspoon minced fresh dill, or ¼ teaspoon dried
3 cups Vegetable Stock (see page 10)
¼ teaspoon salt
White pepper
1 cup soy milk

Heat the oil in a large saucepan over medium heat, add the leeks, cover, and cook, stirring occasionally, for 5 minutes, or until they are softened. Remove the cover, add the mushrooms, and cook, stirring, for 10 minutes. Add the wine, bay leaf, dill, stock, salt, and white pepper to taste, simmer the mixture for 30 minutes, then discard the bay leaf. In a food processor blend the soup in batches until it is smooth and return it to the saucepan. Slowly stir in the soy milk, heat the soup over low heat until it reaches the desired serving temperature, adjust the seasonings, and serve.

4 TO 6 SERVINGS

Calories 184 Kc • Protein 5 Gm • Fat 6 Gm • Percent of calories from fat 31% • Cholesterol 0 mg • Dietary Fiber 3 Gm • Sodium 291 mg • Calcium 83 mg

Cauliflower-Almond Cream Soup

This is another soup that works well served hot or chilled. If serving chilled, I usually use the toasted slivered almonds or some chives for garnish, and save the creamy almond butter for the hot version.

2 tablespoons almond butter
2 tablespoons silken tofu, drained
1 teaspoon low-sodium tamari
1 large head cauliflower, trimmed and broken into florets
1 tablespoon corn oil
3 large shallots, minced
3 cups Vegetable Stock (see page 10)
½ teaspoon salt
⅛ teaspoon cayenne
⅛ teaspoon freshly grated nutmeg
2 cups almond milk
Minced parsley for garnish (optional)
Snipped chives for garnish (optional)
Toasted slivered almonds for garnish (optional)

To make creamy almond butter, in a small bowl combine the almond butter, tofu, and tamari, whisking until thoroughly blended. Set aside for garnish.

Chop the cauliflower into ½-inch pieces and set aside. Heat the oil in a large saucepan over medium heat. Add the shallots, cover, and cook for 3 minutes, or until softened. Add the cauliflower, stock, and salt. Cover and bring to a boil over high heat. Reduce the heat to medium and cook until the vegetables are soft, about 30 minutes. Puree the mixture in a food processor until smooth, working in batches. Transfer the soup back to the saucepan. Add the cayenne and nutmeg, and slowly stir in the almond milk. Reheat to the desired serving temperature and serve garnished with a dollop of creamy almond butter and a sprinkling of parsley, chives, or toasted slivered almonds, if desired.

6 SERVINGS

Calories 181 Kc • Protein 5 Gm • Fat 13 Gm • Percent of calories from fat 60% •
Cholesterol 0 mg • Dietary Fiber 4 Gm • Sodium 360 mg • Calcium 75 mg

Vanilla-scented Carrot Bisque

The hint of vanilla complements the natural sweetness of the carrots in this tasty soup.

1 tablespoon corn oil
5 large carrots, shredded
1 rib celery, minced
1 leek, white part only, minced
2 cups Vegetable Stock (see page 10)
½ teaspoon vanilla extract

½ teaspoon sugar (or a natural sweetener)
½ teaspoon salt
¼ teaspoon freshly ground white pepper
1 cup vanilla or plain rice milk
Chopped parsley for garnish

Heat the oil in a large saucepan over medium heat. Add the carrots, celery, and leek and cook, stirring, for 5 minutes, or until the vegetables begin to soften. Stir in the stock. Bring to a boil over high heat. Reduce the heat to medium, cover, and simmer until the vegetables are very tender, 20 to 25 minutes. Let them cool slightly. Puree the mixture in a food processor and return it to the saucepan. Add the vanilla extract, sugar, salt, and pepper. Slowly stir in the rice milk and cook over low heat, stirring, until warmed through; do not boil. To serve, ladle into bowls and sprinkle with parsley.

4 SERVINGS

Calories 182 Kc • Protein 3 Gm • Fat 6 Gm • Percent of calories from fat 31% • Cholesterol 0 mg • Dietary Fiber 5 Gm • Sodium 477 mg • Calcium 76 mg

Cream of Greens Soup

If it's a green vegetable, it may find its way into this vibrantly colored soup.

1 tablespoon corn oil
½ cup chopped onion
½ cup minced celery
4 cups Vegetable Stock (see page 10)
3 cups chopped green beans
1 bay leaf
2 cups chopped fresh spinach

1 cup frozen peas
½ cup minced scallion
1 tablespoon minced fresh basil, or ½ teaspoon dried
Salt and freshly ground pepper
1 cup soy milk
½ cup chopped fresh parsley

Heat the oil in a large saucepan over medium heat. Add the onion and celery and cook until softened, about 5 minutes. Add the stock, green beans, and bay leaf. Bring the soup to a boil. Reduce the heat, cover, and simmer 20 minutes. Add the spinach, peas, scallion, and basil. Season with salt and pepper to taste, and simmer 10 minutes. Discard the bay leaf. Puree the soup in a food processor, working in batches if necessary. Return the soup to the saucepan and slowly stir in the soy milk. Add the parsley and stir the soup over low heat until warmed to the desired serving temperature.

6 SERVINGS

Calories 181 Kc • Protein 6 Gm • Fat 7 Gm • Percent of calories from fat 32% • Cholesterol 0 mg • Dietary Fiber 7 Gm • Sodium 240 mg • Calcium 117 mg

Gingered Squash and Sweet Potato Soup

I created this soup one day when I prepared too much squash and sweet potatoes for dinner the previous night. Now, I purposely bake extra so I have enough left over to make this rich soup.

1 medium butternut squash, peeled, halved, and seeded
1 large sweet potato or yam, peeled
Salt and freshly ground pepper
1 tablespoon safflower oil
1 medium onion, chopped
1 teaspoon minced garlic
1 tablespoon minced fresh ginger, or 1 teaspoon dried

1 tablespoon sugar (or a natural sweetener)
⅛ teaspoon ground allspice
⅛ teaspoon cayenne
3 cups Vegetable Stock (see page 10)
1 cup soy milk

Preheat the oven to 350 degrees. Lightly oil a large baking dish or coat with cooking spray. Cut the squash and sweet potato into 1- to 2-inch chunks and place in the prepared baking dish. Season lightly with salt and pepper and cover tightly with a lid or foil. Bake until the vegetables are soft, about 45 minutes. Let them cool.

Heat the oil in a large saucepan over medium-high heat. Add the onion and cook until lightly browned, stirring frequently, about 10 minutes. Add the garlic and ginger to the saucepan and stir 1 minute. Add the sugar, allspice, and cayenne and stir to blend. Add the stock and bring to a boil. Simmer for 5 minutes, then let it cool. Puree the soup mixture in a food processor, working in batches, and return it to the saucepan. Puree the baked squash and sweet potato, and add to the saucepan as well. Slowly blend in the soy milk to achieve the desired consistency, adjust the seasoning with salt and pepper, and slowly reheat the soup until hot, being careful not to boil.

6 SERVINGS

Calories 204 Kc • Protein 4 Gm • Fat 9 Gm • Percent of calories from fat 37% • Cholesterol 0 mg • Dietary Fiber 3 Gm • Sodium 184 mg • Calcium 75 mg

Carrot Beet Soup

Lively colors and old-world flavors combine in this hearty soup enhanced by the creaminess of tofu and soy milk.

1 tablespoon safflower oil
2 medium carrots, chopped
1 medium onion, chopped
3 medium beets, peeled and shredded
1 teaspoon minced garlic
3½ cups Vegetable Stock (see page 10)
1 tablespoon brown sugar (or a natural sweetener)

1 tablespoon dry red wine
1 tablespoon lemon juice
¾ teaspoon salt
½ teaspoon cinnamon
⅛ teaspoon freshly ground pepper
½ cup silken tofu, drained
½ cup soy milk

Heat the oil in a large saucepan over medium heat. Add the carrots and onion, cover, and cook 5 minutes or until the vegetables begin to soften. Remove the cover, add the beets and garlic, and cook, stirring, for 2 minutes. Add the stock, cover, and bring to boil over high heat. Reduce the heat to medium and cook until the vegetables are soft, about 45 minutes. Remove from the heat. Puree the mixture in a food processor, working in batches, until smooth. Transfer the mixture to a saucepan, add the brown sugar, wine, lemon juice, salt, cinnamon, and pepper, and blend well. In a small bowl, combine the tofu and soy milk with $1/2$ cup of the soup until smooth. Stir the tofu mixture into the soup, and heat slowly over low heat to the desired serving temperature. Adjust the seasonings.

6 SERVINGS

Calories 193 Kc • Protein 6 Gm • Fat 7 Gm • Percent of calories from fat 33% • Cholesterol 0 mg • Dietary Fiber 5 Gm • Sodium 517 mg • Calcium 77 mg

Parsleyed Potato Soup

To prevent grated potatoes from discoloring, cover tightly with plastic wrap, but it's best to grate them just prior to use.

1 tablespoon corn oil
½ cup minced onion
3 large boiling potatoes, peeled and grated
2 cups Vegetable Stock (see page 10)

1 cup minced fresh parsley
2 cups soy milk
Salt and freshly ground white pepper
Pinch nutmeg

Heat the oil in a large saucepan over medium heat, add the onion, and cook for 5 minutes, stirring occasionally, until the onion softens. Add the grated potato and stir for 2 minutes. Stir in the stock and simmer, stirring occasionally, until the vegetables soften, about 15 minutes. Add ³/₄ cup of the parsley and puree in a food processor, working in batches. Return the soup to the saucepan, add the remaining ¹/₄ cup parsley, slowly stir in the soy milk, and season with salt, pepper, and nutmeg to taste. Slowly heat the soup over low heat, stirring until it is hot, being careful not to boil.

4 TO 6 SERVINGS

Calories 216 Kc • Protein 6 Gm • Fat 6 Gm • Percent of calories from fat 24% • Cholesterol 0 mg • Dietary Fiber 4 Gm • Sodium 137 mg • Calcium 75 mg

Artichoke Hazelnut Soup

Using frozen artichokes is a real time saver for this captivating soup. Avoid using marinated or brine-packed artichokes, as they would be too strong-tasting.

½ pound hazelnuts
2 10-ounce packages frozen
  artichoke hearts, thawed
1 tablespoon corn oil
1 cup chopped onion
4 cups Vegetable Stock (see
  page 10)
1 bay leaf

1 teaspoon salt
⅛ teaspoon freshly ground white
  pepper
1 tablespoon cornstarch
  combined with 1 tablespoon
  dry sherry
1 cup almond milk

Preheat the oven to 350 degrees. Toast the hazelnuts in a shallow baking pan in the oven, shaking the pan occasionally, until browned, about 10 minutes. Transfer the nuts to a strainer; rub the nuts with a cloth to remove the skins. Grind the hazelnuts in a food processor. Set aside, reserving ¼ cup for garnish.

Slice the artichoke hearts and reserve. Heat the oil in large saucepan over medium heat. Add the onion, cover, and cook, stirring occasionally, until the onion is softened, about 5 minutes. Add the stock, bay leaf, sliced artichokes, ground hazelnuts (except for the reserved ¼ cup), salt, and pepper. Heat to boiling. Reduce the heat to low; simmer, covered, until the artichokes are tender, about 20 minutes. Add the cornstarch mixture to the soup, stirring frequently, until the soup is thickened, 6 to 8 minutes. Slowly whisk in the almond milk, and simmer 5 minutes longer. Strain through a fine sieve, discard the solids, and adjust the seasonings. To serve, ladle the soup into bowls and garnish with the reserved ¼ cup hazelnuts.

4 TO 6 SERVINGS

Calories 496 Kc • Protein 13 Gm • Fat 38 Gm • Percent of calories from fat 61% • Cholesterol 0 mg • Dietary Fiber 15 Gm • Sodium 773 mg • Calcium 206 mg

Gingered Broccoli Soup with Sesame Seeds

1 tablespoon safflower oil
¼ cup chopped scallion
1½ teaspoons minced fresh
   ginger, or ½ teaspoon dried
4 cups chopped broccoli
1 tablespoon low-sodium tamari
½ teaspoon freshly ground black
   pepper
2 cups Vegetable Stock (see
   page 10)

½ cup orange juice
1 cup rice milk
2 tablespoons cornstarch
   dissolved in 2 tablespoons
   orange juice
1 tablespoon toasted sesame
   seeds for garnish

Heat the oil in a large saucepan over medium heat. Add the scallion and ginger and cook until fragrant, about 2 minutes. Stir in the broccoli and cook 3 more minutes. Season with the tamari and pepper. Add the stock and orange juice and bring to a boil. Reduce the heat to medium-low, cover, and simmer until the broccoli is tender, about 15 minutes. Cool slightly. Working in batches, puree the mixture in the food processor until smooth. Return to the saucepan, stir in the rice milk, and heat until hot, but not boiling. Stir in the cornstarch mixture and whisk until thickened. Taste and adjust the seasonings. Garnish with the sesame seeds.

4 SERVINGS

Calories 191 Kc • Protein 5 Gm • Fat 7 Gm • Percent of calories from fat 32% •
Cholesterol 0 mg • Dietary Fiber 5 Gm • Sodium 318 mg • Calcium 96 mg

Herbed Root Vegetable Soup

This pleasing soup includes a variety of winter's tasty abundance.

1 tablespoon corn oil
3 large shallots, minced
3 large carrots, shredded
2 parsnips, shredded
1 medium potato, peeled and chopped
4 scallions, minced
1 small clove garlic, minced
4 cups Vegetable Stock (see page 10)

1 teaspoon minced fresh chervil, or ¼ teaspoon dried
1 teaspoon minced fresh tarragon, or ¼ teaspoon dried
¼ teaspoon minced fresh marjoram, or pinch dried
1 cup soy milk
Salt and freshly ground pepper
1 tablespoon minced fresh parsley for garnish

Heat the oil in a large saucepan over medium heat. Add the shallots, carrots, parsnips, and potato, cover, and cook 5 minutes, stirring occasionally. Remove the cover, add the scallions, garlic, stock, chervil, tarragon, and marjoram. Bring to a boil and cook, uncovered, 10 to 15 minutes. Reduce the heat to low and cook another 10 minutes, or until the vegetables are soft. Working in batches, puree the soup in a food processor. Return it to the saucepan, slowly stir in the soy milk, and reheat until it comes to a simmer. Season with salt and pepper to taste and sprinkle with the minced parsley.

6 SERVINGS

Calories 247 Kc • Protein 6 Gm • Fat 8 Gm • Percent of calories from fat 28% • Cholesterol 0 mg • Dietary Fiber 7 Gm • Sodium 244 mg • Calcium 92 mg

Parsnip and Potato Soup

Great served hot or cold. The bright pimiento garnish adds a bold contrast to the light-colored soup.

1 tablespoon corn oil
1 medium leek, white part only, minced
1 large boiling potato, peeled and shredded
1 large parsnip, peeled and shredded
3 cups Vegetable Stock (see page 10)

½ teaspoon salt
⅛ teaspoon freshly ground white pepper
1 cup rice milk
1½ tablespoons minced pimiento for garnish

Heat the oil in a large saucepan. Add the leek, potato, and parsnip and cook over medium heat, stirring occasionally for 5 minutes. Add the stock, cover, and bring to boil over medium-high heat. Reduce the heat to medium and cook until the vegetables are soft, about 30 minutes.

Puree the soup mixture in a food processor, in batches. Return the soup to the saucepan and season with the salt and pepper. Slowly stir in the rice milk and blend well. If serving the soup hot, rewarm it to serving temperature over low heat. If serving it chilled, transfer the soup to a container and refrigerate it for several hours. Before serving, taste it and adjust the seasonings. Garnish with the minced pimiento.

4 SERVINGS

Calories 274 Kc • Protein 5 Gm • Fat 8 Gm • Percent of calories from fat 25% • Cholesterol 0 mg • Dietary Fiber 6 Gm • Sodium 507 mg • Calcium 82 mg

Quick Cream of Mushroom Soup

Chunky with juicy mushroom pieces, this soup has a complex flavor that belies its ease of preparation.

1 tablespoon olive oil
¾ pound mushrooms, sliced (3 cups)
½ cup minced celery leaves
2 tablespoons dry vermouth
3½ cups Vegetable Stock (see page 10)

2 tablespoons minced fresh parsley, or 2 teaspoons dried
½ teaspoon minced fresh thyme, or pinch dried
Salt and freshly ground pepper
1 cup soy milk

Heat the oil in a large saucepan over medium heat. Add the mushrooms and celery leaves and cook, stirring, for 5 minutes. Add the vermouth, stock, parsley, and thyme and simmer for 15 minutes. Season with salt and pepper to taste. Remove from the heat. In a small bowl, combine the soy milk with ½ cup of the soup, blending well. Stir the mixture gently into the soup and serve immediately.

4 SERVINGS

Calories 202 Kc • Protein 6 Gm • Fat 9 Gm • Percent of calories from fat 40% • Cholesterol 0 mg • Dietary Fiber 4 Gm • Sodium 252 mg • Calcium 72 mg

Cream of Spinach Soup

2 tablespoons safflower oil
2 shallots, minced
2 tablespoons all-purpose flour
2 cups Vegetable Stock (see
    page 10)
1 10-ounce package frozen
    chopped spinach, thawed and
    drained

1 cup rice milk
1 cup silken tofu, drained
Salt and freshly ground pepper
Pinch nutmeg

Heat the oil in a large skillet over medium heat. Add the shallots and cook, stirring, for 5 minutes, or until softened. Add the flour and continue stirring for 2 minutes. Slowly add the stock, stirring constantly. Add the spinach and simmer, uncovered, for 10 to 12 minutes. In a food processor, puree the soup mixture, along with the rice milk and tofu, blending until smooth. Return the soup to the saucepan, season with salt and pepper to taste, add the nutmeg, and heat gently until hot. Do not boil.

4 SERVINGS

Calories 221 Kc • Protein 8 Gm • Fat 12 Gm • Percent of calories from fat 46% • Cholesterol 0 mg • Dietary Fiber 4 Gm • Sodium 205 mg • Calcium 158 mg

Winter Squash Bisque

The apple butter adds a richness of flavor and color to this warming winter soup.

1 pound butternut squash
1 tablespoon safflower oil
½ cup chopped onion
3 cups Vegetable Stock (see page 10)

1 cup silken tofu, drained
½ cup soy milk
1 tablespoon apple butter
Salt and freshly ground pepper

Peel, halve, and seed the squash. Cut into 1-inch chunks and set aside. Heat the oil in a large saucepan over medium heat, add the onion, cover, and cook 5 minutes, or until softened. Add the squash and stock, cover, and simmer 15 to 20 minutes, or until the squash is very tender. Puree the squash mixture in a food processor and return it to the saucepan. In the same food processor (don't bother to wash it) combine the tofu, soy milk, and apple butter and blend until well combined. Add ¹/₂ cup of the pureed soup and blend well. Pour the tofu mixture back into the saucepan and stir to combine thoroughly. Season with salt and pepper to taste. If serving the soup chilled, transfer it to a container and refrigerate for several hours. If serving it hot, slowly heat the soup, stirring, being careful not to boil.

4 SERVINGS

Calories 234 Kc • Protein 7 Gm • Fat 10 Gm • Percent of calories from fat 36% • Cholesterol 0 mg • Dietary Fiber 3 Gm • Sodium 203 mg • Calcium 114 mg

Squash Almond Bisque

The use of almonds three ways makes this a decidedly rich and delicious soup, which can be served hot or cold.

1 tablespoon corn oil
1 large onion, sliced
6 medium yellow squash (summer squash)
3 cups Vegetable Stock (see page 10)

1½ cups almond milk
2 tablespoons almond butter
Salt and pepper
2 tablespoons toasted slivered almonds for garnish

Heat the oil in a large saucepan, add the onions, cover, and cook for 5 minutes. Remove the cover, add the squash and stock, and simmer for 15 minutes, or until the vegetables are soft. Puree the mixture in a food processor until smooth, working in batches if necessary. Blend in the almond milk and almond butter, and season with salt and pepper to taste. To serve cold, transfer the soup to a container and refrigerate for several hours. To serve hot, place the soup back in the saucepan and reheat gently, being careful not to boil. Garnish with the slivered almonds.

4 SERVINGS

Calories 297 Kc • Protein 9 Gm • Fat 19 Gm • Percent of calories from fat 55% • Cholesterol 0 mg • Dietary Fiber 7 Gm • Sodium 225 mg • Calcium 136 mg

Fresh Asparagus Cilantro Soup

2 pounds fresh asparagus
1 tablespoon safflower oil
1 small onion, minced
2½ cups Vegetable Stock (see page 10)
2 tablespoons minced fresh cilantro

1 tablespoon lemon juice
½ teaspoon salt
Pinch cayenne
1 cup rice milk

Trim the asparagus and cut it into 1-inch pieces. In a large saucepan, heat the oil, add the onion, and cook over medium heat, stirring occasionally, until the onion is tender, about 5 minutes. Add the stock and asparagus and bring to a boil. Reduce the heat, add the cilantro, lemon juice, salt, and cayenne, and simmer for 8 to 10 minutes, or until the asparagus is tender. Puree the soup in a food processor, working in batches, if necessary. Press through a fine strainer to achieve a smooth consistency. Return to the saucepan, stir in the rice milk, and reheat slowly to desired serving temperature.

4 SERVINGS

Calories 229 Kc • Protein 8 Gm • Fat 12 Gm • Percent of calories from fat 45% • Cholesterol 0 mg • Dietary Fiber 5 Gm • Sodium 492 mg • Calcium 71 mg

Winter Vegetable Chowder

Lovely flecks of green against the rich orange background make this soup as delightful to behold as it is to eat.

1 tablespoon olive oil
½ cup diced onion
½ cup minced celery
1 medium carrot, chopped
1 medium sweet potato, peeled
   and diced
1 cup peeled, diced butternut
   squash
½ cup diced red bell pepper

1 teaspoon minced garlic
3 cups Vegetable Stock (see
   page 10)
½ teaspoon minced fresh thyme,
   or ⅛ teaspoon dried
2 cups finely chopped kale
1 cup soy milk
Salt and freshly ground pepper

Heat the oil in a large saucepan over medium heat and add the onion, celery, and carrot. Cover and cook 5 minutes. Add the sweet potato, squash, bell pepper, garlic, stock, and thyme. Reduce the heat and simmer 20 minutes or until the vegetables are tender. Meanwhile, boil the kale in lightly salted water for 10 minutes, or until tender. Drain and set aside. Puree the soup mixture in a food processor until smooth, return to the saucepan. Stir in the soy milk, cooked kale, and salt and pepper to taste. Slowly heat the soup until it is hot, being careful not to boil.

6 SERVINGS

Calories 169 Kc • Protein 4 Gm • Fat 6 Gm • Percent of calories from fat 29% •
Cholesterol 0 mg • Dietary Fiber 4 Gm • Sodium 173 mg • Calcium 102 mg

Champagne and Cucumber Bisque

This light and elegant soup is a perfect beginning to a special meal. It is delicious served warm or chilled.

1 tablespoon corn oil
1 medium onion, chopped
1 large shallot, chopped
5 to 6 cups peeled, sliced
   cucumbers
¾ teaspoon salt
¼ teaspoon freshly ground white
   pepper

1 cup Vegetable Stock (see page
   10)
1 cup dry champagne
1 cup silken tofu, drained
1 cup soy milk
Minced parsley or scallion for
   garnish

Heat the oil in a large saucepan. Add the onion and shallot, and sauté 5 minutes or until they begin to soften. Add the cucumbers, salt, and pepper and cook 3 minutes over medium heat. Add the stock and champagne and simmer for 10 minutes. Puree the mixture in a food processor with the tofu and soy milk. Return to the saucepan over medium heat, and cook gently for 5 minutes. Garnish with minced parsley or scallions.

6 SERVINGS

Calories 137 Kc • Protein 4 Gm • Fat 5 Gm • Percent of calories from fat 34% • Cholesterol 0 mg • Dietary Fiber 2 Gm • Sodium 355 mg • Calcium 48 mg

Pecan Pumpkin Soup

A family tradition on Thanksgiving and so easy because you can make it a day ahead. To make your work even simpler, substitute canned pumpkin for fresh.

1 cup pecan halves
1 small pie pumpkin (about 2½ cups)
1 tablespoon safflower oil
1 medium onion, chopped
3 cups Vegetable Stock (see page 10)

½ cup silken tofu, drained
½ cup soy milk
2 tablespoons apple juice
Salt, pepper, and nutmeg

Preheat the oven to 375 degrees. Place the pecans on a baking sheet and toast them in the oven for 8 to 10 minutes, stirring 2 or 3 times, until they are lightly browned. Remove from the oven and let them cool. Peel and seed the pumpkin and cut it into 1-inch chunks. Heat the oil in a large saucepan, add the onion and pumpkin, cover, and cook 5 minutes, stirring occasionally. Add the stock, cover again, and cook 20 minutes longer or until the vegetables are tender. Meanwhile, grind the pecans in a food processor until smooth. Add the tofu, soy milk, and apple juice and blend until smooth. Transfer to a small bowl. Let the pumpkin mixture cool slightly and then puree in a food processor, working in batches. Return the soup to the saucepan and slowly stir in the pecan mixture. Season to taste with salt, pepper, and nutmeg. If serving the soup cold, refrigerate it for several hours or overnight to chill thoroughly. If serving it hot, heat slowly, but do not boil.

4 TO 6 SERVINGS

Calories 365 Kc • Protein 8 Gm • Fat 24 Gm • Percent of calories from fat 57% • Cholesterol 0 mg • Dietary Fiber 8 Gm • Sodium 160 mg • Calcium 105 mg

Creamy Cannellini Soup

1 tablespoon olive oil
1 onion, chopped
1 rib celery, chopped
1 leek, white part only, chopped
3 cups Vegetable Stock (see
  page 10)
2 cups cooked (or canned)
  cannellini beans

Pinch sage
Salt and freshly ground pepper
1 cup rice milk (or more as
  needed)
Snipped chives for garnish

Heat the oil in a large saucepan over medium heat. Add the onion, celery, and leek, cover, and cook for 5 minutes. Add the stock, beans, sage, and salt and pepper to taste. Cover and simmer gently for 15 minutes. Puree the soup mixture in a food processor until smooth, working in batches if necessary. Return the soup to the saucepan. Slowly stir in the rice milk and cook over low heat for 5 minutes, or until heated to the desired serving temperature. If the soup is too thick, add more rice milk to achieve the desired consistency. To serve, ladle into bowls and garnish with a sprinkling of chives.

4 SERVINGS

Calories 287 Kc • Protein 11 Gm • Fat 8 Gm • Percent of calories from fat 24% • Cholesterol 0 mg • Dietary Fiber 8 Gm • Sodium 218 mg • Calcium 132 mg

Pureed Pea Soup

The hint of orange complements the natural sweetness of the peas.

3 cups Vegetable Stock (see
   page 10)
4 cups shelled fresh peas, or
   high-quality frozen
Pinch sugar (or a natural
   sweetener)

½ cup orange juice
1 cup almond milk
Salt and freshly ground pepper
Snipped chives for garnish

Heat the stock to a simmer in a small saucepan. Cook the peas and sugar
in the stock, uncovered, until tender, about 10 minutes. Strain the peas,
reserving the stock. Puree the peas in a food processor with the orange
juice until well blended. Return the peas to the stock. Add the almond
milk and salt and pepper to taste. Serve cold or reheat and serve warm,
garnished with chives.

4 SERVINGS

Calories 265 Kc • Protein 12 Gm • Fat 7 Gm • Percent of calories from fat 25% •
Cholesterol 0 mg • Dietary Fiber 12 Gm • Sodium 321 mg • Calcium 96 mg

Chilled Ginger Carrot Soup

1 tablespoon corn oil
1 medium onion, minced
4 medium carrots, shredded
1 Granny Smith apple, peeled,
 cored, and chopped
1 teaspoon minced fresh ginger

3 cups Vegetable Stock (see
 page 10)
¼ teaspoon salt
Pinch cayenne
Pinch turmeric
1 cup rice milk

Heat the oil in a large saucepan over medium heat. Add the onion, cover, and cook 5 minutes. Remove the cover and stir in the carrots, apple, and ginger. Cook another 5 minutes. Stir in the stock, salt, cayenne, and turmeric. Cover and bring to a boil over high heat. Reduce the heat to low and simmer until the vegetables are soft, about 30 minutes. Remove from the heat.

Puree the mixture in a food processor until smooth, working in batches. Transfer the soup to a container, stir in the rice milk, and blend well. Refrigerate the soup several hours to chill thoroughly. Taste and adjust the seasonings before serving.

4 SERVINGS

Calories 243 Kc • Protein 3 Gm • Fat 11 Gm • Percent of calories from fat 39% • Cholesterol 0 mg • Dietary Fiber 6 Gm • Sodium 372 mg • Calcium 70 mg

Chilled Pea Soup with Mint

2 cups frozen peas
2 cups Vegetable Stock (see page 10)
2 lettuce leaves, torn into quarters
3 scallions, chopped
½ cup firm silken tofu, drained

½ cup rice milk
1 tablespoon minced fresh mint, or 1 teaspoon dried
½ teaspoon salt
⅛ teaspoon freshly ground white pepper
Mint sprigs for garnish

Combine the peas, stock, lettuce, and scallions in a medium saucepan over medium heat. Cover and simmer about 5 minutes. Cool to room temperature. Place the mixture in a food processor with the tofu and rice milk, and process until smooth. Transfer to a container and add the minced mint, salt, and pepper. Refrigerate, covered, until well chilled. Serve garnished with sprigs of fresh mint.

4 SERVINGS

Calories 139 Kc • Protein 6 Gm • Fat 4 Gm • Percent of calories from fat 23% • Cholesterol 0 mg • Dietary Fiber 5 Gm • Sodium 476 mg • Calcium 56 mg

Chilled Vegetable Soup with Herbs

1 tablespoon corn oil
1 small onion, chopped
1 leek, white part only, chopped
1 small potato, peeled and
   chopped
½ cup chopped celery
2 tablespoons fresh lemon juice
1 cup shelled fresh green peas
1 cup chopped fresh spinach
1 small cucumber, peeled,
   seeded, and chopped

3 cups Vegetable Stock (see
   page 10)
2 cups soy milk
½ teaspoon salt
⅛ teaspoon freshly ground
   pepper
1 tablespoon minced fresh
   parsley, or 1 teaspoon dried
1 teaspoon minced fresh basil,
   or ¼ teaspoon dried

Heat the oil in a large saucepan over low heat. Add the onion, leek, potato, celery, and lemon juice and cook 8 to 10 minutes, or until the vegetables are tender, stirring occasionally. Add the peas, spinach, cucumber, and stock. Increase the heat and bring to boil. Reduce the heat and simmer until all the vegetables are tender, about 10 minutes.

In a food processor, puree the mixture, in batches if necessary, and strain through a sieve into large bowl. Blend in the soy milk, salt, and pepper. Refrigerate for several hours or overnight. Garnish with the parsley and basil just before serving.

6 TO 8 SERVINGS

Calories 183 Kc • Protein 5 Gm • Fat 7 Gm • Percent of calories from fat 34% •
Cholesterol 0 mg • Dietary Fiber 4 Gm • Sodium 320 mg • Calcium 74 mg

Chilled Spinach-Watercress Soup

The slightly peppery flavor of fresh watercress is showcased in this delicate, lightly seasoned soup.

1 tablespoon corn oil
1 cup minced celery
1 cup minced scallions
3 cups Vegetable Stock (see page 10)
3 cups chopped fresh spinach

2 bunches watercress, tough stems removed
1 cup soy milk
3/4 teaspoon salt
1/2 teaspoon freshly ground black pepper

Heat the oil in a large saucepan over low heat. Add the celery, cover, and cook until softened, about 5 minutes. Add the scallions and cook 2 minutes longer. Stir in the stock and simmer about 10 minutes. Add the spinach and cook 5 more minutes. Remove from the heat. Puree the mixture in a food processor, working in batches. Transfer the pureed soup to a large container. Place the watercress in the food processor and finely mince. Add the soy milk, salt, and pepper and combine with 1/2 cup of the pureed soup. Stir the watercress mixture into the soup. Refrigerate for several hours before serving. When ready to serve, taste and adjust the seasonings.

4 SERVINGS

Calories 215 Kc • Protein 7 Gm • Fat 12 Gm • Percent of calories from fat 48% • Cholesterol 0 mg • Dietary Fiber 5 Gm • Sodium 742 mg • Calcium 172 mg

Chilled Zucchini Soup

A perfect soup for the height of summer when zucchini and basil are at their peak and a chilled soup is just right.

1 tablespoon olive oil
1 large shallot, minced
5 cups chopped zucchini
¼ cup minced scallion
1½ cups Vegetable Stock (see page 10)

1 tablespoon minced fresh basil, or 1 teaspoon dried
1½ cups soy milk
1 teaspoon lemon juice
Salt and freshly ground pepper
Fresh basil leaves for garnish

Heat the oil in a large saucepan over medium heat, add the shallot, zucchini, and scallion and cook, covered, for 5 minutes, stirring occasionally. Remove the cover, add the stock and bring to a boil. Simmer the mixture for 10 minutes, or until the zucchini is very tender. In a food processor, puree the zucchini mixture in batches with the minced basil, soy milk, lemon juice, and salt and pepper to taste. Transfer the soup to a container and refrigerate, covered, for several hours or overnight. To serve, ladle the soup into bowls and garnish with fresh basil leaves.

4 SERVINGS

Calories 156 Kc • Protein 6 Gm • Fat 7 Gm • Percent of calories from fat 40% • Cholesterol 0 mg • Dietary Fiber 3 Gm • Sodium 139 mg • Calcium 70 mg

Summer Medley Vichyssoise

1 tablespoon olive oil
½ cup chopped onion
1 carrot, chopped
1 small white potato, peeled and chopped
2 scallions, chopped
3 cups Vegetable Stock (see page 10)
2 small zucchini, thinly sliced

2 small summer yellow squash, thinly sliced
1 tablespoon lemon juice
¼ cup chopped fresh basil, or 1 tablespoon dried
1 cup soy milk
½ teaspoon salt
⅛ teaspoon cayenne
Fresh basil leaves for garnish

Heat the oil in a large saucepan over medium heat. Add the onion and carrot and cook, covered, for 5 minutes, or until the vegetables begin to soften. Add the potato, scallions, and half the stock, cover, and simmer 10 minutes. Add the remaining stock, zucchini, summer squash, and lemon juice. Cover and simmer 10 minutes, or until the vegetables are tender. In a food processor, puree the soup with the chopped basil in several batches, and return to the saucepan. Slowly stir in the soy milk. Add the salt and cayenne and simmer 5 minutes, being careful not to boil. Transfer to a container and refrigerate, covered, for several hours or overnight. To serve, ladle into bowls and garnish with fresh basil leaves.

4 TO 6 SERVINGS

Calories 178 Kc • Protein 5 Gm • Fat 7 Gm • Percent of calories from fat 33% • Cholesterol 0 mg • Dietary Fiber 4 Gm • Sodium 410 mg • Calcium 67 mg

Chilled Asparagus Bisque

A simple preparation makes a simply elegant soup.

2 pounds fresh asparagus,
 trimmed
1 tablespoon corn oil
1 cup chopped scallion
3½ cups Vegetable Stock (see
 page 10)

1 cup rice milk
Salt and freshly ground white
 pepper

Cut the asparagus into 1-inch pieces and set aside. Heat the oil in a large saucepan over medium heat. Add the scallion and cook, covered, stirring occasionally, for about 3 minutes or until the scallion begins to soften. Add the stock and asparagus. Reduce the heat to medium, cover, and cook until the asparagus is tender, about 5 minutes. Remove from the heat. With a slotted spoon, remove asparagus tips and reserve for garnish.

In a food processor, puree the asparagus mixture, in batches if necessary, and transfer to a container. Refrigerate, covered, for several hours or overnight. Before serving, stir in the rice milk and season to taste with salt and white pepper. Ladle into soup bowls and garnish each serving with the reserved asparagus tips.

4 TO 6 SERVINGS

Calories 181 Kc • Protein 7 Gm • Fat 7 Gm • Percent of calories from fat 36% • Cholesterol 0 mg • Dietary Fiber 5 Gm • Sodium 212 mg • Calcium 80 mg

Chilled Cucumber Soup

1 clove garlic
¾ teaspoon salt
2 cucumbers, peeled, seeded, and chopped
1 cup silken tofu, drained
1 tablespoon lemon juice
1 tablespoon minced fresh dill, or ½ teaspoon dried

1 tablespoon minced fresh parsley, or ½ teaspoon dried
1 cup almond milk
8 thin cucumber slices for garnish
4 dill sprigs for garnish

In a food processor, combine the garlic and salt until garlic is minced. Add the cucumbers, tofu, lemon juice, minced dill, and parsley and process until well combined. Slowly pour in the almond milk until the desired consistency is reached. Transfer the mixture to a container and refrigerate, covered, for several hours or overnight. To serve, ladle the soup into bowls and garnish with the cucumber slices and sprigs of fresh dill.

4 SERVINGS

Calories 91 Kc • Protein 5 Gm • Fat 5 Gm • Percent of calories from fat 50% • Cholesterol 0 mg • Dietary Fiber 2 Gm • Sodium 445 mg • Calcium 58 mg

Chilled Broccoli Soup

1 large head broccoli
2 tablespoons olive oil
1 medium onion, chopped
1 clove garlic, minced
2 tablespoons minced fresh
   tarragon, or 1 teaspoon dried
¾ teaspoon salt

½ teaspoon freshly ground white
   pepper
2 cups Vegetable Stock (see
   page 10)
1 cup rice milk
1 cup silken tofu, drained
1 tablespoon lemon juice

Peel the tough outer layer from the broccoli stalks. Chop the broccoli into ½-inch pieces, reserving 6 small florets for garnish. Lightly steam the reserved florets until just tender. Run under cold water to stop the cooking process and set aside.

Heat the oil in a large saucepan over medium heat. Add the onion, cover, and cook, stirring occasionally, until softened, about 5 minutes. Add the broccoli, garlic, tarragon, ½ teaspoon of the salt, and the pepper and cook 1 minute. Stir in the stock. Reduce the heat and simmer until the broccoli is tender, 15 to 20 minutes. Let it cool. Puree the soup in a food processor, working in batches, until smooth. Strain into a large bowl. In a small bowl, combine the rice milk, tofu, lemon juice, and the remaining ¼ teaspoon of salt and whisk until well blended. Add ⅓ cup of the soup and blend well. Slowly pour the rice milk mixture into the soup and stir until well combined. Cover and refrigerate several hours or overnight. To serve, ladle into bowls and garnish with the reserved broccoli florets.

6 SERVINGS

Calories 144 Kc • Protein 4 Gm • Fat 8 Gm • Percent of calories from fat 46% • Cholesterol 0 mg • Dietary Fiber 3 Gm • Sodium 494 mg • Calcium 61 mg

Puree of Gazpacho Soup with Salsa Cream

A delightfully unexpected way to serve this spicy favorite. Choose a hot or mild salsa, depending on your preference.

½ cup silken tofu, drained
¾ cup bottled salsa
¼ cup rice milk
1 teaspoon lemon juice
¾ teaspoon salt
1 tablespoon olive oil
1 cup chopped onion
1 cup chopped bell pepper

½ cup chopped carrot
1 tablespoon minced garlic
¼ teaspoon cayenne
3 cups Vegetable Stock (see page 10)
4 pounds tomatoes, peeled, seeded, and chopped
¼ cup minced scallion

To make the salsa cream, in a small bowl combine the tofu, salsa, rice milk, lemon juice, and ¼ teaspoon of the salt until well blended. Set aside. Heat the oil in a large saucepan over medium heat. Add the onion, bell pepper, carrot, and garlic. Cover and cook until the vegetables soften, stirring occasionally, about 5 minutes. Remove the cover, add the remaining ½ teaspoon salt, cayenne, and stock and simmer 30 minutes. Increase the heat to high. Add the tomatoes and cook until softened about 10 minutes. Puree the soup in a food processor. Transfer to a large bowl, cover, and refrigerate. At serving time, taste and adjust the seasonings. Ladle into bowls, and swirl about 2 tablespoons of the salsa cream into each bowl. Garnish with the minced scallion.

6 SERVINGS

Calories 207 Kc • Protein 6 Gm • Fat 9 Gm • Percent of calories from fat 35% • Cholesterol 0 mg • Dietary Fiber 6 Gm • Sodium 868 mg • Calcium 67 mg

Chilled Cream of Watercress Soup

1 tablespoon corn oil
1 medium onion, minced
1 rib celery, minced
1 medium potato, peeled and
    chopped
4 cups Vegetable Stock
    (see page 10)

3 cups watercress leaves and
    tender stems, packed
2 cups soy milk
½ teaspoon salt
¼ teaspoon freshly ground
    pepper

Heat the oil in large saucepan over medium heat, add the onion and celery, cover, and cook 5 minutes. Add the potato and stock, cover, and simmer about 15 minutes, or until the vegetables are tender. Add the watercress and cook for 2 minutes. Let the mixture cool. Puree the mixture in a food processor, working in batches. Transfer the soup to a container, stir in the soy milk, and season with the salt and pepper. Refrigerate until ready to serve. Adjust the seasonings before serving.

6 SERVINGS

Calories 209 Kc • Protein 6 Gm • Fat 7 Gm • Percent of calories from fat 30% • Cholesterol 0 mg • Dietary Fiber 4 Gm • Sodium 409 mg • Calcium 84 mg

Puree of Red Pepper Soup

3 red bell peppers
1 tablespoon olive oil
1 medium onion, finely chopped
2 cups tomato puree
½ cup dry red wine
½ teaspoon salt

⅛ teaspoon freshly ground pepper
1 cup soy milk
1 tablespoon minced parsley for garnish

Preheat the broiler. Arrange the peppers on a broiler pan and broil, turning the peppers until blackened on all sides. Place the peppers in paper bag for 10 minutes. Peel the peppers with your fingers, discarding the membranes and seeds. Puree the peppers and reserve.

Heat the oil in a large saucepan over medium heat. Add the onion and cook about 5 minutes, or until softened. Add the pepper puree, tomato puree, wine, salt, and pepper. Bring to a boil. Reduce the heat and simmer 15 minutes, stirring occasionally. Remove from the heat and let the mixture come to room temperature. Stir in the soy milk. Cover and refrigerate several hours or overnight. Garnish with the minced parsley.

4 SERVINGS

Calories 189 Kc • Protein 5 Gm • Fat 8 Gm • Percent of calories from fat 38% • Cholesterol 0 mg • Dietary Fiber 4 Gm • Sodium 354 mg • Calcium 32 mg

Chilled Leek and Pear Soup

1 tablespoon corn oil
3 leeks, white part only, chopped
2 ripe pears, peeled, cored, and
   sliced
3 cups Vegetable Stock (see
   page 10)
1 tablespoon balsamic vinegar
1 teaspoon cinnamon
1 tablespoon minced fresh
   parsley, or 1 teaspoon dried

1 tablespoon minced fresh mint,
   or 1 teaspoon dried
1 cup almond milk
1 teaspoon sugar (or a natural
   sweetener)
Salt and freshly ground pepper
Fresh mint sprigs for garnish

Heat the oil in a large saucepan over low heat. Add the leeks, cover, and cook until tender, about 5 minutes. Remove the cover, add the pears, stock, vinegar, and cinnamon, increase the heat to high and bring to a boil. Reduce the heat to low, cover, and simmer until the pears are very soft, about 10 minutes. Let the mixture cool. Puree the mixture in a food processor with the parsley, minced mint, almond milk, and sugar until smooth. Transfer to a container, season with salt and pepper to taste, and refrigerate for several hours until chilled. Garnish with sprigs of fresh mint and serve.

4 TO 6 SERVINGS

Calories 238 Kc • Protein 4 Gm • Fat 11 Gm • Percent of calories from fat 41% • Cholesterol 0 mg • Dietary Fiber 5 Gm • Sodium 161 mg • Calcium 102 mg

Chilled Melon Soup

This celebration of summer melons makes a refreshing first course at a Sunday brunch.

½ cup apple juice
½ cup almond milk
1 cup firm silken tofu, drained
1½ cups freshly squeezed orange juice
2 cups chopped honeydew
2 cups chopped cantaloupe

¼ cup fresh lime juice
⅓ cup honey (or a natural sweetener)
2 tablespoons minced fresh mint, or 1 teaspoon dried, crumbled
Fresh mint sprigs for garnish

In a food processor, combine the apple juice, almond milk, and tofu until well blended. Transfer to a small bowl and set aside. In the food processor, puree the orange juice, honeydew, cantaloupe, and lime juice. Add the honey and minced mint. Pour into a serving bowl and carefully stir in the reserved mixture. Cover and refrigerate several hours before serving. Garnish with mint sprigs.

4 TO 6 SERVINGS

Calories 186 Kc • Protein 6 Gm • Fat 2 Gm • Percent of calories from fat 12% • Cholesterol 0 mg • Dietary Fiber 1 Gm • Sodium 45 mg • Calcium 45 mg

Chilled Plum Soup

I like to serve this soup for dessert after a fiery dinner of Thai or Szechwan food, but it also makes a delightful starter.

1 30-ounce can purple plums
1 cup apple juice
2 tablespoons sugar (or a natural sweetener)
½ teaspoon ground cinnamon
2 tablespoons lemon juice
Pinch of salt
⅛ teaspoon freshly ground white pepper

1 tablespoon cornstarch combined with 1 tablespoon water
½ cup almond milk
1 cup firm silken tofu, drained
⅓ cup black raspberry liqueur
Mint leaves for garnish

Drain the plums and reserve the syrup. Pit the plums, chop, and combine with the reserved syrup, apple juice, sugar, cinnamon, lemon juice, salt, and pepper in a large saucepan and bring to boil over medium heat. Reduce the heat to low and simmer 5 minutes. Whisk in the cornstarch mixture, stirring until thickened, about 2 minutes. Remove from the heat and set aside. In a small bowl, combine the almond milk, tofu, and liqueur, with ½ cup of the soup and whisk together until thoroughly blended. In a food processor, puree the plum soup until smooth. Combine the soup and tofu mixture in a container, blend well, cover, and refrigerate several hours or overnight. To serve, ladle soup into bowls and garnish with fresh mint leaves.

6 SERVINGS

Calories 177 Kc • Protein 4 Gm • Fat 2 Gm • Percent of calories from fat 10% • Cholesterol 0 mg • Dietary Fiber 2 Gm • Sodium 32 mg • Calcium 38 mg

Chilled Ginger Peach Soup

Canned peaches also make a flavorful soup when fresh peaches are not in season.

1 pound fresh peaches, peeled, pitted, and sliced, or 2 cups canned
1 cup silken tofu, drained
1 cup fresh orange juice
½ cup almond milk
1 tablespoon mirin (or dry white wine)

1 tablespoon lemon juice
½ teaspoon powdered ginger
½ teaspoon sugar (or a natural sweetener)
Fresh mint leaves for garnish

Puree the peaches in a food processor until smooth. Add all of the remaining ingredients and blend well, working in batches if necessary. Transfer to a glass or plastic container and refrigerate several hours or overnight until chilled. Serve chilled garnished with fresh mint leaves.

4 SERVINGS

Calories 114 Kc • Protein 4 Gm • Fat 3 Gm • Percent of calories from fat 22% • Cholesterol 0 mg • Dietary Fiber 2 Gm • Sodium 7 mg • Calcium 32 mg

2
Salads and Salad Dressings

This chapter is replete with amazingly rich adaptations of old family favorites such as Dijon Potato Salad and Caraway Coleslaw, as well as some intriguing new creations such as Curried Tempeh Salad with Papaya and Grapes. Each recipe uses one or more dairy alternatives to produce flavorful results.

Additionally, to insure that you will never be without a well-dressed salad, this chapter includes numerous velvety dressings such as Creamy Raspberry Vinaigrette and Sesame-Chive Dressing that are guaranteed to lure you away from fatty dairy-based dressings.

Dijon Potato Salad

1 pound small new potatoes,
  scrubbed
2 carrots, finely grated
½ cup minced scallion
3 tablespoons minced fresh
  parsley, or 1 tablespoon dried
3 tablespoons minced fresh
  dill, or 1 tablespoon dried
¼ cup silken tofu, drained

¼ cup soy milk
2 tablespoons lemon juice
1 tablespoon olive oil
2 tablespoons Dijon mustard
1 teaspoon sugar (or a natural
  sweetener)
Salt and freshly ground white
  pepper

Heat a large saucepan of salted water over high heat to boiling; add the potatoes. Reduce the heat to maintain a steady simmer, cook the potatoes, covered, until tender, about 10 minutes. Drain in a colander and rinse under cold running water. When cool, cut the potatoes into $1/4$-inch slices and place in a large bowl. Add the carrots to the potatoes in the bowl. Combine the scallion, parsley, dill, tofu, soy milk, lemon juice, olive oil, mustard, and sugar in a food processor; process until well blended, and pour the dressing over the potatoes and carrots. Toss gently until the ingredients are thoroughly coated with the dressing; season with salt and pepper to taste. Refrigerate the salad, covered, several hours or overnight. Serve chilled, or bring to room temperature before serving.

6 SERVINGS

Calories 110 Kc • Protein 3 Gm • Fat 3 Gm • Percent of calories from fat 26% • Cholesterol 0 mg • Dietary Fiber 2 Gm • Sodium 47 mg • Calcium 35 mg

Potato Salad Niçoise

This flavorful potato salad can be prepared several hours ahead and refrigerated before serving. Serve chilled or at room temperature.

2 pounds boiling potatoes
2 tablespoons dry white wine
1 tablespoon olive oil
2 tablespoons minced scallion
1 cup Tofu Mayonnaise (see page 258)

1 tablespoon Dijon mustard
2 tablespoons Niçoise olives, pitted
2 tablespoons chopped, oil-packed, sun-dried tomatoes
Salt and freshly ground pepper

Place the potatoes in a large saucepan with enough salted cold water to cover, and bring to a boil. Reduce the heat, cover, and simmer until the potatoes are tender, about 25 minutes. In a small bowl combine the wine, oil, scallion, Tofu Mayonnaise, mustard, olives, tomatoes, and salt and pepper to taste. Whisk until blended and set aside. Drain the potatoes, peel, and cut into medium dice. Transfer to a medium bowl, let them cool slightly, and pour the dressing mixture over the potatoes. Toss gently until thoroughly blended. Season with more salt and freshly ground pepper to taste.

4 TO 6 SERVINGS

Calories 222 Kc • Protein 7 Gm • Fat 8 Gm • Percent of calories from fat 32% • Cholesterol 0 mg • Dietary Fiber 3 Gm • Sodium 312 mg • Calcium 42 mg

Minted New Potato Salad

4 pounds new potatoes,
  quartered
1 cup packed fresh mint leaves
4 tablespoons white wine
  vinegar
3 tablespoons Dijon mustard
1 teaspoon salt

¼ teaspoon freshly ground
  pepper
1¼ cups silken tofu, drained
2 cups frozen peas, thawed and
  drained
Salt and freshly ground pepper
Mint sprigs for garnish

Place the potatoes in a large saucepan. Add cold salted water to cover. Bring to a boil and simmer until the potatoes are just tender, about 10 minutes. Combine the mint leaves, vinegar, mustard, salt, and pepper in a food processor. Blend 1 minute. Add the tofu and blend well. Adjust the seasonings. Drain and rinse the potatoes under cold water until cool. Drain well. Transfer to a large bowl, add the peas and enough dressing to coat. Season with salt and pepper to taste. Garnish with mint sprigs and serve.

8 SERVINGS

Calories 231 Kc • Protein 10 Gm • Fat 2 Gm • Percent of calories from fat 9% • Cholesterol 0 mg • Dietary Fiber 6 Gm • Sodium 368 mg • Calcium 66 mg

Mustard-Tarragon New Potato Salad

This flavorful salad may be served chilled or at room temperature. You can eliminate the horseradish and add more mustard if you prefer a more pronounced mustard flavor.

1 pound new potatoes
½ cup silken tofu, drained
1 tablespoon Dijon mustard
1 teaspoon prepared horseradish
2 tablespoons lemon juice

2 tablespoons minced fresh
   tarragon, or 2 teaspoons dried
1 tablespoon minced fresh
   parsley, or 1 teaspoon dried
Salt and freshly ground pepper

Bring a large pot of salted water to a rapid boil over high heat. Add the potatoes, reduce the heat to medium and simmer until tender but still firm, 10 to 12 minutes. Drain well and let the potatoes cool. Do not peel. Cut the potatoes into thin slices. In large bowl, combine the tofu, mustard, horseradish, lemon juice, tarragon, parsley, and salt and pepper to taste, and blend well. Add the potato slices and toss to coat with the dressing. Cover and refrigerate before serving.

4 SERVINGS

Calories 108 Kc • Protein 5 Gm • Fat 2 Gm • Percent of calories from fat 13% • Cholesterol 0 mg • Dietary Fiber 2 Gm • Sodium 31 mg • Calcium 30 mg

Sweet Potato Salad

Volunteer to bring potato salad to your next gathering. With Sweet Potato Salad, friends who expect the "same old thing" will be pleasantly surprised.

6 medium-size sweet potatoes
2 cups frozen peas, thawed and
  blanched
1 cup Tofu Mayonnaise (see page
  258)
4 minced scallions

2 tablespoons chopped fresh
  parsley, or 2 teaspoons dried
2 tablespoons sweet pickle relish
1 teaspoon lemon juice
Salt and freshly ground pepper

Cover the potatoes with cold water, bring to a boil, and cook until tender, about 20 minutes. Let them cool, then peel and dice. Combine the potatoes and peas in a large bowl. In a separate bowl, combine all of the remaining ingredients and mix well. Add to the potato mixture and toss gently. Serve at room temperature or chilled.

8 SERVINGS

Calories 155 Kc • Protein 5 Gm • Fat 3 Gm • Percent of calories from fat 15% • Cholesterol 0 mg • Dietary Fiber 5 Gm • Sodium 227 mg • Calcium 46 mg

Provençal Potato Salad

1 medium red bell pepper
1 medium yellow bell pepper
2 pounds boiling potatoes
¼ cup Niçoise olives, pitted
2 tablespoons chopped oil-
   packed, sun-dried tomatoes
1 cup Tofu Mayonnaise (see page
   258)

2 tablespoons snipped fresh
   chives, or 2 teaspoons dried
1 tablespoon Dijon mustard
1 tablespoon capers
Salt and freshly ground pepper

Preheat the broiler. Place the peppers about 2 inches from the heat source and broil until charred and blistered, turning often, about 10 minutes. Close the peppers inside a paper or plastic bag for about 10 minutes. Peel with your fingers, halve, and seed the peppers. Slice the peppers into 1-inch dice and reserve.

Place the potatoes in a large saucepan with salted cold water to cover and bring to a boil. Reduce the heat, cover, and simmer until the potatoes are tender, about 25 minutes. Drain, cool, peel, and cut into medium dice. Transfer to a medium bowl, add the reserved peppers, olives, and tomatoes. Toss gently until combined. In a small bowl blend together the Tofu Mayonnaise, chives, mustard, and capers. Add the dressing to the potato mixture and toss gently until well combined. Season with salt and pepper to taste.

4 TO 6 SERVINGS

Calories 210 Kc • Protein 7 Gm • Fat 6 Gm • Percent of calories from fat 25% • Cholesterol 0 mg • Dietary Fiber 4 Gm • Sodium 485 mg • Calcium 55 mg

Radish Slaw

The peppery bite of the radish is tempered by the creamy dressing in this unusual slaw.

2 cups finely chopped white cabbage
1½ cups grated red radishes (12 to 15)
1 cup grated daikon (Japanese radish) (about 5 ounces)
½ cup grated carrot
1 small onion, minced

½ cup silken tofu, drained
¼ cup soy milk
1 tablespoon cider vinegar
1 teaspoon sugar (or a natural sweetener)
½ teaspoon celery seed
Salt and freshly ground pepper

Combine the cabbage, radishes, daikon, carrot, and onion in a medium bowl. In a small bowl, combine the tofu, soy milk, vinegar, sugar, celery seed, and salt and pepper to taste. Stir until well blended. Add the dressing to the slaw and toss thoroughly to coat. Taste and adjust the seasonings. Refrigerate, covered, until ready to serve.

4 TO 6 SERVINGS

Calories 57 Kc • Protein 2 Gm • Fat 1 Gm • Percent of calories from fat 20% • Cholesterol 0 mg • Dietary Fiber 2 Gm • Sodium 30 mg • Calcium 46 mg

Confetti Coleslaw

1 cup silken tofu, drained
½ cup soy milk
¼ cup sugar (or a natural
    sweetener)
2 tablespoons lemon juice
1 tablespoon Dijon mustard
½ teaspoon dried basil
⅛ teaspoon Tabasco sauce
3 cups shredded white cabbage
1 cup shredded red cabbage

1 unpeeled apple, chopped, and
    tossed with 1 teaspoon lemon
    juice
1 carrot, grated
¼ cup minced scallion
2 tablespoons minced fresh
    parsley, or 2 teaspoons dried
Salt and freshly ground pepper
    to taste

Combine the tofu, soy milk, sugar, lemon juice, mustard, basil, and Tabasco in a small bowl and reserve. Meanwhile, in a large bowl combine the white cabbage, red cabbage, apple, carrot, scallion, and parsley and mix well. Add the dressing, and stir to combine well. Season with salt and pepper to taste. Cover and refrigerate for several hours. Serve chilled.

6 TO 8 SERVINGS

Calories 88 Kc • Protein 3 Gm • Fat 2 Gm • Percent of calories from fat 17% • Cholesterol 0 mg • Dietary Fiber 1 Gm • Sodium 34 mg • Calcium 47 mg

Caraway Coleslaw

Cabbage and caraway are a natural combination in this crisp coleslaw.

1½ pounds cabbage, cored and
 shredded
1 carrot, grated
1 tablespoon caraway seed
1 cup silken tofu, drained
2 tablespoons lemon juice

1 tablespoon sugar (or a natural
 sweetener)
¾ teaspoon salt
¼ teaspoon freshly ground
 pepper

In a large bowl, combine the cabbage, carrot, and caraway seed. In a small bowl combine the tofu, lemon juice, sugar, salt, and pepper, and mix until well blended. Add the sauce to the slaw and toss until thoroughly combined. Serve at once or refrigerate, covered, until serving time.

8 SERVINGS

Calories 54 Kc • Protein 4 Gm • Fat 1 Gm • Percent of calories from fat 15% • Cholesterol 0 mg • Dietary Fiber 2 Gm • Sodium 257 mg • Calcium 60 mg

Vegetable Slaw

2 cups shredded white cabbage
1 cup shredded red cabbage
1 carrot, grated
¼ pound mushrooms, sliced thin (1 cup)
½ green bell pepper, minced
2 scallions, minced
1 sweet gherkin, chopped
¾ cup Tofu Mayonnaise (see page 258)

1 tablespoon lemon juice
1 teaspoon minced fresh dill, or ¼ teaspoon dried
½ teaspoon minced fresh chervil, or pinch dried
½ teaspoon salt
¼ teaspoon pepper

Place the cabbages, carrot, mushrooms, bell pepper, scallions, and gherkin in a large bowl and toss gently to combine. In a small bowl, combine the Tofu Mayonnaise with the lemon juice, dill, chervil, salt, and pepper, mixing until well blended. Pour the dressing over the slaw, and toss gently to coat. Cover and refrigerate for at least an hour before serving to let the flavors blend.

4 TO 6 SERVINGS

Calories 82 Kc • Protein 3 Gm • Fat 3 Gm • Percent of calories from fat 33% • Cholesterol 0 mg • Dietary Fiber 2 Gm • Sodium 486 mg • Calcium 66 mg

Fruit and Vegetable Slaw

This deliciously different slaw, studded with sweet bites of fruit, provides a welcome change from the usual coleslaw.

2 cups shredded white cabbage
1 carrot, grated
2 scallions, minced
1 Red Delicious apple, unpeeled and diced
½ cup pineapple chunks (fresh or canned)

¾ cup silken tofu, drained
¼ cup almond milk
¼ cup pineapple juice
2 tablespoons lemon juice
½ teaspoon salt
⅛ teaspoon freshly ground pepper

In a large bowl combine the cabbage, carrot, scallions, apple, and pineapple, and set aside. In a small bowl combine the tofu, almond milk, pineapple juice, lemon juice, salt, and pepper, mixing until well combined. Pour the dressing over the slaw and toss gently to coat. Taste and adjust the seasonings. Cover and refrigerate at least 1 hour before serving.

4 TO 6 SERVINGS

Calories 75 Kc • Protein 3 Gm • Fat 2 Gm • Percent of calories from fat 24% • Cholesterol 0 mg • Dietary Fiber 2 Gm • Sodium 246 mg • Calcium 40 mg

Salad of Torn Greens
with Creamy Mustard Vinaigrette

The creamy tanginess of the dressing is the perfect enhancement to the fresh salad greens.

2 scallions, minced
2 tablespoons minced parsley
¼ cup silken tofu, drained
¼ cup soy milk
2 tablespoons Dijon mustard
1 tablespoon cider vinegar
Salt and freshly ground pepper

1 small head radicchio, torn into bite-size pieces
½ small head Boston lettuce, torn into bite-size pieces
½ small head red or green leaf lettuce, torn into bite-size pieces

In a food processor, combine the scallions, parsley, tofu, soy milk, mustard, vinegar, and salt and pepper to taste. Carefully wash and dry the lettuces, and place in a serving bowl. Just before serving, drizzle the dressing over the lettuces and toss the salad.

4 SERVINGS

Calories 37 Kc • Protein 2 Gm • Fat 1 Gm • Percent of calories from fat 34% • Cholesterol 0 mg • Dietary Fiber 1 Gm • Sodium 57 mg • Calcium 44 mg

Summer Vegetable Salad
with Creamy Dill Sauce

2 cups broccoli florets
2 cups cauliflower florets
1 cup cherry tomatoes, halved
1 large carrot, peeled and
  grated
3 minced scallions
1 cucumber, sliced thin

1 cup silken tofu, drained
1 cup soy milk
¼ cup Dijon mustard
¼ cup chopped fresh dill, or
  1 tablespoon dried
Salt and freshly ground pepper

Bring a large pot of salted water to a boil. Add the broccoli and cauli-flower and cook 1 to 2 minutes. Drain in a colander and rinse under cold running water to stop the cooking. Drain well. Transfer the broccoli and cauliflower to a large bowl, add the tomatoes, carrot, scallions, and cucumber, cover and refrigerate. In a small bowl, combine the tofu, soy milk, mustard, and dill until well blended. Pour the sauce over the vegetables, and toss gently to combine. Season with salt and pepper to taste.

6 TO 8 SERVINGS

Calories 77 Kc • Protein 5 Gm • Fat 3 Gm • Percent of calories from fat 29% • Cholesterol 0.15 mg • Dietary Fiber 2 Gm • Sodium 77 mg • Calcium 55 mg

Brown Rice and Vegetable Salad

This hearty salad is a complete meal in itself.

4 cups cooked brown rice
12 cherry tomatoes, halved
1 small zucchini, cut into ¼-inch
    rounds
1 small yellow (summer) squash,
    cut into ¼-inch rounds
1 red bell pepper, cored, seeded,
    and cut into ¼-inch dice
1 carrot, grated
1 rib celery, chopped
1 cup frozen peas, thawed

¼ cup minced scallion
1 cup silken tofu, drained
¼ cup fresh lemon juice
2 tablespoons olive oil
¾ teaspoon salt
1 tablespoon minced fresh
    parsley, or 1 teaspoon dried
2 teaspoons minced fresh basil,
    or pinch dried
¼ teaspoon freshly ground
    pepper

In a large bowl, combine the rice, tomatoes, zucchini, squash, bell pepper, carrot, celery, peas, and scallion and set aside. In a small bowl, combine the tofu, lemon juice, oil, salt, parsley, basil, and pepper and mix thoroughly. Pour the dressing over the rice and vegetables, toss to coat. Chill 1 to 2 hours or until ready to serve.

4 TO 6 SERVINGS

Calories 303 Kc • Protein 9 Gm • Fat 8 Gm • Percent of calories from fat 25% • Cholesterol 0 mg • Dietary Fiber 7 Gm • Sodium 378 mg • Calcium 63 mg

Pasta Salad with Creamy Tarragon Dressing

½ pound small pasta shells
1 teaspoon toasted sesame oil
½ pound asparagus, stems peeled
3 medium tomatoes, peeled, seeded, and chopped
½ cup silken tofu, drained
2 tablespoons tahini (sesame paste)
2 tablespoons soy milk
2 tablespoons fresh lemon juice

1 tablespoon snipped fresh chives, or 1 teaspoon dried
1 tablespoon Dijon mustard
1 tablespoon low-sodium tamari
1 teaspoon grated lemon zest
1 tablespoon minced fresh tarragon, or large pinch dried, crumbled
Watercress sprigs for garnish
Cherry tomatoes for garnish

Bring a large pot of salted water to a boil. Add the pasta shells, stir, and cook, uncovered, until just tender but firm, about 8 minutes. Drain, run under cold water, and drain well. Place the pasta in a large bowl and toss with the sesame oil. Meanwhile, bring a pot of salted water to a boil. Add the asparagus and cook until crisp-tender, about 2 minutes. Drain and run under cold water to stop the cooking process. Drain well. Cut the asparagus diagonally into 1-inch pieces. Add the asparagus to the pasta. Add the tomatoes, and set aside. In a food processor, combine the tofu, tahini, soy milk, lemon juice, chives, mustard, tamari, lemon zest, and tarragon until creamy and well blended. Pour the dressing over the pasta salad and toss gently. Cover the salad and refrigerate until it is chilled, 1 to 2 hours. To serve, divide the pasta salad among individual plates. Garnish with watercress and cherry tomatoes.

4 TO 6 SERVINGS

Calories 267 Kc • Protein 11 Gm • Fat 7 Gm • Percent of calories from fat 24% • Cholesterol 0 mg • Dietary Fiber 2 Gm • Sodium 156 mg • Calcium 48 mg

Tropical Pasta Salad

An ambrosial combination of color, texture, and flavor. Make a bowl for your next gathering and enjoy the raves.

8 ounces radiatore, or other small shaped pasta
1 teaspoon olive oil
1 cup snow peas, blanched
12 spinach leaves, torn into pieces
½ cup chopped celery
1 6-ounce jar marinated artichoke hearts, liquid reserved
2 minced scallions
½ cucumber, peeled, seeded, and sliced
1 kiwi, peeled and sliced

1 cup seedless red grapes
1 cup pineapple chunks (canned or fresh)
½ cup golden raisins
½ cup silken tofu, drained
¼ cup tahini (sesame paste)
¼ cup soy milk
¼ cup fresh lemon juice
¼ cup sugar (or a natural sweetener)
Salt and freshly ground white pepper
¼ cup toasted sesame seeds

Cook the pasta in a pot of boiling, salted water, uncovered, until tender but firm to the bite. Drain and rinse with cold water. Place the cooked pasta in a large serving bowl and toss with the olive oil. Add the snow peas, spinach, celery, artichokes with marinade, scallions, cucumber, kiwi, grapes, pineapple, and raisins and toss gently to combine. In a small bowl, combine the tofu, tahini, soy milk, lemon juice, sugar, and salt and white pepper to taste. Pour the dressing over the pasta salad and toss gently until coated. Taste and adjust the seasonings. Sprinkle with the sesame seeds and serve.

6 SERVINGS

Calories 385 Kc • Protein 11 Gm • Fat 12 Gm • Percent of calories from fat 27% • Cholesterol 0 mg • Dietary Fiber 5 Gm • Sodium 92 mg • Calcium 123 mg

Baked Tofu and Tomato Salad with Creamy Peppercorn Dressing

Baked tofu can be found in the refrigerated case of natural food stores . This salad is best when made with garden fresh, very ripe tomatoes.

1 cup silken tofu, drained
¼ cup soy milk
2 tablespoons fresh lemon juice
2 teaspoons coarsely cracked
   pepper
1 teaspoon Worcestershire sauce
1 teaspoon Dijon mustard
1 teaspoon low-sodium tamari

½ teaspoon salt or to taste
1 small head romaine lettuce
2 large ripe tomatoes
8 ounces baked tofu
4 marinated artichoke hearts
½ cup thinly sliced mushrooms
12 pitted black olives

To make the dressing, in a medium bowl combine the silken tofu, soy milk, lemon juice, pepper, Worcestershire, mustard, tamari, and salt and whisk to blend. Transfer to a container, cover, and refrigerate for several hours. Meanwhile, to prepare the salad, wash the romaine and cut the head crosswise into 1/4-inch-wide ribbons called chiffonade. Divide the chiffonade among 4 serving plates. Cut the tomatoes into thin slices, and arrange the slices in a circle on each plate. Cut the baked tofu into 1/2-inch-wide by 1/4-inch-thick slices. Arrange in a spoke design on each plate. Place an artichoke heart in the center of each plate. Divide the mushrooms and olives among the plates. Drizzle with the salad dressing and serve.

4 SERVINGS

Calories 132 Kc • Protein 10 Gm • Fat 6 Gm • Percent of calories from fat 39% • Cholesterol 0 mg • Dietary Fiber 2 Gm • Sodium 572 mg • Calcium 80 mg

Spiced Tofu Salad

1 tablespoon corn oil
1 pound extra-firm tofu, cut into
    1-inch cubes
4 tablespoons fresh lime juice
3 tablespoons honey (or a natural
    sweetener)
1 tablespoon low-sodium tamari
2 tablespoons minced fresh
    ginger, or 2 teaspoons dried
¼ teaspoon ground cardamom
⅛ teaspoon allspice

1 cup Tofu Mayonnaise (see page
    258)
Salt and freshly ground pepper
½ honeydew melon, scooped into
    balls with a melonball cutter
1 mango, peeled and diced
2 tablespoons minced fresh mint,
    or 2 teaspoons dried
1 head Boston lettuce, torn into
    pieces
1 bunch watercress, trimmed

Heat the oil in a skillet over medium heat. Add the cubed tofu and sprinkle with 1 tablespoon of the lime juice, 1 tablespoon of the honey, the tamari, 1 tablespoon of the ginger, $1/8$ teaspoon of the cardamom, and the allspice. Cook for 5 minutes, tossing gently to coat the tofu. Remove from the heat and let it cool. In a medium bowl, combine the Tofu Mayonnaise with the remaining 2 tablespoons honey, 3 tablespoons lime juice, 1 tablespoon ginger, $1/8$ teaspoon cardamom, and salt and pepper to taste, whisking until well blended. Add the cooled tofu, honeydew, mango, and mint, and toss gently to coat. Refrigerate at least 1 hour before serving. To serve, line 4 serving plates with the lettuce and watercress, and mound the salad in the center of each plate.

4 SERVINGS

Calories 288 Kc • Protein 13 Gm • Fat 11 Gm • Percent of calories from fat 33% • Cholesterol 0 mg • Dietary Fiber 2 Gm • Sodium 549 mg • Calcium 120 mg

Mediterranean Salad with Cannellini Beans

Cannellini beans are Italian white kidney beans. They are creamy and delicious and are widely available canned in most supermarkets or Italian specialty stores.

2 tablespoons olive oil
2 cloves garlic, minced
¼ cup dry white wine
1 bunch of broccoli
1 cup Tofu Mayonnaise (see page 258)
1 tablespoon fresh lemon juice
¼ teaspoon dried basil
¼ teaspoon dried oregano

½ teaspoon salt
½ teaspoon freshly ground pepper
2 cups canned cannellini beans
½ cup chopped red onion
Halved cherry tomatoes for garnish
Pitted oil-cured black olives for garnish

Heat the oil in a large skillet over low heat. Add the garlic and cook over low heat for about 30 seconds; add the wine and cook about 1 minute. Set aside to cool. Separate the broccoli tops into small florets, peel the stems and cut them into 1/4-inch slices. In a medium saucepan of boiling salted water, blanch the broccoli, uncovered, until bright green, about 30 seconds. Drain and rinse under cold running water until cool; drain well.

In a small bowl, combine the Tofu Mayonnaise, lemon juice, basil, and oregano; blend well. Whisk in the garlic and the wine. Season with the salt and pepper.

In a large bowl, combine the beans, broccoli, and onion. Add the dressing and toss well. Cover and refrigerate several hours, or overnight. Garnish with cherry tomatoes and black olives before serving.

4 TO 6 SERVINGS

Calories 240 Kc • Protein 11 Gm • Fat 10 Gm • Percent of calories from fat 36% • Cholesterol 0 mg • Dietary Fiber 7 Gm • Sodium 956 mg • Calcium 89 mg

Lima Bean Salad
with Horseradish Mayonnaise

An updated dairy-free version of an old family recipe.

2 pounds frozen lima beans
1 cup chopped scallion
1 cup firm silken tofu, drained
3 tablespoons cider vinegar
2 tablespoons prepared
   horseradish

1 tablespoon sugar (or a natural
   sweetener)
¾ teaspoon salt
¼ teaspoon white pepper
¼ cup chopped fresh parsley, or 1
   tablespoon dried

Cook the lima beans according to package directions. Drain and run under cold water to cool. Place the beans in a bowl and combine with the scallion. In a small bowl, combine the tofu, vinegar, horseradish, sugar, salt, and pepper, and stir gently into the beans and scallion. Refrigerate several hours or overnight. Before serving, sprinkle with the chopped parsley.

4 TO 6 SERVINGS

Calories 111 Kc • Protein 6 Gm • Fat 4 Gm • Percent of calories from fat 31% • Cholesterol 2 mg • Dietary Fiber 15 Gm • Sodium 570 mg • Calcium 108 mg

Tempeh Strips with Orange Mayonnaise

2 cups water
½ cup fresh orange juice
3 tablespoons grated orange
   rind
¼ teaspoon dried mint, or 1
   teaspoon fresh
1 pound tempeh

1½ cups Tofu Mayonnaise (see
   page 258)
1 tablespoon snipped fresh
   chives or green part of scallion
Salt and freshly ground pepper
1 small head romaine lettuce
2 navel oranges

Place the water in a saucepan over medium-high heat with ¼ cup of the orange juice, 2 tablespoons of the orange rind, and the mint, and bring to a boil. Add the tempeh, reduce the heat to medium, and simmer for 10 minutes. Remove the tempeh from the saucepan with a slotted spoon and let it cool. In a bowl, combine the Tofu Mayonnaise with the remaining ¼ cup orange juice, 1 tablespoon orange rind, and the chives, and season with salt and pepper to taste. Slice the tempeh in ½-inch strips, place in a bowl, and coat with half the Tofu Mayonnaise, tossing gently. Cut the lettuce in ¼-inch horizontal strips and line a serving platter with it. Arrange the tempeh on top of the lettuce. Peel and section the oranges, removing the membranes, and arrange the orange sections on the platter as a garnish. Pass the remaining mayonnaise separately.

4 SERVINGS

Calories 363 Kc • Protein 29 Gm • Fat 16 Gm • Percent of calories from fat 39% • Cholesterol 0 mg • Dietary Fiber 11 Gm • Sodium 458 mg • Calcium 103 mg

Cilantro Tempeh Salad

For a colorful presentation, serve this hearty salad on a bed of lettuce and garnish with alternating slices of tomato and avocado.

1 pound tempeh
1 tablespoon olive oil
2 ribs celery, thinly sliced
2 scallions, chopped
¼ cup minced red bell pepper
2 tablespoons chopped fresh
  cilantro

1 tablespoon lemon juice
½ cup Tofu Mayonnaise (see page
  258)
Salt and freshly ground pepper
3 tablespoons chopped
  peanuts

Place the tempeh in a saucepan with enough water to cover it and poach for 10 minutes. Drain, pat dry, and cut into ¹/₂-inch dice. Heat the oil in a medium skillet over medium-high heat. Add the tempeh and cook until lightly browned, about 5 minutes per side, and let it cool. In a large bowl, combine the tempeh with the celery, scallions, bell pepper, cilantro, and lemon juice. Stir in the Tofu Mayonnaise. Season with salt and pepper to taste. Cover and refrigerate at least 1 hour. Sprinkle the salad with the peanuts before serving.

4 SERVINGS

Calories 332 Kc • Protein 27 Gm • Fat 18 Gm • Percent of calories from fat 47% • Cholesterol 0 mg • Dietary Fiber 10 Gm • Sodium 172 mg • Calcium 59 mg

Curried Tempeh Salad with Papaya and Grapes

1 pound tempeh
1 cup Tofu Mayonnaise (see page 258)
¼ cup almond milk
1 tablespoon lemon juice
1 teaspoon honey (or a natural sweetener)

1 teaspoon curry powder
6 cups thinly sliced romaine lettuce
2 papayas, peeled and sliced
1 cup seedless green grapes

Place the tempeh in a saucepan with enough water to cover it and simmer over medium heat for 10 minutes. Remove the tempeh from the heat, drain, and let it cool. Cut the tempeh into 1-inch cubes and reserve. In a small bowl, whisk together the Tofu Mayonnaise, almond milk, lemon juice, honey, and curry powder until well blended. Pour the dressing on the tempeh and toss to coat. Divide the lettuce among 4 serving plates, arrange the papaya slices in a spoke design on the lettuce, and mound the tempeh in the center of each plate. Scatter grapes over all 4 salads.

4 SERVINGS

Calories 342 Kc • Protein 28 Gm • Fat 15 Gm • Percent of calories from fat 37% • Cholesterol 0 mg • Dietary Fiber 12 Gm • Sodium 313 mg • Calcium 97 mg

Citrus Tempeh Salad

1 pound tempeh
½ cup silken tofu, drained
¼ cup rice milk
1 tablespoon orange juice
1 tablespoon lemon juice
1 tablespoon lime juice
½ teaspoon salt
⅛ teaspoon freshly ground
  pepper

½ cup diced celery
¼ cup diced green bell pepper
¼ cup diced water chestnuts
2 minced scallions
2 oranges, peeled and
  segmented
6 cups fresh spinach, washed and
  torn

Place the tempeh in a medium saucepan with enough water to cover it and poach over medium heat for 10 minutes. Remove it from the heat, drain, and let it cool. In a small bowl, combine the tofu, rice milk, orange juice, lemon juice, lime juice, salt, and pepper, stirring until well blended. Cut the tempeh into 1-inch pieces and place in a large bowl. Add the celery, bell pepper, water chestnuts, scallions, and orange segments and toss gently. Add enough dressing to coat, tossing gently. Divide the spinach among 4 serving plates and mound the salad on top of the spinach.

4 SERVINGS

Calories 318 Kc • Protein 29 Gm • Fat 10 Gm • Percent of calories from fat 27% • Cholesterol 0 mg • Dietary Fiber 14 Gm • Sodium 389 mg • Calcium 166 mg

Curried Rice Salad

4 cups water
2 cups rice
1 tablespoon minced candied
  ginger
2 teaspoons curry powder
¼ teaspoon turmeric
2 tablespoons corn oil
3 tablespoons lemon juice
Salt and freshly ground pepper
1 cup frozen peas, thawed

1 cup golden raisins
½ cup chopped red bell pepper
½ cup toasted slivered almonds
½ cup firm silken tofu, drained
¼ cup almond milk
1 tablespoon almond butter
1 teaspoon sugar (or a natural
  sweetener)
1 teaspoon low-sodium tamari
⅛ teaspoon cayenne

Bring the water to a boil in a large saucepan, add the rice, ginger, curry powder, and turmeric. Reduce the heat to low, cover, and simmer until the rice is tender and all the liquid is absorbed, about 30 minutes. Transfer to a large bowl. Add the oil and 2 tablespoons of the lemon juice and toss well. Season with salt and pepper to taste. Cover and refrigerate several hours or overnight. Add the peas, raisins, bell pepper, and almonds and toss gently. In a small bowl or food processor, combine the tofu, almond milk, almond butter, remaining 1 tablespoon lemon juice, sugar, tamari, and cayenne. Pour the dressing over the rice salad and toss to combine well. Taste and adjust the seasonings. Cover and refrigerate until ready to serve.

8 SERVINGS

Calories 375 Kc • Protein 8 Gm • Fat 11 Gm • Percent of calories from fat 26% •
Cholesterol 0 mg • Dietary Fiber 4 Gm • Sodium 117 mg • Calcium 53 mg

Cantaloupe Kiwi Salad

½ cup firm silken tofu, drained
1 tablespoon fresh lime juice
1 tablespoon honey (or a natural sweetener)
¼ teaspoon ground cardamom

1 cantaloupe, scooped into balls with a melonball cutter
2 kiwi, peeled and sliced
Fresh mint leaves for garnish

In a serving bowl whisk together the tofu, lime juice, honey, and cardamom until well blended. Add the cantaloupe and kiwi, and stir gently to combine well. Garnish with fresh mint leaves.

4 SERVINGS

Calories 155 Kc • Protein 4 Gm • Fat 1 Gm • Percent of calories from fat 7% • Cholesterol 0 mg • Dietary Fiber 5 Gm • Sodium 66 mg • Calcium 60 mg

Creamy Green Bean and Tomato Salad

1½ pounds green beans, trimmed
2 ripe tomatoes, peeled, seeded, and chopped
½ cup soy milk

¼ cup silken tofu, drained
¼ cup balsamic vinegar
2 tablespoons minced fresh chervil, or 2 teaspoons dried
Salt and freshly ground pepper

Bring a pot of salted water to a boil, add the beans, and boil them for 5 to 7 minutes, or until crisp-tender. Drain the beans and run cold water over them to stop the cooking process. Pat the beans dry, cut into 2-inch pieces, and place them in a serving bowl. Add the tomatoes and set aside. In a food processor combine the soy milk, tofu, vinegar, and chervil until well blended. Pour the dressing over the salad, season with salt and pepper to taste, stirring to combine.

4 SERVINGS

Calories 115 Kc • Protein 5 Gm • Fat 2 Gm • Percent of calories from fat 13% • Cholesterol 0 mg • Dietary Fiber 6 Gm • Sodium 29 mg • Calcium 97 mg

Seitan Salad with
Tarragon Walnut Mayonnaise

Seitan, or "wheat meat," can be purchased in the refrigerated case of most natural food stores. It is also available in a dry mix that is more economical and easier than making it from scratch.

1¼ cups Tofu Mayonnaise (see page 258)
¼ cup capers
1 tablespoon minced fresh tarragon, or 1 teaspoon dried
1 tablespoon tarragon vinegar
½ teaspoon salt
⅛ teaspoon cayenne
2 cups cooked seitan
½ cup walnut halves
¼ cup minced celery
¼ cup minced scallion
6 cups salad greens

In a large bowl combine the Tofu Mayonnaise with the capers, tarragon, vinegar, salt, and cayenne. Add the seitan, walnuts, celery, and scallion and toss well to combine. Adjust the seasonings. Refrigerate for at least 1 hour or more so the flavors can mingle. To serve, divide the salad greens among 4 serving plates and place the salad mixture on top of the greens.

4 SERVINGS

Calories 419 Kc • Protein 38 Gm • Fat 17 Gm • Percent of calories from fat 36% • Cholesterol 0 mg • Dietary Fiber 6 Gm • Sodium 1038 mg • Calcium 111 mg

Sesame-Chive Dressing

This robust dressing stands up well to the spicy bite of watercress.

2 cups silken tofu, drained
½ teaspoon minced garlic
1 tablespoon Dijon mustard
1½ teaspoons lemon juice
½ teaspoon Tabasco sauce
1 teaspoon toasted sesame oil

2 tablespoons snipped fresh
   chives, or 2 teaspoons dried
1 tablespoon chopped fresh
   parsley, or 1 teaspoon dried
½ teaspoon salt
¼ teaspoon freshly ground pepper

In a medium bowl combine the tofu, garlic, mustard, lemon juice, and Tabasco sauce with a wire whisk until well blended. Drizzle in the sesame oil, whisking constantly. Fold in the chives, parsley, salt, and pepper. Cover and refrigerate until chilled. Refrigerated and tightly covered, this dressing will keep for up to 1 week.

MAKES ABOUT 2 CUPS

Calories 24 Kc • Protein 2 Gm • Fat 1 Gm • Percent of calories from fat 52% • Cholesterol 0 mg • Dietary Fiber 0 Gm • Sodium 81 mg • Calcium 13 mg

Creamy Raspberry Vinaigrette

The aromatic balsamic vinegar perfectly complements the raspberries in a delightful dressing that can adorn either green salads or fresh fruit.

1 10-ounce package of frozen
   raspberries in syrup, drained
6 tablespoons olive oil
¼ cup silken tofu, drained

2 tablespoons balsamic vinegar
¼ teaspoon salt
⅛ teaspoon freshly ground
   pepper

Puree the raspberries in a food processor. Strain into a small bowl, discarding the seeds. Place the oil, tofu, vinegar, salt, and pepper in food processor and mix well. Add the raspberry puree and process until well combined. Refrigerate, covered, until ready to use. Refrigerated and tightly covered, this dressing will keep for up to 1 week.

MAKES ABOUT 2 CUPS

Calories 67 Kc • Protein 0 Gm • Fat 5 Gm • Percent of calories from fat 68% • Cholesterol 0 mg • Dietary Fiber 1 Gm • Sodium 37 mg • Calcium 4 mg

Creamy Herb Dressing

Experiment with different herbs in this dressing, according to your own taste.

2 tablespoons chopped scallion
1 tablespoon chopped fresh parsley, or 1 teaspoon dried
1 teaspoon chopped fresh basil, or ¼ teaspoon dried
1 teaspoon snipped fresh chives, or ¼ teaspoon dried
½ teaspoon chopped fresh thyme, or pinch dried

1 cup silken tofu, drained
1 tablespoon olive oil
1 teaspoon cider vinegar
½ teaspoon fresh lemon juice
¼ teaspoon salt
⅛ teaspoon freshly ground pepper

Combine the scallion, parsley, basil, chives, and thyme in a food processor and mix until smooth. Add the tofu, oil, vinegar, lemon juice, salt, and pepper and process until well combined. Refrigerate, covered, until ready to serve. Refrigerated and tightly covered, this dressing will keep for up to 1 week.

MAKES ABOUT 1¹/₂ CUPS

Calories 22 Kc • Protein 1 Gm • Fat 2 Gm • Percent of calories from fat 70% • Cholesterol 0 mg • Dietary Fiber 0 Gm • Sodium 50 mg • Calcium 9 mg

Creamy Pesto Dressing

A delicious way to dress pasta or potato salads, this flavorful dressing also makes a good topping for baked potatoes or steamed vegetables.

2 cloves garlic, halved
2 cups firmly packed fresh basil leaves
1 cup silken tofu, drained
1 tablespoon olive oil

1 tablespoon cider vinegar
1 teaspoon salt or to taste
¼ teaspoon freshly ground pepper
¼ cup soy milk (optional)

Combine the garlic and basil in a food processor and mince well. Add the tofu, oil, vinegar, salt, and pepper and blend until well combined. To thin, add the soy milk and blend again. Refrigerate, covered, until ready to serve. Refrigerated and tightly covered, this dressing will keep for up to 1 week.

MAKES ABOUT 2 CUPS

Calories 18 Kc • Protein 1 Gm • Fat 1 Gm • Percent of calories from fat 64% • Cholesterol 0 mg • Dietary Fiber 0 Gm • Sodium 146 mg • Calcium 14 mg

Walnut-Dill Dressing

1 cup silken tofu, drained
¼ cup soy milk
1 tablespoon lemon juice
2 tablespoons chopped toasted walnuts

2 tablespoons chopped fresh dill, or 2 teaspoons dried
½ teaspoon salt
⅛ teaspoon freshly ground pepper

In a medium bowl, whisk together the tofu with the soy milk and lemon juice until well blended. Add the walnuts, dill, salt, and pepper and blend well. Refrigerate, covered, until serving. Refrigerated and tightly covered, this dressing will keep for up to 1 week.

MAKES ABOUT 1½ CUPS

Calories 23 Kc • Protein 1 Gm • Fat 1 Gm • Percent of calories from fat 57% • Cholesterol 0 mg • Dietary Fiber 0 Gm • Sodium 101 mg • Calcium 9 mg

Creamy Tarragon Vinaigrette

1 tablespoon chopped shallot
1 tablespoon minced fresh
   tarragon, or 1 teaspoon dried
1 cup silken tofu, drained
¼ cup soy milk
4 tablespoons tarragon vinegar
1 tablespoon olive oil

1 teaspoon Dijon mustard
¾ teaspoon salt
¼ teaspoon sugar (or a natural
   sweetener)
⅛ teaspoon freshly ground
   pepper

In a food processor, combine the shallot and tarragon until finely minced. Add the remaining ingredients and process until smooth. Adjust the seasonings. Refrigerate, covered, until serving. Refrigerated and tightly covered, this dressing will keep for up to 1 week.

MAKES ABOUT 1¹/₂ CUPS

Calories 27 Kc • Protein 1 Gm • Fat 2 Gm • Percent of calories from fat 60% • Cholesterol 0 mg • Dietary Fiber 0 Gm • Sodium 151 mg • Calcium 13 mg

Guacamole Goddess Dressing

Great on a salad made with crisp romaine and ripe tomatoes, this dressing can also double as a dip for chips or crudités.

1 scallion, chopped
1 tablespoon chopped fresh
    parsley, or 1 teaspoon dried
1 small clove garlic, chopped
2 cups silken tofu, drained
2 tablespoons fresh lemon juice
1 tablespoon cider vinegar
2 teaspoons Worcestershire
    sauce

½ teaspoon sugar (or a natural
    sweetener)
½ teaspoon Dijon mustard
¼ teaspoon celery salt
⅛ teaspoon freshly ground
    pepper
⅛ teaspoon Tabasco sauce
1 large ripe avocado, peeled,
    pitted, and chopped

In a food processor, combine the scallion, parsley, and garlic, until finely minced. Add the tofu, lemon juice, vinegar, Worcestershire, sugar, mustard, celery salt, pepper, and Tabasco and blend well. Add the avocado, and pulse to combine. Transfer to a small bowl and refrigerate, covered, until ready to serve. Refrigerated and tightly covered, this dressing will keep for up to 1 week.

MAKES ABOUT 2³/₄ CUPS

Calories 28 Kc • Protein 1 Gm • Fat 2 Gm • Percent of calories from fat 66% • Cholesterol 0 mg • Dietary Fiber 1 Gm • Sodium 32 mg • Calcium 10 mg

Ginger-Wasabi Dressing

The fiery wasabi and spicy ginger are mellowed by the creamy Tofu Mayonnaise in this unusual dressing. For an added Asian touch, garnish your salad with tiny enoki mushrooms.

1½ cups Tofu Mayonnaise (see page 258)
1 large scallion, minced
1 clove garlic, minced
2 tablespoons chopped fresh cilantro

1 tablespoon minced fresh ginger, or 1 teaspoon dried
2 tablespoons lemon juice
1 tablespoon toasted sesame oil
1 teaspoon low-sodium tamari
1 teaspoon wasabi powder

Combine all of the ingredients in a food processor and mix until thoroughly blended. Refrigerate, covered, until ready to serve. Refrigerated and tightly sealed, this dressing will keep for up to 1 week.

MAKES ABOUT 3 CUPS

Calories 22 Kc • Protein 1 Gm • Fat 2 Gm • Percent of calories from fat 71% • Cholesterol 0 mg • Dietary Fiber 0 Gm • Sodium 85 mg • Calcium 6 mg

Creamy Lime Dressing with Fresh Dill

½ cup silken tofu, drained
¼ cup soy milk
¼ cup fresh lime juice
1 tablespoon minced onion
2 tablespoons minced fresh dill,
  or 2 teaspoons dried

½ teaspoon salt, or to taste
⅛ teaspoon freshly ground white
  pepper

Place all of the ingredients in a small bowl, and whisk together until thoroughly blended. Refrigerate, covered, until serving. Refrigerated and tightly covered, this dressing will keep for up to 1 week.

MAKES ABOUT 1 CUP

Calories 16 Kc • Protein 1 Gm • Fat 0 Gm • Percent of calories from fat 34% • Cholesterol 0 mg • Dietary Fiber 0 Gm • Sodium 150 mg • Calcium 8 mg

Thousand Island Dressing

A classic dressing updated with dairy alternatives. Serve with iceberg or romaine lettuce, or use as a tasty sauce for veggie burgers.

½ cup Tofu Mayonnaise (see
  page 258)
¼ cup ketchup
¼ cup minced dill pickle
1 tablespoon minced scallion

1 tablespoon minced fresh
  parsley, or 1 teaspoon dried
1 teaspoon minced capers
  (optional)
½ teaspoon Tabasco sauce

Combine all of the ingredients in a food processor, mixing until well combined. Cover and chill until serving. Refrigerated and tightly covered, this dressing will keep for up to 1 week.

MAKES ABOUT 1 CUP

Calories 21 Kc • Protein 1 Gm • Fat 1 Gm • Percent of calories from fat 54% • Cholesterol 0 mg • Dietary Fiber 0 Gm • Sodium 180 mg • Calcium 11 mg

"Buttermilk" Dressing

A dairy-free alternative to ranch-style dressings. Use on your favorite mixed greens.

½ cup Tofu Mayonnaise (see page 258)
1 teaspoon minced onion
¼ teaspoon minced garlic
½ cup soy milk
1 teaspoon Dijon mustard
2 tablespoons safflower oil

1 tablespoon chopped fresh parsley, or 1 teaspoon dried
1 tablespoon lemon juice
½ teaspoon salt
¼ teaspoon paprika
¼ teaspoon freshly ground pepper

Combine all of the ingredients in a small bowl and stir or whisk until smooth and well combined. Cover and refrigerate until chilled. Refrigerated and tightly covered, this dressing will keep for up to 1 week.

MAKES ABOUT 1 ¼ CUPS

Calories 45 Kc • Protein 1 Gm • Fat 4 Gm • Percent of calories from fat 78% • Cholesterol 0 mg • Dietary Fiber 0 Gm • Sodium 186 mg • Calcium 8 mg

Lemon Cream Dressing

A cool and refreshing dressing for most salads, as well as steamed vegetables. Decrease the amount of liquid for a fabulous dipping sauce.

1 cup firm silken tofu, drained
½ cup tahini (sesame paste)
2 tablespoons minced onion
¼ cup lemon juice
¼ cup almond milk
2 tablespoons sugar (or a natural sweetener)

1 tablespoon cider vinegar
1 tablespoon lemon zest
½ teaspoon salt
Pinch of cayenne

Place all of the ingredients in a food processor and process until the mixture is smooth. Refrigerate, covered, for at least 1 hour before using to let the flavors blend. Refrigerated and tightly covered, this dressing will keep for up to 1 week.

MAKES ABOUT 2 CUPS

Calories 75 Kc • Protein 3 Gm • Fat 6 Gm • Percent of calories from fat 66% • Cholesterol 0 mg • Dietary Fiber 0 Gm • Sodium 83 mg • Calcium 29 mg

Creamy Poppy Seed Dressing

¼ cup tahini (sesame paste)
¼ cup almond milk
2 tablespoons minced onion
3 tablespoons poppy seeds
1 teaspoon minced garlic
3 tablespoons cider vinegar
3 tablespoons lemon juice

1 tablespoon celery seed
1 teaspoon dry mustard
2 tablespoons sugar (or a natural sweetener)
½ teaspoon salt
Pinch cayenne
¾ cup safflower oil

Place all of the ingredients except the oil in a food processor and blend until smooth and well combined. Still processing, gradually add the oil. Refrigerate the dressing in a tightly covered jar and chill until ready to use. Refrigerated and tightly covered, this dressing will keep for up to 1 week.

MAKES ABOUT 1½ CUPS

Calories 182 Kc • Protein 2 Gm • Fat 18 Gm • Percent of calories from fat 88% • Cholesterol 0 mg • Dietary Fiber 1 Gm • Sodium 104 mg • Calcium 56 mg

Carrot Ginger Dressing

¼ cup chopped cooked carrots
¾ cup soy milk
½ cup firm silken tofu, drained
¼ cup orange juice
3 tablespoons cider vinegar

½ teaspoon salt
½ teaspoon powdered ginger
⅛ teaspoon freshly ground white
   pepper

Place all of the ingredients in a food processor and blend until smooth and well combined. Refrigerate, covered, until serving. Refrigerated and tightly covered, this dressing will keep for up to 1 week.

MAKES ABOUT 2 CUPS

Calories 16 Kc • Protein 1 Gm • Fat 0 Gm • Percent of calories from fat 29% • Cholesterol 0 mg • Dietary Fiber 0 Gm • Sodium 80 mg • Calcium 7 mg

Fresh Herb Dressing

1 cup firm silken tofu, drained
½ cup rice milk
2 scallions, minced
½ cup minced fresh parsley, or
   2½ tablespoons dried
¼ cup minced fresh basil, or 1
   tablespoon dried
¼ cup minced fresh marjoram,
   or 1 tablespoon dried

2 tablespoons snipped fresh
   chives, or 2 teaspoons dried
2 tablespoons minced capers
1 tablespoon Dijon mustard
¼ cup lemon juice
½ teaspoon salt
¼ teaspoon freshly ground
   pepper

Combine all of the ingredients in a food processor and blend until well combined. Refrigerate, covered, until ready to serve. This dressing is best made several hours ahead to allow the flavors to mingle. Refrigerated and tightly covered, this dressing will keep for up to 1 week.

MAKES ABOUT 2 CUPS

Calories 16 Kc • Protein 1 Gm • Fat 1 Gm • Percent of calories from fat 32% • Cholesterol 0 mg • Dietary Fiber 0 Gm • Sodium 102 mg • Calcium 16 mg

Fresh Vegetable Dressing

½ cucumber, peeled and
  seeded
½ green bell pepper, seeded
1 small onion, chopped
1 cup firm silken tofu, drained
¼ cup soy milk
1 tablespoon minced fresh
  parsley, or 1 teaspoon dried

1 teaspoon Dijon mustard
1 tablespoon lemon juice
½ teaspoon salt
⅛ teaspoon freshly ground
  pepper

Place the cucumber, bell pepper, and onion in a food processor and process until minced. Drain the liquid from the processed vegetables, add the tofu, soy milk, parsley, mustard, lemon juice, salt, and pepper and process until well combined. Transfer to a small bowl and refrigerate, covered, until ready to use. Refrigerated and tightly covered, this dressing will keep for up to 1 week.

MAKES ABOUT 2 CUPS

Calories 20 Kc • Protein 2 Gm • Fat 0 Gm • Percent of calories from fat 23% • Cholesterol 0 mg • Dietary Fiber 0 Gm • Sodium 89 mg • Calcium 12 mg

Gingered Chutney Dressing

A bottled chutney works just fine for this flavorful dressing. Try it on a salad of mixed greens sprinkled with chopped apples, peanuts, and raisins.

1 cup Tofu Mayonnaise (see page 258)
¼ cup chutney
½ teaspoon curry powder

⅛ teaspoon ground ginger
2 tablespoons apple juice (optional)

In a food processor, combine the Tofu Mayonnaise, chutney, curry powder, and ginger until well blended. If a thinner dressing is desired, add the apple juice. Refrigerate until ready to use. Refrigerated and tightly covered, this dressing will keep for up to 1 week.

MAKES ABOUT 1¼ CUPS

Calories 41 Kc • Protein 1 Gm • Fat 2 Gm • Percent of calories from fat 43% • Cholesterol 0 mg • Dietary Fiber 0 Gm • Sodium 123 mg • Calcium 8 mg

Horseradish Dressing

This dressing is ideal for composed salads which use strips of seitan or other meat alternatives.

1 cup Tofu Mayonnaise (see page 258)
¼ cup drained prepared horseradish
¼ cup soft tofu

2 tablespoons minced fresh parsley, or 2 teaspoons dried
1 teaspoon Dijon mustard
Salt and freshly ground pepper

In a small bowl, combine the Tofu Mayonnaise with the horseradish and soft tofu, whisking until well blended. Add the parsley and mustard, and season to taste with salt and pepper. Refrigerated and tightly closed, this dressing will keep for up to 1 week.

MAKES ABOUT 1 ½ CUPS

Calories 25 Kc • Protein 1 Gm • Fat 2 Gm • Percent of calories from fat 63% • Cholesterol 0 mg • Dietary Fiber 0 Gm • Sodium 109 mg • Calcium 12 mg

Creamy Lemon-Walnut Vinaigrette

Try this flavorful dressing on a salad of bitter greens.

½ cup soft silken tofu,
  drained
¼ cup chopped walnuts
¼ cup lemon juice
2 tablespoons minced shallot

2 tablespoons minced fresh
  parsley, or 2 teaspoons dried
½ teaspoon salt
⅛ teaspoon freshly ground pepper
½ cup walnut oil

In a food processor, combine the tofu, walnuts, lemon juice, shallot, parsley, salt, and pepper, mixing until well blended. With the machine running, add the walnut oil in a stream, processing until emulsified. Refrigerate dressing until ready to serve. Refrigerated and tightly covered, this dressing will keep for up to 1 week.

MAKES ABOUT 1¹/₂ CUPS

Calories 104 Kc • Protein 1 Gm • Fat 11 Gm • Percent of calories from fat 92% • Cholesterol 0 mg • Dietary Fiber 0 Gm • Sodium 98 mg • Calcium 7 mg

Creamy "Bacon" Dressing

Imagine a creamy bacon dressing with no cholesterol. If tempeh bacon is unavailable, add ¹/₂ cup of soy bacon bits to the dressing. This dressing is great on a spinach salad.

2 tablespoons safflower oil
¹/₂ pound tempeh bacon, chopped
1 cup soft silken tofu, drained
2 tablespoons fresh lemon juice
1 tablespoon Dijon mustard
¹/₂ teaspoon salt
¹/₄ teaspoon freshly ground pepper
¹/₄ cup corn oil

Heat the oil in a medium skillet, add the tempeh bacon and cook over medium heat, stirring occasionally, until crisp. Reserve. In a food processor, combine the tofu, lemon juice, mustard, salt, and pepper. With the machine running, add the corn oil in a stream until well blended. Transfer the dressing to a bowl and stir in the reserved tempeh bacon. Refrigerate until ready to serve. Refrigerated and tightly covered, this dressing will keep for up to 1 week.

MAKES ABOUT 1¹/₄ CUPS

Calories 159 Kc • Protein 3 Gm • Fat 16 Gm • Percent of calories from fat 85% • Cholesterol 0 mg • Dietary Fiber 0 Gm • Sodium 458 mg • Calcium 15 mg

Avocado Dressing

Especially good with fresh ripe tomatoes and your favorite salad greens.

1 scallion, chopped
¼ cup peeled, seeded, and cubed cucumber
1 small avocado, pitted and peeled

½ cup soy milk
¼ cup fresh lemon juice
1 tablespoon olive oil
Salt
Cayenne

In a food processor, combine the scallion and cucumber until finely minced. Add the avocado, soy milk, lemon juice, oil, and salt and cayenne to taste, processing until the dressing is smooth. Refrigerate until ready to serve. Refrigerated and tightly covered, this dressing will keep for up to 1 week.

MAKES ABOUT 1 1/2 CUPS

Calories 41 Kc • Protein 0 Gm • Fat 4 Gm • Percent of calories from fat 82% • Cholesterol 0 mg • Dietary Fiber 2 Gm • Sodium 6 mg • Calcium 6 mg

Greener Goddess Dressing

¼ cup chopped fresh parsley leaves, or 1 tablespoon dried
2 scallions, minced
1 clove garlic, minced
1 teaspoon capers

1 cup Tofu Mayonnaise (see page 258)
1 teaspoon balsamic vinegar
Salt and freshly ground pepper

In a food processor, mix the parsley, scallions, garlic, and capers until finely minced. Add the Tofu Mayonnaise and vinegar and process to mix well. Season the dressing with salt and pepper to taste, and refrigerate, covered, until ready to serve. Refrigerated and tightly covered, this dressing will keep for up to 1 week.

MAKES ABOUT 1 1/4 CUPS

Calories 14 Kc • Protein 0 Gm • Fat 1 Gm • Percent of calories from fat 62% • Cholesterol 0 mg • Dietary Fiber 0 Gm • Sodium 72 mg • Calcium 7 mg

Lemon Pepper Dressing

A perfect accompaniment to fresh steamed asparagus. Served chilled or at room temperature, this dressing is also sublime on a salad of Boston lettuce mixed with watercress.

¾ cup soft tofu, drained
3 tablespoons fresh lemon juice
1 tablespoon Dijon mustard
¼ teaspoon salt

1½ teaspoons coarsely ground pepper, or to taste
¼ cup olive oil

In a food processor, combine the tofu, lemon juice, mustard, salt, and pepper until well mixed. With the machine running, add the oil in a stream, until well blended. Refrigerate, covered, until ready to use. Refrigerated and tightly covered, this dressing will keep for up to 1 week.

MAKES ABOUT 1 CUP

Calories 75 Kc • Protein 1 Gm • Fat 7 Gm • Percent of calories from fat 87% • Cholesterol 0 mg • Dietary Fiber 0 Gm • Sodium 85 mg • Calcium 11 mg

Creamy Mustard Dressing

A rich, flavorful dressing with only two tablespoons of oil. Perfect for a crisp salad of romaine and leaf lettuce.

1 cup soft silken tofu, drained
2 tablespoons Dijon mustard
1 tablespoon lemon juice
1 teaspoon finely minced garlic

½ teaspoon salt
¼ teaspoon freshly ground
   pepper
2 tablespoons olive oil

In a bowl combine the tofu, mustard, lemon juice, garlic, salt, and pepper, whisking until well blended. Whisk in the oil until incorporated. Adjust the seasonings. Refrigerate, covered, until ready to use. Refrigerated and tightly covered, this dressing will keep for up to 1 week.

MAKES ABOUT 1¼ CUPS

Calories 42 Kc • Protein 1 Gm • Fat 4 Gm • Percent of calories from fat 76% • Cholesterol 0 mg • Dietary Fiber 0 Gm • Sodium 135 mg • Calcium 12 mg

3

Appetizers, Spreads, and Dips

Many of the recipes in this chapter, such as Savory Mushroom Strudel or Broiled Artichoke Toasts, can be used as first course appetizers, light lunches, or supper entrees. They also adapt well to a party buffet. The versatile spreads such as Chickpea-Watercress Tapenade and Spicy Almond Spread are equally at home filling croustades on an hors d'oeuvre tray, as a dip for crudités, or as tasty sandwich fillings. Best of all, there's not a speck of dairy product in any of the recipes.

Crostini with Olives and Capers

½ teaspoon fennel seeds
1 tablespoon olive oil
¼ pound tofu sausage, crumbled
1 tablespoon minced shallot
2 tablespoons dry white wine
½ pound firm tofu, well drained

6 oil-cured black olives, pitted
  and thinly sliced
2 tablespoons capers
Salt and freshly ground pepper
1 10-inch-long French baguette
¼ cup minced fresh parsley

Preheat the oven to 400 degrees. Crush the fennel seeds in a mortar or with a spice mill. Heat the oil in a medium skillet over medium heat. Add the fennel seeds and stir until aromatic, about 2 minutes. Add the sausage and cook 5 minutes, breaking up with spoon. Add the shallot and cook until softened, stirring frequently, about 3 minutes. Transfer the mixture to a food processor using a slotted spoon. Add the wine to the skillet and bring to a boil, scraping up any browned bits. Add to the sausage mixture. Add the tofu, olives, 1 tablespoon of the capers, salt and pepper to taste, and blend until well combined. Cut baguette into 16 $1/2$-inch rounds. Spread the sausage mixture on the bread rounds. Arrange on a baking sheet. Bake until heated through, about 3 minutes, or until the tops are light brown. Garnish the top of each crostini with the remaining 1 tablespoon capers and the parsley and serve.

6 TO 8 SERVINGS

Calories 62 Kc • Protein 3 Gm • Fat 3 Gm • Percent of calories from fat 40% • Cholesterol 0 mg • Dietary Fiber 0 Gm • Sodium 176 mg • Calcium 11 mg

Herbed Tofu Crostini

This recipe can be doubled or tripled to accommodate longer baguettes.

¾ cup shredded soy mozzarella
¼ cup firm tofu, well drained
1 tablespoon fresh minced basil,
   or 1 teaspoon dried
1 teaspoon fresh minced oregano,
   or ½ teaspoon dried

Salt and freshly ground
   pepper
1 8-inch-long French baguette
1 tablespoon olive oil

Preheat the oven to 400 degrees. In a small bowl, combine the soy cheese, tofu, basil, oregano, and salt and pepper to taste and set aside. Slice the bread diagonally into about 12 ½-inch-thick rounds. Brush with the olive oil and spread with the tofu mixture. Arrange on a baking sheet and bake for 3 to 5 minutes or until the cheese melts.

4 SERVINGS

Calories 188 Kc • Protein 10 Gm • Fat 7 Gm • Percent of calories from fat 36% • Cholesterol 0 mg • Dietary Fiber 1 Gm • Sodium 292 mg • Calcium 86 mg

Broiled Artichoke Toasts

1 10-ounce package frozen
  artichoke hearts
1 tablespoon corn oil
½ cup minced onion
½ cup Tofu Mayonnaise (see page
  258)

2 tablespoons minced fresh
  parsley, or 2 teaspoons dried
Salt and freshly ground pepper
6 slices good quality bread of
  choice

Cook the artichoke hearts according to the package directions. Drain, chop, and set aside. Heat the oil in a small skillet, add the onion and cook over medium heat, for 5 minutes, or until softened, stirring occasionally. Add the chopped artichokes, Tofu Mayonnaise, parsley, and salt and pepper to taste and mix well. Toast the bread lightly, trim the crusts and cut the toast in half diagonally. Divide the artichoke mixture among the toasts, and broil about 4 inches from the heat source until lightly browned and slightly puffed.

4 SERVINGS

Calories 269 Kc • Protein 10 Gm • Fat 13 Gm • Percent of calories from fat 39% • Cholesterol 0 mg • Dietary Fiber 2 Gm • Sodium 406 mg • Calcium 32 mg

Artichoke Dip

This simple but tasty dip pulls together in seconds and is great served with crackers or crudités. Spoon into some pre-made croustades and warm in the oven—your guests will think you spent all day in the kitchen!

1 14-ounce can brine-packed
    artichoke hearts, drained
1/4 cup silken tofu, drained
1 tablespoon lemon juice

1/8 teaspoon dried oregano
Salt and freshly ground white
    pepper

Combine the artichoke hearts, tofu, lemon juice, and oregano in a food processor and puree until smooth. Season with salt and pepper to taste.

MAKES ABOUT 1 1/2 CUPS

Calories 15 Kc • Protein 1 Gm • Fat 0 Gm • Percent of calories from fat 10% • Cholesterol 0 mg • Dietary Fiber 1 Gm • Sodium 23 mg • Calcium 12 mg

Sesame "Cheese" Dip

1 cup firm tofu, well drained
1/3 cup tahini (sesame paste)
1 tablespoon lemon juice
1 tablespoon low-sodium tamari
1 tablespoon toasted sesame oil
1 tablespoon minced scallion

1 tablespoon minced fresh
    parsley, or 1 teaspoon dried
1/4 teaspoon salt
1/8 teaspoon cayenne
2 tablespoons toasted sesame
    seeds

In a food processor, combine all of the ingredients except the sesame seeds and process until smooth. Transfer the mixture to a small serving bowl, top with the sesame seeds, and serve with crackers or crudités.

MAKES ABOUT 1 1/2 CUPS

Calories 79 Kc • Protein 4 Gm • Fat 6 Gm • Percent of calories from fat 73% • Cholesterol 0 mg • Dietary Fiber 0 Gm • Sodium 113 mg • Calcium 41 mg

Sun-dried Tomato and Olive Dip

1 cup oil-cured black olives
1 cup firm tofu, drained
¼ cup chopped oil-packed
   sun-dried tomatoes
1 tablespoon lemon juice
2 tablespoons minced fresh
   parsley, or 2 teaspoons dried

Salt and freshly ground black
   pepper
4 cherry tomatoes, quartered
Fresh parsley sprig for garnish

Remove the pits from the olives and reserve 6 halves. Chop the remaining olives and set aside. Combine the tofu, tomatoes, and lemon juice in a food processor and process until the mixture is smooth and well blended. Transfer the mixture to a small bowl and stir in the minced parsley and chopped olives, mixing until well combined. Season to taste with salt and pepper. Transfer the dip to a small serving bowl, smoothing the top with a knife. To garnish, cut the reserved olive halves in half lengthwise. Arrange a circle of alternating olives and cherry tomato pieces. Place a sprig of fresh parsley in center of the bowl. To serve, place the bowl in center of a serving tray and surround with crackers or crudités.

MAKES ABOUT 2¹/₃ CUPS

Calories 10 Kc • Protein 1 Gm • Fat 1 Gm • Percent of calories from fat 52% • Cholesterol 0 mg • Dietary Fiber 0 Gm • Sodium 38 mg • Calcium 6 mg

Almost-Instant Guacamole

1 cup firm silken tofu, drained
1 large ripe avocado, peeled and
seeded

½ cup green chili salsa
2 tablespoons lemon juice
½ teaspoon salt

Place all of the ingredients in a food processor and blend until well combined. Taste to adjust the seasonings. Refrigerate, covered, until ready to serve.

MAKES 2 CUPS

Calories 30 Kc • Protein 1 Gm • Fat 2 Gm • Percent of calories from fat 61% • Cholesterol 0 mg • Dietary Fiber 0 Gm • Sodium 140 mg • Calcium 8 mg

Watercress-Walnut Pesto Dip

1 cup firm silken tofu, drained
2 cups chopped watercress
¼ cup walnut pieces
¼ cup almond milk
1 clove garlic

1 tablespoon lemon juice
1 tablespoon fresh chopped
basil, or 1 teaspoon dried
½ teaspoon salt
Dash of Tabasco sauce

Combine all of the ingredients in a food processor and process until well combined. Refrigerate, covered, until ready to serve.

MAKES 2 CUPS

Calories 25 Kc • Protein 2 Gm • Fat 2 Gm • Percent of calories from fat 58% • Cholesterol 0 mg • Dietary Fiber 0 Gm • Sodium 85 mg • Calcium 14 mg

Hot Spinach Dip

The "hot" in this spinach dip can be taken two ways—depending on the amount of chili peppers you add. For a mild version, decrease the peppers, or omit entirely. Serve with tortilla chips or pita wedges.

1 tablespoon olive oil
2 or 3 hot green chili peppers, seeded and chopped
1 small onion, minced
2 tomatoes, peeled, seeded, and chopped
1 10-ounce package frozen chopped spinach, thawed and squeezed dry

1 tablespoon red wine vinegar
8 ounces extra-firm silken tofu, drained
1 cup grated soy cheddar cheese
1 cup soy milk
Salt and freshly ground pepper

Preheat the oven to 375 degrees. Heat the oil in a small skillet over medium heat. Add the peppers and onion and cook, stirring, for 5 minutes, or until the onion is softened. Add the tomatoes, and cook 2 minutes longer, stirring occasionally. Transfer the mixture to a bowl and mix in the spinach, vinegar, tofu, soy cheddar, soy milk, and salt and pepper to taste, stirring well to combine. Transfer the dip to a lightly oiled 10-inch glass pie plate or gratin dish and bake for 20 minutes or until hot.

8 TO 10 SERVINGS

Calories 100 Kc • Protein 7 Gm • Fat 4 Gm • Percent of calories from fat 40% • Cholesterol 0 mg • Dietary Fiber 2 Gm • Sodium 89 mg • Calcium 112 mg

Lemony Spinach Dip

2 cups silken tofu, drained
1 10-ounce package frozen chopped spinach, thawed and squeezed dry
1 8-ounce can water chestnuts, drained

¼ cup chopped scallion
2 tablespoons lemon juice
½ teaspoon salt
¼ teaspoon freshly ground pepper
¼ teaspoon celery salt

Place all of the ingredients in a food processor and pulse until well combined. Refrigerate, covered, until ready to serve.

MAKES ABOUT 3 CUPS

Calories 21 Kc • Protein 2 Gm • Fat 0 Gm • Percent of calories from fat 21% • Cholesterol 0 mg • Dietary Fiber 0 Gm • Sodium 87 mg • Calcium 10 mg

Herbed Veggie Dip

A flavorful dip for crudités. Change the herbs to suit your taste.

2 ribs celery
2 medium dill pickles
1 scallion, trimmed
2 cups firm silken tofu, drained
3 tablespoons fresh lemon juice
1 tablespoon tomato paste
1 tablespoon Dijon mustard
3 tablespoons drained capers

½ cup minced fresh parsley, or 3 tablespoons dried
¼ cup fresh dill, or 1 tablespoon dried
1 teaspoon paprika
½ teaspoon salt
⅛ teaspoon cayenne

In a food processor, finely mince the celery, pickles, and scallion. Add the remaining ingredients and pulse until well combined. Refrigerate, covered, until ready to serve.

MAKES ABOUT 2½ CUPS

Calories 20 Kc • Protein 2 Gm • Fat 0 Gm • Percent of calories from fat 27% • Cholesterol 0 mg • Dietary Fiber 0 Gm • Sodium 223 mg • Calcium 17 mg

Spinach Triangles

⅔ cup whole wheat flour
⅔ cup all-purpose flour
1 stick margarine (½ cup)
¼ teaspoon salt
2 tablespoons ice water (or more)
Filling:
2 tablespoons olive oil
1 cup minced onion
2 cups chopped mushrooms
  (about ⅓ pound)

2 10-ounce packages frozen
  spinach, thawed and squeezed
  dry
1 tablespoon low-sodium tamari
2 cups firm tofu, drained and
  pressed
Salt and freshly ground pepper
Nutmeg

Preheat the oven to 400 degrees. Place the flours, margarine, and salt in a food processor and process in short on/off pulses until crumbly. Pulsing, add enough of the water to form a dough. Roll out the dough on a floured surface to about 12 × 15 inches and cut into 16 to 20 small squares. Heat the oil in a large skillet over medium heat, add the onion, cover, and cook until softened, about 5 minutes. Add the mushrooms and cook 3 minutes longer, uncovered. Chop the spinach and add to the onion mixture, along with the tamari. Cook until all the liquid is absorbed. Transfer the spinach mixture to a food processor and pulse with the tofu to mix well. Add the salt, pepper, and nutmeg to taste. Spoon a small amount of filling on each pastry square, until all the filling is used. Fold the pastry over the filling to form triangles. Place the pastries on a baking sheet that has been sprayed with cooking spray. Prick holes in the tops of the pastries with a fork, and bake for 15 minutes or until golden brown.

MAKES 16 TO 20

Calories 99 Kc • Protein 5 Gm • Fat 5 Gm • Percent of calories from fat 44% • Cholesterol 0 mg • Dietary Fiber 1 Gm • Sodium 134 mg • Calcium 20 mg

Artichoke Phyllo Rolls

1 14-ounce can artichoke hearts, drained and rinsed
½ cup silken tofu, well drained
1 teaspoon lemon juice
1 teaspoon Dijon mustard
¾ teaspoon salt

⅛ teaspoon cayenne
2 cloves garlic, minced
½ teaspoon dried oregano
15 phyllo pastry sheets
6 tablespoons margarine, melted

Preheat the oven to 375 degrees. Squeeze the artichoke hearts to remove excess liquid, and finely chop. Place the artichokes in a medium bowl and combine with the tofu, lemon juice, mustard, salt, cayenne, garlic, and oregano.

Stack the phyllo between 2 sheets of wax paper and cover with a damp cloth to keep it from drying out. On a work surface brush 1 sheet of the phyllo lightly with some of the melted margarine, cover it with a second sheet of phyllo, and brush the top lightly with some of the remaining melted margarine. Brush the margarine on 3 more phyllo sheets and layer in the same manner, for a total of 5 layers. Spread one third of the artichoke mixture in a strip along one long side of the prepared phyllo layers about 1 inch from the edge and roll up the phyllo, beginning at the filled edge and tucking in the sides as you proceed. Arrange the roll seam side down on a baking sheet sprayed with non-stick cooking spray, and brush the roll with some of the melted margarine. Working quickly, make 2 more rolls with the remaining phyllo, filling, and margarine. Bake for 20 to 25 minutes, or until golden. Let the rolls cool and cut them with a serrated knife into bite-size pieces.

MAKES ABOUT **36** PIECES

Calories 40 Kc • Protein 1 Gm • Fat 1 Gm • Percent of calories from fat 35% • Cholesterol 0 mg • Dietary Fiber 0 Gm • Sodium 107 mg • Calcium 8 mg

Savory Mushroom Strudel

½ cup olive oil
¼ cup minced onion
¼ cup minced celery
2 cups sliced mushrooms
   (½ pound)
1 large clove garlic, minced
1 tablespoon dry sherry
1 teaspoon low-sodium tamari
½ cup shredded soy mozzarella
½ cup silken tofu, well drained

½ cup dried bread crumbs
2 tablespoons minced fresh
   parsley, or 2 teaspoons dried
1 tablespoon lemon juice
1 teaspoon minced fresh thyme,
   or ¼ teaspoon dried
⅛ teaspoon freshly ground
   pepper
Pinch cayenne
12 phyllo pastry sheets

Heat 1 tablespoon of the olive oil in a large skillet over medium-high heat. Add the onion and celery and cook for 5 minutes, stirring frequently. Add the mushrooms, garlic, sherry, and tamari, and continue cooking until the vegetables are tender and the liquid has evaporated. Remove from the heat and drain well. Return the mushroom mixture to the skillet. Add the soy mozzarella, tofu, bread crumbs, parsley, lemon juice, thyme, pepper, and cayenne. Taste and adjust the seasonings. Preheat the oven to 375 degrees. Lightly oil a large baking sheet or coat with nonstick cooking spray and set aside.

Stack the phyllo between two sheets of wax paper and cover with a damp cloth. Place one sheet of phyllo on a work surface and brush with some of the olive oil. Top with a second sheet of phyllo and brush with oil. Repeat to form a stack of 12 sheets, brushing each layer with oil. Spoon the mushroom mixture along one long edge of the phyllo stack, leaving a 2-inch border at each end. Carefully roll up the phyllo around the filling and tuck in the ends. Place the strudel on the prepared baking sheet, seam side down. Brush with oil, and bake until crisp and lightly browned, about 20 minutes. Let it cool slightly before slicing.

6 TO 8 SERVINGS

Calories 305 Kc • Protein 6 Gm • Fat 21 Gm • Percent of calories from fat 62% •
Cholesterol 0 mg • Dietary Fiber 1 Gm • Sodium 234 mg • Calcium 49 mg

Stuffed Mushrooms

Tofu sausage is available in natural food stores.

2 dozen large, firm mushrooms
2 tablespoons olive oil
¼ pound tofu sausage
2 minced shallots
1 clove garlic, minced
½ teaspoon dried basil
¼ teaspoon dried oregano
¼ teaspoon hot red pepper flakes

¼ teaspoon fennel seeds, crushed
½ teaspoon salt
⅛ teaspoon freshly ground pepper
⅓ cup fine dry bread crumbs
¼ cup grated soy mozzarella
2 tablespoons dry white wine

Preheat the oven to 400 degrees. Clean and trim the mushrooms, separate the stems from the caps, and reserve the caps. Mince the stems and reserve. Heat 1 tablespoon of the oil in a large skillet over medium heat, add the tofu sausage, and cook, crumbling into small pieces, until browned, about 5 minutes. Add the shallots and garlic; sauté, stirring frequently, until the shallots are softened, about 3 minutes. Stir in the reserved mushroom stems, basil, oregano, pepper flakes, fennel, salt, and pepper, and sauté about 5 minutes. Add the bread crumbs and soy cheese, stirring until well combined. Add the wine; stir to moisten the mixture, remove it from the heat, and let it cool. Gently press the stuffing mixture into the mushroom caps, dividing it evenly. Drizzle the caps with the remaining 1 tablespoon of oil. Arrange the caps on a baking sheet; bake until the stuffing is bubbly and the mushrooms are browned, about 5 to 7 minutes. Arrange on a serving platter and serve immediately.

MAKES 2 DOZEN

Calories 31 Kc • Protein 2 Gm • Fat 2 Gm • Percent of calories from fat 57% • Cholesterol 0 mg • Dietary Fiber 0 Gm • Sodium 86 mg • Calcium 12 mg

Cannellini-stuffed Avocados

1 cup shelled fresh peas

1 medium carrot, grated

2 cups cooked or canned cannellini beans

2 oranges, peeled, segmented, and coarsely chopped

3 scallions, minced

2 tablespoons balsamic vinegar

¼ cup silken tofu, well drained

2 tablespoons soy milk

1 tablespoon lemon juice

2 tablespoons chopped fresh parsley, or 2 teaspoons dried

1 tablespoon snipped chives, or 1 teaspoon dried

1 teaspoon sugar (or a natural sweetener)

½ teaspoon salt

⅛ teaspoon freshly ground black pepper

⅛ teaspoon Tabasco sauce

2 ripe avocados

In a small saucepan of salted boiling water, blanch the peas until tender, 3 to 5 minutes. Remove with a slotted spoon, drain, and let cool. Add the carrot to the same saucepan and boil until tender, about 1 minute. Drain and cool. In a medium bowl, combine the beans with the peas, carrot, orange pieces, and scallions. Add the vinegar and toss to coat. Cover and refrigerate at least 1 hour. In a small bowl, combine the tofu, soy milk, lemon juice, parsley, chives, sugar, salt, pepper, and Tabasco. Blend well. Add to the salad and toss to combine well. Adjust the seasonings. Halve the avocados and remove the pits. Spoon the salad into the avocado halves, and serve.

4 SERVINGS

Calories 401 Kc • Protein 16 Gm • Fat 16 Gm • Percent of calories from fat 35% • Cholesterol 0 mg • Dietary Fiber 12 Gm • Sodium 904 mg • Calcium 127 mg

Stuffed Cherry Tomatoes

These little stuffed tomato cups are pretty enough for an elegant party yet simple enough for an informal occasion.

½ cup firm tofu, drained
1 tablespoon chopped capers
1 tablespoon minced scallions
1 teaspoon minced pimiento
½ teaspoon salt
⅛ teaspoon freshly ground black pepper

24 cherry tomatoes, stems removed
1 tablespoon minced fresh parsley, or 1 teaspoon dried
Fresh parsley sprigs or watercress for garnish

In a small bowl, combine the tofu, capers, scallions, pimiento, salt, and pepper. Refrigerate while preparing the tomatoes. Cut a thin slice off the bottom of a tomato. Using the tip of a knife, scoop out the pulp and gently squeeze out the seeds and juice. Discard the sliced-off piece, juice, and seeds. Repeat with the remaining tomatoes. Using a teaspoon handle, stuff each tomato with some of the tofu mixture. Chill the tomatoes at least 30 minutes so the flavors can blend, but bring tomatoes back to room temperature before serving for the best flavor. Sprinkle with the minced parsley, and arrange on a serving platter garnished with fresh parsley or watercress.

MAKES 24

Calories 7 Kc • Protein 0 Gm • Fat 0 Gm • Percent of calories from fat 25% • Cholesterol 0 mg • Dietary Fiber 0 Gm • Sodium 63 mg • Calcium 3 mg

Stuffed Radishes and Snow Peas

2 cups firm tofu, well drained
1 tablespoon fresh lemon
   juice
1 tablespoon Dijon mustard
1 tablespoon minced
   scallion

1 tablespoon minced fresh
   parsley, or 1 teaspoon dried
½ teaspoon salt
¼ teaspoon Tabasco sauce
8 large radishes
8 large snow peas

Combine the tofu, lemon juice, mustard, scallion, parsley, salt, and Tabasco in a food processor. Taste, adjust the seasonings, and refrigerate while preparing the vegetables. Cut ¼ inch from the tops of the radishes, reserving the tops if desired, and scoop out the inside of the radishes with a small melonball cutter. Trim and string the peas, being careful not to tear the pod. If stringing the snow peas hasn't opened up one side of the pod, use a small sharp knife to do so. Fill a pastry bag (using a star tip) with the tofu mixture, and fill the radishes and pea pods. Replace the reserved tops on the radishes, if using, and arrange the radishes and pea pods decoratively on a serving tray.

MAKES 16

Calories 23 Kc • Protein 3 Gm • Fat 1 Gm • Percent of calories from fat 29% • Cholesterol 0 mg • Dietary Fiber 0 Gm • Sodium 100 mg • Calcium 14 mg

Mushroom Spread

This spread is wonderful served warm with crackers or sliced French bread rounds. Vegetarian Worcestershire sauce is available in natural food stores. The regular variety contains anchovies.

2 tablespoons olive oil
3 cups chopped mushrooms
  (about ½ pound)
1 cup minced onion
1 clove garlic, minced
2 tablespoons all-purpose flour
⅛ teaspoon freshly ground pepper

½ cup grated soy mozzarella
1 tablespoon vegetarian
  Worcestershire sauce
1 teaspoon low-sodium tamari
½ cup silken tofu, well drained
1 teaspoon fresh lemon juice

Heat the oil in a large skillet over medium heat. Add the mushrooms, onion, and garlic and sauté about 5 minutes, stirring. Stir in the flour and pepper and mix well. Add the soy mozzarella, Worcestershire sauce, and tamari and continue cooking until the soy cheese is melted. Blend in the tofu and lemon juice, and cook until heated through. Do not boil. Serve warm.

MAKES ABOUT 3 CUPS

Calories 26 Kc • Protein 1 Gm • Fat 2 Gm • Percent of calories from fat 56% • Cholesterol 0 mg • Dietary Fiber 0 Gm • Sodium 22 mg • Calcium 13 mg

Chick-pea–Watercress Tapenade

Canned chick-peas work fine for this tasty spread, particularly when served with crackers or crudités.

1¼ cups cooked or canned chick-peas
¾ cup firm silken tofu, well drained
¼ cup tahini (sesame paste)
2 tablespoons fresh lemon juice
2 cups chopped watercress, leaves and tender stems

4 scallions, minced
3 tablespoons capers
½ teaspoon salt
¼ teaspoon freshly ground pepper

Combine the chick-peas, tofu, tahini, and lemon juice in a food processor and blend until smooth. Add the watercress, scallions, capers, salt, and pepper and process until well blended. Transfer to a serving bowl. Cover and refrigerate for several hours before serving to allow the flavors to blend.

MAKES ABOUT 2 CUPS

Calories 50 Kc • Protein 3 Gm • Fat 3 Gm • Percent of calories from fat 52% • Cholesterol 0 mg • Dietary Fiber 1 Gm • Sodium 199 mg • Calcium 27 mg

Spicy Almond Spread

Use as a zesty spread for tea sandwiches or to fill zucchini cups or cherry tomatoes. Thin with a little almond milk to use as a dip for crudités.

1½ cups firm tofu, well drained
⅓ cup almond butter
3 tablespoons almond milk
1 tablespoon olive oil
1 tablespoon Dijon mustard
1½ teaspoons Tabasco sauce
½ cup minced onion
½ cup minced celery

¼ cup minced green bell pepper
¼ cup minced fresh tarragon, or 1 tablespoon dried
¼ cup minced fresh parsley, or 1 tablespoon dried
½ teaspoon paprika
Salt
Cayenne

In a food processor, combine the tofu, almond butter, almond milk, olive oil, mustard, and Tabasco until well blended. Add the onion, celery, bell pepper, tarragon, parsley, paprika, and salt and cayenne to taste, depending on the degree of spiciness desired. Taste and adjust the seasonings. If a thinner spread is desired, add more almond milk.

MAKES ABOUT 3 CUPS

Calories 39 Kc • Protein 2 Gm • Fat 3 Gm • Percent of calories from fat 64% • Cholesterol 0 mg • Dietary Fiber 0 Gm • Sodium 19 mg • Calcium 20 mg

Sun-dried Tomato and "Cheese" Spread

Use this flavorful spread in tea sandwiches or to fill cherry tomatoes.

1 tablespoon olive oil
¼ cup minced onion
1 cup silken tofu, well drained
¼ cup snipped fresh chives, or
   1 tablespoon dried
¼ cup chopped oil-packed sun-
   dried tomatoes

1 tablespoon lemon juice
1 teaspoon Dijon mustard
¼ teaspoon salt
Pinch cayenne

Heat the oil in a small skillet over medium heat. Add the onion and cook until tender, about 5 minutes. Let cool. In a medium bowl, combine the tofu, chives, tomatoes, lemon juice, mustard, salt, and cayenne. Add the onions and mix well. Stored tightly covered in the refrigerator, this spread will keep for several days.

MAKES ABOUT 1³/₄ CUPS

Calories 24 Kc • Protein 1 Gm • Fat 2 Gm • Percent of calories from fat 63% •
Cholesterol 0 mg • Dietary Fiber 0 Gm • Sodium 50 mg • Calcium 8 mg

Herbed Tofu Spread

1 pound firm tofu, drained
¼ cup minced fresh parsley
2 tablespoons snipped fresh
   chives, or 2 teaspoons dried
2 tablespoons olive oil
1 tablespoon lemon juice

1 teaspoon salt
1 tablespoon fresh thyme,
   or 1 teaspoon dried
1½ teaspoons fresh basil,
   or ½ teaspoon dried
Pinch cayenne

Place the tofu in a food processor with the parsley, chives, oil, lemon juice, salt, thyme, basil, and cayenne and blend until smooth. Transfer to a bowl and refrigerate for several hours or overnight.

MAKES ABOUT 1 CUP

Calories 66 Kc • Protein 5 Gm • Fat 4 Gm • Percent of calories from fat 61% •
Cholesterol 0 mg • Dietary Fiber 0 Gm • Sodium 328 mg • Calcium 30 mg

Dilled Mushroom Jalapeño Spread

To diffuse the heat of the jalapeños and cayenne, I generally serve this spread on a cushion of French bread or in a croustade.

1 tablespoon olive oil
1 cup chopped mushrooms
   (about ¼ pound)
2 jalapeño peppers, seeded
   and minced
½ cup minced scallion
2 tablespoons lemon juice

½ teaspoon salt
⅛ teaspoon cayenne
½ cup silken tofu, drained
¼ cup soy milk
¼ cup tahini (sesame paste)
2 tablespoons chopped fresh dill,
   or 2 teaspoons dried

Heat the oil in a medium skillet over medium heat. Add the mushrooms, jalapeños, and scallion and cook for 5 minutes. Add the lemon juice, salt, and cayenne. Cook 2 minutes longer, stirring occasionally. Remove from the heat. In a small bowl combine the tofu, soy milk, tahini, and dill, whisking until thoroughly blended. Stir the tofu mixture into the mushroom mixture and blend well. Transfer to a serving bowl, or spoon into croustades and serve.

4 SERVINGS

Calories 179 Kc • Protein 7 Gm • Fat 14 Gm • Percent of calories from fat 71% • Cholesterol 0 mg • Dietary Fiber 1 Gm • Sodium 512 mg • Calcium 76 mg

Elegant Asparagus Timbales

1½ pounds fresh asparagus
spears, trimmed
¼ cup firm silken tofu, well
drained
1 tablespoon almond butter
½ teaspoon salt
¼ teaspoon freshly grated nutmeg

⅛ teaspoon cayenne
4 cherry tomatoes, cut into thin
slices
1 tablespoon chopped fresh
parsley, or 1 teaspoon dried
8 sprigs watercress for
garnish

Preheat the oven to 400 degrees. Lightly oil 4 custard cups or coat with nonstick cooking spray. Cook the asparagus in enough boiling water to cover, until tender, about 5 minutes. Drain well. Cut off 4 tips and set aside. Place the remaining asparagus in a food processor and puree until smooth. Add the tofu, almond butter, salt, nutmeg, and cayenne, and process until well blended. Spoon into the prepared cups, and place in a 9 × 9-inch baking pan. Add 1 inch of boiling water to the pan. Bake until set, about 30 minutes. Just before serving, warm the reserved asparagus tips in simmering water until heated through. Invert the timbales onto serving plates. Top each timbale with a fan of three cherry tomato slices and 1 of the reserved asparagus tips. Sprinkle with the chopped parsley, arrange a sprig of watercress on either side of the timbale, and serve.

4 SERVINGS

Calories 80 Kc • Protein 7 Gm • Fat 4 Gm • Percent of calories from fat 42% • Cholesterol 0 mg • Dietary Fiber 2 Gm • Sodium 329 mg • Calcium 46 mg

Eggplant Pâté

A firm, almost pâté-like version of Baba Ganouj, the popular Middle Eastern eggplant spread.

1 cup almonds
1 large eggplant
1 tablespoon olive oil
½ cup minced onion
1 teaspoon minced garlic
½ cup almond butter or tahini
   (sesame paste)
1 cup firm tofu, well drained

¼ cup minced fresh parsley, or 1
   tablespoon dried
1 tablespoon low-sodium tamari
1 teaspoon lemon juice
¼ teaspoon allspice
½ teaspoon salt
⅛ teaspoon cayenne

Preheat the oven to 350 degrees. Spread the almonds on a baking sheet and bake for 10 minutes. Finely grind in a food processor. Increase the oven temperature to 375 degrees. Halve the eggplant and bake, cut side down, on a lightly oiled baking pan until tender, about 30 minutes. Scoop out the pulp and set aside. Reduce the oven temperature to 350 degrees. Heat the oil in a small skillet over medium heat, add the onion, cover, and cook until tender, about 5 minutes. Add the garlic and cook 1 minute longer. Place the eggplant pulp in a food processor, add the cooked onion mixture and the almond butter, tofu, parsley, tamari, lemon juice, allspice, salt, and cayenne, and process until well blended. Taste and adjust the seasonings. Lightly oil a small loaf pan or coat with nonstick cooking spray. Fill with the eggplant mixture and cover loosely with aluminum foil. Bake for about 1 hour and 20 minutes, or until firm. Let it cool completely before removing it from the pan. Refrigerate several hours or overnight before serving.

8 SERVINGS

Calories 254 Kc • Protein 8 Gm • Fat 21 Gm • Percent of calories from fat 69% • Cholesterol 0 mg • Dietary Fiber 3 Gm • Sodium 380 mg • Calcium 113 mg

4

Pasta Dishes

Everyone loves pasta. There are so many wonderful ways to enjoy it that it has become a mainstay of many people's diet, not just vegetarians'.

However, making the decision to give up dairy products raises some serious questions, such as: "What about lasagne?" or "How do I make my macaroni and cheese?" Once again, a trusty arsenal of dairy alternatives can put creamy pasta dishes on the table that are sure to satisfy. Along with dairy-free versions of the "classics" come such intriguing temptations as Rigatoni with Vodka Tomato Cream, Rotini with Creamy Mushroom Sauce, and Ziti with Tarragon-Walnut Pesto. With pasta dishes like these, you'll never miss the dairy products.

Tofu Lasagne

A dairy-free version of everyone's favorite. This dish alone has won many of my friends and cooking students over to dairy-free cooking.

1 tablespoon olive oil
1 medium onion, minced
1 teaspoon minced garlic
4 cups tomato puree
1 tablespoon dried basil
1 teaspoon dried oregano
1 bay leaf
1½ teaspoons salt
½ teaspoon freshly ground pepper

3 cups firm tofu, drained and crumbled
¼ cup minced fresh parsley, or 1 tablespoon dried
8 ounces lasagna noodles, cooked and drained
1 cup shredded soy mozzarella cheese

Heat the oil in a large saucepan over medium heat. Add the onion, cover, and cook 5 minutes, stirring occasionally. Remove the lid, add the garlic, tomato puree, basil, oregano, bay leaf, $1/2$ teaspoon of the salt, and $1/4$ teaspoon of the pepper. Simmer for 20 to 30 minutes to allow the flavors to blend. Discard the bay leaf. Preheat the oven to 375 degrees. In a large bowl, combine the tofu with the parsley, the remaining 1 teaspoon of salt, and the remaining $1/4$ teaspoon of pepper, mixing until well combined. Spread a thin layer of the tomato sauce in the bottom of a shallow rectangular baking dish. Arrange a layer of the cooked lasagna noodles in the bottom of the pan, and top with a layer of the tofu mixture. Repeat with alternating layers, ending with a layer of the tomato sauce. Top with the soy cheese, and bake for 30 to 40 minutes, or until heated through. Let stand for 5 minutes before cutting.

8 SERVINGS

Calories 261Kc • Protein 15 Gm • Fat 6 Gm • Percent of calories from fat 20% • Cholesterol 0 mg • Dietary Fiber 4 Gm • Sodium 557 mg • Calcium 106 mg

Tofu Ravioli

Serve these flavorful packets cloaked with your favorite tomato sauce. Although tofu ravioli are available commercially prepared, they are easy to make yourself and far more economical.

3½ cups all-purpose flour
⅛ teaspoon salt
1 cup warm water (approximately)
3 cups firm tofu, drained and crumbled

2 tablespoons minced fresh parsley, or 2 teaspoons dried
¾ teaspoon salt
¼ teaspoon freshly ground black pepper

Mix the flour and salt together in a bowl and add just enough of the water to make a soft dough. Knead well, about 5 minutes, and set aside. Place the tofu in a mixing bowl, add the parsley, salt, and pepper; mix well and set aside. Divide the dough into 4 equal pieces and roll out on a floured board. Cut into 3 × 5-inch rectangles. Place a heaping teaspoon of the tofu mixture onto each rectangle, fold the dough over the filling to cover, aligning the edges of the dough to form a square. Seal all round the edges with a fork to secure the filling inside. Drop the squares into a large pan of salted boiling water, a few at a time, and cook for 10 minutes, or until the ravioli float to the surface. Drain well, and serve with your favorite tomato sauce.

MAKES ABOUT 48 RAVIOLI, OR 8 TO 10 SERVINGS

Calories 223 Kc • Protein 11 Gm • Fat 2 Gm • Percent of calories from fat 9% • Cholesterol 0 mg • Dietary Fiber 2 Gm • Sodium 277 • Calcium 83 mg

Rigatoni with Artichoke Carrot Sauce

1 tablespoon safflower oil
½ cup minced onion
1 teaspoon minced garlic
3 large carrots, peeled and grated
1 (10-ounce) package frozen artichoke hearts, thawed and sliced
1½ cups Vegetable Stock (see page 10)

¾ teaspoon salt
½ teaspoon freshly ground white pepper
1 teaspoon minced fresh thyme, or ⅛ teaspoon dried
1½ cups soy milk
1 pound rigatoni, or other tubular pasta

Heat the oil in a large saucepan over medium heat. Add the onion and cook, covered, for 5 minutes, or until soft. Remove the lid, stir in the garlic, carrots, and artichokes, and cook for 5 minutes. Add the stock, increase the heat to medium high, and bring to a boil. Add the salt, pepper, and thyme, reduce the heat to low, and simmer for 15 minutes. Remove from the heat and slowly stir in the soy milk. While the sauce is simmering, cook the rigatoni in a pot of boiling salted water until tender but firm to the bite. Drain and toss with the sauce.

4 SERVINGS

Calories 524 Kc • Protein 18 Gm • Fat 10 Gm • Percent of calories from fat 17% • Cholesterol 0 mg • Dietary Fiber 8 Gm • Sodium 541 mg • Calcium 97 mg

Linguine with Lime Cilantro Sauce

2 tablespoons olive oil
1 cup minced onion
1 red bell pepper, seeded and
 cut in ½-inch dice
1 yellow bell pepper, seeded and
 cut in ½-inch dice
2 tablespoons all-purpose
 flour
2 cups soy milk

1 tomato, peeled, seeded, and
 chopped
1 tablespoon minced garlic
2 tablespoons fresh lime juice
1 tablespoon minced fresh ginger
¼ teaspoon hot red pepper flakes
2 tablespoons minced cilantro
1 pound linguine

Heat the oil in a large skillet over medium heat. Add the onion and bell peppers, and cook until softened, about 5 minutes. Stir in the flour and gradually add the soy milk, stirring constantly until smooth. Cook for 2 minutes longer over very low heat. Add the tomato, garlic, lime juice, ginger, and pepper flakes, and stir until well combined. Add the cilantro, and continue cooking and stirring over low heat, for 3 to 5 minutes. Meanwhile, cook the linguine in a large pot of boiling salted water until tender but still firm to the bite. Drain the pasta and place in a serving bowl, add the sauce and toss. Serve immediately.

4 SERVINGS

Calories 486 Kc • Protein 16 Gm • Fat 9 Gm • Percent of calories from fat 17% • Cholesterol 0 mg • Dietary Fiber 4 Gm • Sodium 57 mg • Calcium 57 mg

Lemon-Tarragon Pasta Spirals

1 tablespoon corn oil
2 shallots, minced
1 clove garlic, minced
1 pound firm tofu, drained and
  crumbled
½ cup chopped fresh tarragon
½ cup fresh bread crumbs
2 tablespoons lemon juice
1 teaspoon salt
⅛ teaspoon cayenne
½ cup soy milk
9 lasagna noodles

Sauce:
1 tablespoon corn oil
2 shallots, minced
1 16-ounce can tomatoes,
  drained
2 tablespoons tomato paste
1 teaspoon lemon juice
1 cup soy milk mixed with 2
  tablespoons cornstarch
1 teaspoon brandy
Salt and freshly ground pepper
Fresh tarragon sprigs for garnish

Heat the oil in a small skillet over medium heat, add the shallots and the garlic and cook about 5 minutes, stirring frequently, until softened. Let cool, and then transfer to a food processor and add the tofu, tarragon, bread crumbs, lemon juice, salt, and cayenne, and puree until well blended. Add the soy milk and puree to blend. Transfer to a bowl and refrigerate 30 minutes.

To assemble, cook the lasagna noodles in a large pot of boiling salted water until al dente. Drain, separate onto a work surface, and pat dry. Divide the filling among the lasagna noodles, and spread over the surface of each noodle. Starting at one short end, roll the noodles up tightly, in a jelly roll fashion. Preheat the oven to 350 degrees.

For the sauce, heat the oil in a medium skillet over medium-low heat. Add the shallots and cook 5 minutes, stirring frequently. In a food processor, puree the tomatoes with the tomato paste and lemon juice until blended. Add the pureed mixture to the shallots. Simmer the sauce for 10 minutes. Stir in the soy milk mixture and simmer, stirring, until thickened, about 5 minutes. Stir in the brandy and season with salt and pepper to taste.

Place the pasta rolls in a lightly oiled shallow baking pan, seam side down. Lightly coat the pasta rolls with 1 cup of the sauce. Cover loosely and bake 15 minutes to heat through. Remove the rolls from the pan and cut each into 2 slices and stand upright. Spread a small amount of sauce on each plate, and arrange 3 slices on top of the sauce. Spoon the remaining sauce over each plate and garnish with tarragon sprigs.

6 SERVINGS

Calories 258 Kc • Protein 11 Gm • Fat 8 Gm • Percent of calories from fat 29% • Cholesterol 0 mg • Dietary Fiber 2 Gm • Sodium 670 mg • Calcium 94 mg

Pesto

Soy Parmesan is available in natural food stores. If unavailable, substitute grated soy mozzarella, miso paste, or soft tofu and a little extra salt.

1½ cups packed fresh basil leaves
½ cup pine nuts (or almonds)
3 large cloves garlic

⅓ cup grated soy Parmesan
⅓ cup olive oil
½ teaspoon salt

Place the basil, pine nuts, and garlic in a food processor and puree until smooth. Add the Parmesan, oil, and salt and puree to a smooth paste.

MAKES 2 CUPS

Calories 72 Kc • Protein 2 Gm • Fat 7 Gm • Percent of calories from fat 83% • Cholesterol 0 mg • Dietary Fiber 0 Gm • Sodium 103 mg • Calcium 36 mg

Pesto Lasagne

A nice change from regular lasagne, and a real crowd-pleaser.

1 tablespoon olive oil
1 medium onion, chopped
1 green bell pepper, seeded and chopped
2 cloves garlic, minced
2 cups sliced mushrooms (about ½ pound)
1 28-ounce can whole tomatoes, drained

1 6-ounce can tomato paste
1 small bay leaf
1 8-ounce package lasagna noodles
2 cups Pesto (recipe on page 151)
1 pound firm tofu, drained and crumbled
8 ounces grated soy mozzarella

Heat the oil in a large saucepan over medium heat. Add the onion, bell pepper, and garlic and cook until softened, about 5 minutes. Add the mushrooms and cook 3 minutes longer, stirring occasionally. Add the tomatoes, tomato paste, and bay leaf. Reduce the heat to low, cover, and simmer 45 minutes, stirring occasionally. Discard the bay leaf.

While the sauce is cooking, bring a pot of salted water to a boil and cook the lasagna noodles according to the package directions. Drain in a colander and run under cold water. Reserve. Preheat the oven to 350 degrees. Mix the pesto and tofu in a medium bowl. Spoon a thin layer of tomato sauce into bottom of a 9 × 13-inch baking dish. Top with a layer of noodles. Spread some of the pesto mixture evenly over the top. Sprinkle with some of the mozzarella. Repeat the layering. Cover with foil and bake for 30 minutes. Remove the foil and bake 10 minutes longer, until top is golden brown.

8 SERVINGS

Calories 428 Kc • Protein 21 Gm • Fat 22 Gm • Percent of calories from fat 45% • Cholesterol 0 mg • Dietary Fiber 5 Gm • Sodium 493 mg • Calcium 232 mg

Santa Fe Pasta Bake

1 10-ounce package frozen
spinach, thawed
1 cup firm silken tofu, drained
½ cup rice milk
½ teaspoon dried oregano
1 tablespoon olive oil
2 cloves garlic, minced
2 cups cooked pinto beans
2 cups picante sauce

1 6-ounce can tomato paste,
blended with 1 cup water
1 tablespoon chili powder (or to
taste)
8 ounces penne pasta, cooked
and drained
1 cup shredded soy Cheddar
cheese

Preheat the oven to 350 degrees. Squeeze the liquid out of the spinach and place in a food processor with the tofu, rice milk, and oregano and process until well blended. Set aside. Heat the oil in a large skillet over low heat, add the garlic and cook until fragrant, being careful not to burn. Add the pinto beans, picante sauce, tomato paste mixture, and chili powder and mix well. Bring to a boil. Reduce the heat and simmer, uncovered, 5 minutes. Add the pasta and mix well. Lightly oil a large baking dish or coat it with nonstick cooking spray and spoon half of the pasta mixture into the dish, spreading it evenly. Spread the spinach mixture evenly on top of the pasta layer. Top with the remaining pasta mixture. Bake, covered, for 25 minutes. Uncover and sprinkle with the soy cheese; continue baking 5 minutes. Let stand several minutes before serving.

4 SERVINGS

Calories 446 Kc • Protein 23 Gm • Fat 11 Gm • Percent of calories from fat 20% • Cholesterol 0 mg • Dietary Fiber 9 Gm • Sodium 1278 mg • Calcium 262 mg

Mediterranean Pasta Bake

An Italian version of macaroni and cheese.

1 tablespoon olive oil
4 minced scallions
2 cloves garlic, minced
2 tablespoons chopped fresh parsley, or 2 teaspoons dried
1 tablespoon chopped fresh basil, or 1 teaspoon dried
¾ teaspoon salt
½ teaspoon freshly ground black pepper
1 pound shell pasta, cooked and drained

2 cups firm tofu, drained and crumbled
2 tablespoons lemon juice
1 tablespoon chopped capers
2 cups diced ripe tomatoes
2 cups soy milk
2 tablespoons cornstarch combined with 2 tablespoons water
½ cup silken tofu, drained
½ cup grated soy mozzarella cheese

Preheat the oven to 375 degrees. Heat the oil in a large skillet, add the scallions and cook over medium heat for 3 minutes. Add the garlic, parsley, basil, salt, and black pepper, and cook 2 minutes longer. Combine the scallion mixture with the cooked pasta in a large bowl. Add the crumbled tofu, lemon juice, capers, and tomatoes and mix well. Spray a shallow baking dish with nonstick cooking spray. Spread the pasta mixture evenly in the dish, and set aside. Heat the soy milk in a saucepan over medium high heat, being careful not to boil. Whisk in the cornstarch mixture and stir 2 to 3 minutes, until thickened. Remove from the heat, whisk in the silken tofu, and pour the sauce over the top of the casserole. Sprinkle the top with the grated soy cheese. Bake, uncovered, for 30 minutes.

6 SERVINGS

Calories 467 Kc • Protein 23 Gm • Fat 9 Gm • Percent of calories from fat 17% • Cholesterol 0 mg • Dietary Fiber 3 Gm • Sodium 474 mg • Calcium 117 mg

Fettuccine with Artichoke Caper Sauce

2 tablespoons olive oil
2 tablespoons all-purpose flour
2 cups soy milk
1 clove garlic, crushed
2 tablespoons minced fresh
   parsley, or 2 teaspoons dried
1 tablespoon fresh lemon juice

Salt and freshly ground white
   pepper
1 14-ounce can artichoke hearts
   in brine, drained and sliced
1½ tablespoons capers, rinsed
   and drained
1 pound fettuccine

Heat the oil in a small saucepan over medium heat. Add the flour and cook, stirring constantly, about 2 minutes. Blend in the soy milk, stirring until thickened, about 1 minute. Reduce the heat to low. Add the garlic, 1 tablespoon of the parsley, the lemon juice, salt and pepper to taste and cook about 5 minutes, stirring constantly. Blend in the artichokes and capers. Simmer over low heat about 5 minutes. Meanwhile, cook the fettuccine in a large pot of boiling salted water until tender but firm to the bite. Drain the fettuccine and place in a serving bowl, add the sauce, and toss lightly. Garnish with the remaining 1 tablespoon of parsley.

4 SERVINGS

Calories 513 Kc • Protein 15 Gm • Fat 14 Gm • Percent of calories from fat 25% • Cholesterol 0 mg • Dietary Fiber 5 Gm • Sodium 372 mg • Calcium 47 mg

Ziti with Tarragon-Walnut Pesto

Green peppercorns are packed in vinegar and available in 3-ounce jars in the gourmet section of most supermarkets.

1 pound ziti, or other tubular
   pasta
1 cup packed fresh tarragon
   leaves
2 large cloves garlic
½ teaspoon salt
1 tablespoon green peppercorns,
   drained

1 cup walnut halves
½ cup firm tofu, drained and
   crumbled
1 tablespoon fresh lemon juice
½ cup olive oil
¼ cup hot soy milk

Cook the ziti in a large pot of boiling salted water until tender, but still firm to the bite. While the ziti cooks, prepare the sauce. In a food processor, combine the tarragon and the garlic and puree to a paste. Add the salt, green peppercorns, walnuts, and tofu and process until smooth. Add the lemon juice and continue processing until blended. With the machine running, add the oil in a slow steady stream, followed by the hot soy milk, added slowly, processing until the mixture is smooth and creamy. Adjust the seasonings.

   Drain the pasta and toss with the sauce. Serve immediately.

4 SERVINGS

**Calories 710 Kc • Protein 18 Gm • Fat 39 Gm • Percent of calories from fat 48%
• Cholesterol 0 mg • Dietary Fiber 3 Gm • Sodium 264 mg • Calcium 70 mg**

Farmer's Market Rotini

2 tablespoons olive oil
1 cup chopped onion
1 cup eggplant, cut into julienne
  strips
1 red or yellow bell pepper,
  seeded and cut into julienne
  strips
2 cups zucchini, cut into julienne
  strips (2-inches long and ⅛-inch
  thick)
2 cloves garlic, minced

1 16-ounce can Italian-style plum
  tomatoes, chopped, liquid
  reserved
½ cup soy milk
Salt and freshly ground black
  pepper
1 pound rotini, cooked al dente,
  drained
¼ cup minced fresh basil or
  parsley, or 1 tablespoon dried
½ cup grated soy mozzarella

Heat the oil in a large skillet over medium heat, add the onion, and cook for 5 minutes. Add the eggplant, bell pepper, zucchini, and garlic and cook for 10 minutes, stirring occasionally. Add the tomatoes to the pan with their liquid. Lower the heat to a simmer and continue to cook 5 more minutes. Slowly stir in the soy milk. Blend well and season with salt and pepper to taste. Place the cooked pasta in a large serving bowl. Pour the sauce over the pasta. Sprinkle with the basil and soy mozzarella. Serve immediately.

4 SERVINGS

Calories 593 Kc • Protein 21 Gm • Fat 12 Gm • Percent of calories from fat 18% • Cholesterol 0 mg • Dietary Fiber 7 Gm • Sodium 69 mg • Calcium 111 mg

Rotini with Creamy Mushroom Sauce

2 tablespoons olive oil
1 medium onion, chopped
2 cloves garlic, minced
1½ cups sliced portobello
    mushrooms (about ⅓ pound)
1½ cups sliced white mushrooms
    (about ⅓ pound)
2 tablespoons all-purpose flour
2 cups almond milk

4 drained canned artichoke
    hearts, sliced
1 tablespoon minced fresh basil,
    or ½ teaspoon dried
¼ teaspoon hot red pepper flakes
1 tablespoon balsamic vinegar
1 pound rotini or other spiral
    pasta

Heat the olive oil in a large saucepan over medium heat. Add the onion and sauté 5 minutes or until softened. Add the garlic and mushrooms and cook 1 minute. Stir in the flour and cook 1 minute. Reduce the heat to low. Slowly add the almond milk, stirring constantly, to achieve a smooth sauce, about 2 minutes. Add the artichokes, basil, pepper flakes, and vinegar and simmer 10 minutes to allow the flavors to blend. Meanwhile, cook the rotini in a large pot of boiling salted water until tender. Drain and place the pasta in a serving bowl, add the sauce, and toss lightly.

6 SERVINGS

Calories 410 Kc • Protein 13 Gm • Fat 11 Gm • Percent of calories from fat 24% • Cholesterol 0 mg • Dietary Fiber 4 Gm • Sodium 38 mg • Calcium 50 mg

Spinach-stuffed Manicotti with Tomato Cream Sauce

12 manicotti, cooked al dente
2 10-ounce packages frozen chopped spinach, thawed
2 cups firm tofu, drained and crumbled
2 scallions, minced
2 tablespoons fresh lemon juice
1 teaspoon minced fresh dill, or ¼ teaspoon dried
¼ teaspoon ground nutmeg

Salt and freshly ground pepper
2 tablespoons corn oil
2 tablespoons flour
2½ cups hot rice milk
2 tablespoons tomato paste
1 cup silken tofu, drained
1 cup fresh bread crumbs
2 tablespoons margarine, melted
1 cup grated soy mozzarella

Drain the cooked manicotti in a colander and run under very cold water to stop cooking process. Reserve. Squeeze the spinach in a towel to remove as much liquid as possible. Place in a bowl, add the firm tofu, scallions, lemon juice, ½ teaspoon of the dill, nutmeg, and salt and pepper to taste. Heat the oil in a medium saucepan over medium heat, stir in the flour, and cook 2 minutes. Reduce the heat to low. Whisk in the hot rice milk and tomato paste. Cook 2 minutes longer. Stir in the silken tofu, remaining ½ teaspoon dill, and salt and pepper to taste. Remove the sauce from the heat. Preheat the oven to 350 degrees. Spray a 9 × 13-inch baking dish with vegetable cooking spray. Spread a layer of the sauce in the dish. Stuff the manicotti with the spinach mixture, using a small spoon, being careful not to overstuff. Place the stuffed manicotti in a single layer in the prepared dish. Spoon the remaining sauce over the manicotti. In a small bowl, combine the bread crumbs and margarine with a fork; blend in the soy cheese. Sprinkle over the casserole. Cover with foil, and bake for 30 minutes. Uncover, and bake 10 more minutes to allow the top to become golden brown.

4 SERVINGS

Calories 672 Kc • Protein 36 Gm • Fat 22 Gm • Percent of calories from fat 28% • Cholesterol 0 mg • Dietary Fiber 8 Gm • Sodium 624 mg • Calcium 470 mg

Penne from Heaven

This heavenly pasta dish is penne and broccoli in a creamy sauce, studded with chopped fresh tomatoes.

2 tablespoons corn oil
½ cup chopped onion
2 scallions, minced
2 tablespoons all-purpose flour
2 cups soy milk
2 large tomatoes, peeled, seeded, and chopped
1 tablespoon chopped capers

Salt and freshly ground black pepper
2 cups broccoli florets, coarsely chopped
1 pound penne or other tubular pasta
1 cup grated soy Parmesan cheese
1 tablespoon olive oil

Heat the oil in large skillet over medium heat. Add the onion and scallions, and cook until softened, about 5 minutes. Add the flour and cook, stirring, for 2 minutes. Slowly add the soy milk, stirring constantly, to make a smooth sauce. Add the tomatoes and capers and cook 2 minutes, stirring. Season with salt and pepper to taste. Remove the sauce from the heat and keep warm. Bring a large pot of salted water to boil over high heat. Add the broccoli and cook 3 to 4 minutes. Remove with a slotted spoon and drain well. Transfer the cooked broccoli to a large bowl. Cook the pasta in the boiling salted water until tender. Drain. Add the cooked pasta to the broccoli in the bowl, along with the soy cheese and olive oil, and toss to blend. Add the sauce and toss gently. Season with salt and pepper. Serve immediately.

4 SERVINGS

Calories 561 Kc • Protein 21 Gm • Fat 15 Gm • Percent of calories from fat 25% • Cholesterol 0 mg • Dietary Fiber 5 Gm • Sodium 182 mg • Calcium 146 mg

Radiatore with Mushroom Caper Sauce

The tomato paste adds a rosy blush to the sauce.

2 tablespoons olive oil
2 cups chopped mushrooms
  (about ⅓ pound)
¼ cup minced scallion
2 tablespoons all-purpose flour
2 cups soy milk
2 tablespoons drained capers,
  chopped

1 tablespoon tomato paste
1 tablespoon minced fresh
  parsley, or 1 teaspoon dried
Salt and freshly ground
  pepper
1 pound radiatore pasta or other
  small pasta

Heat the oil in a large skillet over medium heat, add the mushrooms and scallion, and cook 5 minutes, stirring occasionally. Add the flour and cook, stirring for 2 minutes. Slowly stir in the soy milk and cook, stirring constantly for 2 minutes to make a smooth sauce. Stir in the capers, tomato paste, parsley, and salt and pepper to taste. Meanwhile, cook the pasta in a large pot of boiling salted water until tender, and drain. Place the cooked pasta in a serving bowl, add the sauce, and toss well.

4 SERVINGS

Calories 584 Kc • Protein 19 Gm • Fat 11 Gm • Percent of calories from fat 18%
• Cholesterol 0 mg • Dietary Fiber 4 Gm • Sodium 151 mg • Calcium 68 mg

Perciatelli and Tempeh Bacon with Creamy Almond Sauce

Perciatelli can be described as "thick spaghetti," but that doesn't really do it justice. Its delightful chewiness makes it one of my favorite pastas. If you can't find it in the grocery store, try an Italian market.

2 tablespoons corn oil
¼ cup minced onion
2 tablespoons minced shallot
2 tablespoons minced red bell pepper
2 teaspoons minced garlic
2 tablespoons all-purpose flour
2 cups almond milk
½ cup chopped toasted almonds

¼ cup firm tofu, drained and crumbled
2 tablespoons minced fresh parsley
Salt and freshly ground pepper
1 pound perciatelli, (or spaghetti or fettuccine)
4 ounces tempeh bacon, cooked and chopped

Heat the oil in a large skillet over medium heat. Add the onion, shallot, bell pepper, and garlic and sauté until softened, about 5 minutes. Add the flour and cook, stirring, for 2 minutes. Reduce the heat to low. Slowly add the almond milk, stirring constantly, and cook for 2 minutes. Mix in the almonds, tofu, parsley, and salt and pepper to taste. Set the sauce aside and keep warm. Meanwhile, cook the pasta in a large pot of boiling, salted water until tender but still firm to the bite. Drain. Place the cooked pasta in a serving bowl, add the sauce and toss gently. Sprinkle the tempeh bacon on top of the pasta.

4 SERVINGS

Calories 599 Kc • Protein 20 Gm • Fat 24 Gm • Percent of calories from fat 35% • Cholesterol 0 mg • Dietary Fiber 5 Gm • Sodium 462 mg • Calcium 105 mg

Paglia e Fieno

A dairy-free version of the classic pasta dish named for the combination of green and yellow noodles which resemble "straw and hay."

2 tablespoons corn oil
4 ounces tempeh bacon, finely minced
1 10-ounce package frozen peas, thawed
1 cup soy milk
1 cup grated soy Parmesan cheese

Pinch ground nutmeg
Salt and freshly ground pepper
½ pound spinach linguine, cooked al dente, drained
½ pound regular linguine, cooked al dente, drained

Heat the oil in a large saucepan over medium-high heat. Add the tempeh bacon and sauté 2 to 3 minutes. Reduce the heat to low, stir in the peas, soy milk, $1/2$ cup of the soy cheese, nutmeg, and salt and pepper to taste, mixing well. Add the linguine and toss until well combined. Transfer to a serving bowl, sprinkle with the remaining $1/2$ cup soy cheese and serve immediately.

4 SERVINGS

Calories 475 Kc • Protein 20 Gm • Fat 18 Gm • Percent of calories from fat 33%
• Cholesterol 15 mg • Dietary Fiber 6 Gm • Sodium 463 mg • Calcium 127 mg

Capellini with Garlicky Walnut Sauce

2 tablespoons olive oil
4 cloves garlic, chopped
1 cup chopped walnuts
½ cup silken tofu, drained
¼ cup soy milk
12 ounces capellini, or other thin
  pasta

½ cup grated soy Parmesan
  cheese
Salt and freshly ground black
  pepper

Heat the oil in a medium skillet over medium heat, add the garlic and walnuts, and cook, stirring until fragrant, about 1 minute. Remove from the heat. In a small bowl, combine the tofu with the soy milk until well blended, and stir into the walnut mixture. Set aside. Cook the capellini in a large pot of boiling salted water until tender but still firm to the bite. Place the hot cooked pasta in a serving bowl, toss with the sauce, add the soy cheese, and season with salt and black pepper to taste. Serve immediately.

4 SERVINGS

Calories 632 Kc • Protein 20 Gm • Fat 30 Gm • Percent of calories from fat 42%
• Cholesterol 0 mg • Dietary Fiber 4 Gm • Sodium 51 mg • Calcium 112 mg

Linguine with Creamy Red Pepper Sauce

2 tablespoons olive oil
1 onion, chopped
4 large red bell peppers, diced
3 ripe tomatoes, diced
3 cloves garlic, chopped
Salt and freshly ground black
  pepper

½ cup silken tofu, drained
½ cup soy milk
1 pound linguine, cooked al
  dente and drained
2 tablespoons minced fresh
  parsley, or 2 teaspoons dried

Heat the oil in a large skillet over low heat. Add the onion, bell peppers, tomatoes, and garlic, cover and cook 15 minutes, stirring occasionally. Season with salt and pepper to taste, cover and cook 10 minutes longer, or until the vegetables are very tender. Transfer the cooked vegetables to a food processor and puree until smooth. Add the tofu and soy milk and process until smooth. Press the sauce through a fine sieve to achieve a smooth consistency. Adjust the seasonings. Place the hot cooked pasta in a serving bowl, add the sauce and toss to combine. Adjust the seasonings and sprinkle with the minced parsley. Serve immediately.

4 SERVINGS

Calories 466 Kc • Protein 15 Gm • Fat 9 Gm • Percent of calories from fat 16% • Cholesterol 0 mg • Dietary Fiber 5 Gm • Sodium 30 mg • Calcium 53 mg

Rigatoni with Vodka Tomato Cream

2 tablespoons olive oil
3 cloves garlic, chopped
¼ teaspoon hot red pepper flakes
2 tablespoons vodka
3 cups diced ripe tomatoes
½ cup silken tofu, drained

½ cup soy milk
Salt and freshly ground black
    pepper
1 pound rigatoni, or other
    tubular pasta

Heat the oil in a large skillet over medium heat. Add the garlic and hot pepper flakes and cook 1 minute, or until the garlic is fragrant, but not brown. Remove from the heat and carefully add the vodka. Return the pan to the heat and add the tomatoes. Cook over high heat to evaporate the alcohol until the liquid is reduced by half. Transfer the tomato mixture to a food processor, add the tofu and soy milk, and puree to produce a smooth sauce. Season with salt and pepper to taste. Meanwhile, cook the rigatoni in a large pot of boiling salted water until tender but still firm to the bite. Drain and toss the hot cooked pasta with the sauce in a serving bowl.

4 SERVINGS

Calories 460 Kc • Protein 15 Gm • Fat 9 Gm • Percent of calories from fat 17% • Cholesterol 0 mg • Dietary Fiber 4 Gm • Sodium 32 mg • Calcium 41 mg

Fettuccine in a Creamy Tarragon Tomato Sauce

2 tablespoons olive oil
1 small onion, chopped
2 cloves garlic, chopped
1 cup chopped mushrooms
2 cups chopped ripe tomatoes
2 tablespoons tomato paste
1 cup Vegetable Stock (see page 10)

1 cup soy milk
⅓ cup silken tofu, drained
3 tablespoons chopped fresh tarragon, or 1 tablespoon dried
Salt and freshly ground black pepper
1 pound fettuccine, cooked al dente and drained

Heat the oil in a large skillet over medium heat. Add the onion, and cook for 5 minutes. Add the garlic and mushrooms, and cook another 3 minutes or until the vegetables have softened. Add the tomatoes, tomato paste, and stock and cook for 10 minutes, stirring occasionally. Remove from the heat and slowly stir in the soy milk, tofu, 2 tablespoons of the tarragon, and salt and pepper to taste. Toss the hot cooked pasta with the sauce in a serving bowl and sprinkle with remaining 1 tablespoon of tarragon.

4 SERVINGS

Calories 463 Kc • Protein 16 Gm • Fat 9 Gm • Percent of calories from fat 17% • Cholesterol 0 mg • Dietary Fiber 4 Gm • Sodium 45 mg • Calcium 57 mg

Ziti Florentine

1 10-ounce package frozen
   chopped spinach, thawed
1 tablespoon olive oil
¼ cup minced shallots
1 tablespoon all-purpose flour
1 cup hot rice milk
1 cup firm tofu, drained and
   crumbled
½ cup grated soy mozzarella
   cheese

1 tablespoon chopped fresh
   basil, or 1 teaspoon dried
Pinch nutmeg
Salt and freshly ground black
   pepper
1 pound ziti, or other tubular
   pasta

Squeeze the spinach in a towel to remove as much liquid as possible and set aside. Heat the oil in a medium skillet, add the shallots, and cook over medium heat for 5 minutes, or until soft. Stir in the flour and cook, stirring, for 2 minutes. Reduce the heat to low, stir in the rice milk, and cook to produce a smooth sauce, about 3 minutes. Add the spinach, stirring to blend, then add the tofu, soy cheese, basil, nutmeg, and salt and pepper to taste. Meanwhile, cook the pasta in a large pot of boiling salted water until tender, but still firm to the bite. Drain the pasta and toss with the hot sauce. Serve immediately.

4 SERVINGS

Calories 459 Kc • Protein 20 Gm • Fat 7 Gm • Percent of calories from fat 14% • Cholesterol 0 mg • Dietary Fiber 3 Gm • Sodium 114 mg • Calcium 137 mg

Orrechiette and Asparagus with Lemon-Tarragon Pesto

Orrechiette means "little ears" in Italian. If unavailable, substitute radiatore or small shells.

1 cup packed fresh tarragon
  leaves
¼ cup almonds
2 large cloves garlic
¼ cup olive oil
1 tablespoon lemon juice
1 teaspoon minced lemon zest
1 teaspoon white miso paste
¼ cup silken tofu, drained

¼ cup almond milk
12 ounces fresh asparagus,
  trimmed and cut into 2-inch
  lengths
1 pound orrechiette, or other
  small pasta
Salt and freshly ground black
  pepper

Place the tarragon, almonds, and garlic in a food processor and puree until smooth. Add the olive oil, lemon juice, zest, and miso and puree to a smooth paste. Add the tofu and almond milk and set aside. Cook the asparagus in boiling salted water until the asparagus is crisp-tender, about 3 minutes; drain. Meanwhile, cook the pasta in a large pot of boiling salted water until tender; drain. Toss the hot cooked pasta and asparagus with the tarragon mixture, season with salt and pepper to taste, and serve immediately.

4 SERVINGS

Calories 508 Kc • Protein 16 Gm • Fat 17 Gm • Percent of calories from fat 30% • Cholesterol 0 mg • Dietary Fiber 5 Gm • Sodium 52 mg • Calcium 73 mg

Fusilli with Tarragon Mushroom Sauce

2 tablespoons olive oil
½ cup chopped onions
2 cloves garlic, minced
2 cups sliced mushrooms (about
    ½ pound)
3 tablespoons chopped fresh
    tarragon, or 1 tablespoon dried
3 cups tomato puree

Salt and freshly ground black
    pepper
1 cup firm tofu, drained and
    crumbled
¼ cup soy milk
1 pound fusilli, or other spiral
    pasta

Heat the oil in a large skillet over medium heat, add the onions, and
cook until softened, about 5 minutes. Add the garlic, mushrooms, and 2
tablespoons of the tarragon and cook 3 minutes longer. Add the tomato
puree, salt and pepper to taste, and bring to a boil, then reduce the heat
and simmer for 5 to 10 minutes. Meanwhile, combine the tofu and soy
milk with the remaining 1 tablespoon of tarragon, and salt and pepper
to taste; set aside. Cook the pasta in a large pot of boiling salted water
until tender but firm to the bite; drain well. Combine the hot cooked
pasta with the mushroom sauce in a large serving bowl and toss. Divide
the pasta among 4 serving plates, and top each with a spoonful of the
tofu-tarragon cream.

4 SERVINGS

Calories 499 Kc • Protein 19 Gm • Fat 9 Gm • Percent of calories from fat 15%
• Cholesterol 0 mg • Dietary Fiber 6 Gm • Sodium 76 mg • Calcium 72 mg

Fettuccine with Creamy Pumpkin and Red Pepper Sauce

The vivid color and intense flavor of this sauce are an exciting change from tomato sauce.

1 tablespoon corn oil
1 onion, chopped
1 clove garlic, chopped
1 pound pie pumpkin, seeded, peeled and diced
1 red bell pepper, diced
1 cup Vegetable Stock (see page 10)

1 cup soy milk mixed with 1 tablespoon cornstarch
Salt and freshly ground pepper
⅛ teaspoon cayenne
1 pound fettuccine
2 tablespoons minced fresh parsley, or 2 teaspoons dried

Heat the oil in a large saucepan over medium heat. Add the onion, cover, and cook 5 minutes or until softened. Add the garlic and pumpkin and cook 5 minutes longer, covered, stirring occasionally. Add the red bell pepper and continue cooking for 5 minutes, or until the vegetables are tender. Add the stock, increase the heat to high, and cook until the liquid is reduced by half. Transfer the mixture to a food processor and puree until smooth. Return the mixture to a saucepan over low heat, and slowly add the soy milk mixture, heat through, stirring constantly until thickened, and season with salt and pepper to taste and the cayenne. Keep warm. Meanwhile, cook the fettuccine in a large pot of boiling salted water until tender but firm to the bite; drain. Toss the pasta with the sauce, and sprinkle with the parsley.

4 SERVINGS

Calories 485 Kc • Protein 15 Gm • Fat 6 Gm • Percent of calories from fat 12% • Cholesterol 0 mg • Dietary Fiber 4 Gm • Sodium 125 mg • Calcium 68 mg

Linguine with Cognac Portobello Cream

This elegant sauce will elevate your pasta to new heights.

½ cup pecan halves
2 shallots
1 clove garlic
2 tablespoons olive oil
2 cups chopped portobello
  mushrooms (about ⅓ pound)
¼ cup cognac (or brandy)

Salt and freshly ground black
  pepper
1 cup silken tofu, drained
¼ cup soy milk (or more)
1 pound linguine, cooked al
  dente and drained

Preheat the oven to 375 degrees. Spread the pecans on a baking sheet and bake for 5 to 8 minutes. Set aside and allow to cool. In a food processor, mince the shallots and garlic, add the toasted pecans and process until finely ground. Heat the oil in a large skillet over medium heat, add the pecan mixture and cook, stirring, until fragrant. Add the mushrooms, and cook 3 minutes until the mushrooms begin to soften. Add the cognac and cook, stirring for 2 minutes. Season with salt and pepper to taste. Remove from the heat and gradually stir in the tofu and soy milk to make a thick creamy sauce. If the sauce is too thick, add more soy milk until the desired consistency is reached. Adjust the seasonings. Combine the hot cooked pasta with the sauce, tossing to mix well, and serve immediately.

4 SERVINGS

Calories 527 Kc • Protein 16 Gm • Fat 16 Gm • Percent of calories from fat 27% • Cholesterol 0 mg • Dietary Fiber 3 Gm • Sodium 16 mg • Calcium 41 mg

Fettuccine with Curried Broccoli and Chick-peas

This dish draws on Italian, Indian, and Middle Eastern cuisines for a delightful flavor all its own.

2 cups broccoli florets
2 tablespoons corn oil
1 medium onion, minced
2 cloves garlic, minced
1 tablespoon minced fresh
 ginger, or 1 teaspoon dried
1½ teaspoons curry powder
2 cups cooked or canned chick-
 peas, drained

½ cup Vegetable Stock (see
 page 10)
1 cup silken tofu, drained
¼ cup soy milk
2 tablespoons lemon juice
½ teaspoon salt
⅛ teaspoon cayenne
1 pound fettuccine, cooked and
 drained

Place the broccoli in a small pot of boiling salted water and cook until crisp-tender, about 5 minutes. Drain and run under cold water to stop the cooking process and set aside. Heat the oil in a large skillet over medium heat. Add the onion and cook 5 minutes, then add the garlic, ginger, and curry powder, and cook 2 minutes longer, stirring occasionally. Add the chick-peas and cook for 2 minutes, then stir in the stock, and bring to a boil, cooking until the liquid is reduced by half. Remove from the heat. In a small bowl combine the tofu, soy milk, lemon juice, salt, and cayenne until well blended. Slowly whisk into the chick-pea mixture. Add the broccoli and stir to combine. Toss the hot cooked pasta with the chick-pea sauce in a serving bowl and serve.

4 SERVINGS

Calories 505 Kc • Protein 18 Gm • Fat 10 Gm • Percent of calories from fat 18%
• Cholesterol 0 mg • Dietary Fiber 7 Gm • Sodium 464 mg • Calcium 87 mg

Rotini with Curried Tofu Sauce

1 tablespoon olive oil
1 cup chopped onion
1 medium carrot, chopped
1 red bell pepper, seeded and
  chopped
2 cloves garlic, minced
1 teaspoon minced fresh ginger,
  or ¼ teaspoon dried
1½ teaspoons curry powder
1 cup firm tofu, drained and
  crumbled

1 cup soy milk
1 cup silken tofu, drained
2 tablespoons lemon juice
2 tablespoons minced fresh
  cilantro
½ teaspoon salt
⅛ teaspoon cayenne
1 pound rotini, or other spiral
  pasta

Heat the oil in a large skillet over medium heat, add the onion, carrot, and bell pepper, and cook for 5 minutes or until the vegetables begin to soften. Add the garlic, ginger, and curry powder and cook 2 minutes longer. Stir in the crumbled firm tofu and the soy milk, mixing well. Reduce the heat to very low and cook slowly for 10 to 15 minutes. Remove from the heat and set aside. In a small bowl, combine the silken tofu, lemon juice, cilantro, salt, and cayenne. Stir the mixture into the curry sauce until well blended. Meanwhile, cook the pasta in a large pot of boiling salted water until tender but firm to the bite; drain well. To serve, combine the hot cooked pasta and the curried tofu sauce in a serving bowl, tossing well.

4 SERVINGS

Calories 481 Kc • Protein 23 Gm • Fat 8 Gm • Percent of calories from fat 15% • Cholesterol 0 mg • Dietary Fiber 4 Gm • Sodium 316 mg • Calcium 89 mg

Udon and Spinach with Peanut Sauce

Udon are whole wheat Japanese noodles that can be found in Asian grocery stores or natural food stores.

½ cup silken tofu, drained
½ cup creamy peanut butter
⅓ cup almond milk (or more)
1 tablespoon lemon juice
1 tablespoon low-sodium tamari
¼ teaspoon cayenne

2 tablespoons corn oil
1 cup chopped onions
4 cups trimmed fresh spinach
   leaves
12 ounces udon noodles, cooked
   and drained

In a food processor, combine the tofu, peanut butter, almond milk, lemon juice, tamari, and cayenne, processing to make a smooth sauce. Taste and adjust the seasonings. If too thick, add more almond milk. Set aside. Heat the oil in a large skillet over medium-high heat. Add the onions, and cook, stirring occasionally, until softened and lightly browned, about 5 minutes. Reduce the heat to low, add the spinach, cover, and cook until the spinach is tender, about 5 minutes, stirring occasionally. Add the cooked pasta and the reserved sauce, toss to combine, and serve immediately.

4 SERVINGS

Calories 596 Kc • Protein 24 Gm • Fat 27 Gm • Percent of calories from fat 38% • Cholesterol 0 mg • Dietary Fiber 7 Gm • Sodium 1117 mg • Calcium 92 mg

Ziti with Sun-dried Tomato Cream

1 pound ziti, or other tubular
  pasta
1 cup chopped oil-marinated sun-
  dried tomatoes
1 cup firm silken tofu, drained
  and crumbled
3 cloves garlic, chopped
¼ cup chopped fresh basil, or 1
  tablespoon dried

2 tablespoons balsamic vinegar
½ teaspoon salt
⅛ teaspoon freshly ground
  pepper
2 tablespoons olive oil
2 tablespoons minced fresh
  parsley, or 2 teaspoons dried

Cook the ziti in a large pot of boiling salted water until tender but firm to the bite. Meanwhile, in a food processor, combine the tomatoes, tofu, garlic, basil, vinegar, salt, pepper, and olive oil. Process to a smooth consistency. Drain the pasta and toss in a serving bowl with the sauce. Sprinkle with the minced parsley and serve.

4 SERVINGS

Calories 470 Kc • Protein 17 Gm • Fat 11 Gm • Percent of calories from fat 21% • Cholesterol 0 mg • Dietary Fiber 2 Gm • Sodium 332 mg • Calcium 54 mg

Rotini with Oranges and Black Olives

A favorite accompaniment to pasta dishes during my childhood was a salad made of orange slices, olive oil, and black olives. Here, I've incorporated those elements into the pasta sauce itself.

1 orange, peeled and segmented
2 tablespoons olive oil
¼ cup minced shallots
1 tablespoon minced garlic
2 cups firm silken tofu, drained
1 tablespoon capers, drained
1 tablespoon lemon juice
1 tablespoon orange juice
1 teaspoon chopped fresh rosemary, or ⅛ teaspoon dried

Salt and freshly ground black pepper
1 pound rotini, or other spiral pasta
1 cup pitted and diced oil-cured black olives
1 tablespoon snipped fresh chives, or 1 teaspoon dried

Chop the orange segments into a small dice and set aside. Heat the oil in a large skillet over medium heat. Add the shallots and cook 5 minutes, stirring occasionally. Add the garlic and cook 1 minute longer. Place the shallots and garlic in a food processor and puree with the tofu, capers, lemon juice, orange juice, rosemary, and salt and pepper to taste. Meanwhile, cook the rotini in a large pot of boiling salted water until tender but firm to the bite, and drain. Toss the hot cooked pasta with the sauce and serve immediately, sprinkled with olives, orange pieces, and chives.

4 SERVINGS

Calories 478 Kc • Protein 19 Gm • Fat 11 Gm • Percent of calories from fat 20% • Cholesterol 0 mg • Dietary Fiber 2 Gm • Sodium 251 mg • Calcium 98 mg

Macaroni and Cheese Revisited

The ultimate comfort food—without dairy products. A perfect meal for a blustery evening or "just because." Serve with stewed tomatoes for a real trip down memory lane.

2 tablespoons corn oil
½ cup minced onion
2 tablespoons all-purpose flour
2 cups hot soy milk
½ teaspoon salt
⅛ teaspoon freshly ground pepper

⅛ teaspoon ground nutmeg
1 pound pasta elbows, cooked and drained
2 cups grated soy Cheddar cheese

Preheat the oven to 375 degrees. Heat the oil in a saucepan over medium heat, add the onion, and cook 5 minutes. Stir in the flour and cook for 2 minutes, then reduce the heat to very low, and slowly whisk in the hot soy milk. Continue to cook, stirring, for about 3 minutes, or until the mixture thickens. Season with the salt, pepper, and nutmeg. Combine the sauce with the cooked pasta, and 1 cup of the soy cheese. Spoon into a baking dish and top with the remaining 1 cup soy cheese. Bake for 30 to 40 minutes, or until heated through.

4 SERVINGS

Calories 573 Kc • Protein 24 Gm • Fat 15 Gm • Percent of calories from fat 24% • Cholesterol 0 mg • Dietary Fiber 4 Gm • Sodium 605 mg • Calcium 207 mg

Linguine Primavera

A creamy sauce studded with colorful vegetables—a dairy-free version of this "first of spring" classic.

2 tablespoons olive oil
½ cup minced onion
½ cup diced red bell pepper
½ cup sliced mushrooms
¼ cup minced scallion
1 tablespoon minced garlic
2 tablespoons all-purpose flour
2½ cups hot soy milk
1 tablespoon minced fresh basil, or ½ teaspoon dried
1 teaspoon salt

¼ teaspoon black pepper
1 cup asparagus pieces, cut on the diagonal, steamed 4 minutes
1 cup sliced carrots, steamed 6 minutes
1 pound linguine, cooked al dente and drained
2 tablespoons minced fresh parsley, or 2 teaspoons dried

Heat the oil in a large skillet over medium heat. Add the onion, and cook for 3 minutes. Add the bell pepper, mushrooms, scallion, and garlic and cook 5 minutes longer, stirring occasionally. Stir in the flour and cook for 2 minutes. Reduce the heat to low and slowly add the hot soy milk, basil, salt, and pepper, continuing to stir for 3 minutes. Add the asparagus and carrots, and continue to cook for 3 minutes over low heat. Adjust the seasonings. Divide the hot cooked pasta among 4 serving plates and top with the sauce. Sprinkle with the parsley.

4 SERVINGS

Calories 511 Kc • Protein 17 Gm • Fat 10 Gm • Percent of calories from fat 17% • Cholesterol 0 mg • Dietary Fiber 5 Gm • Sodium 548 mg • Calcium 83 mg

Fusilli and Oyster Mushrooms with Creamy Watercress Sauce

The chewiness of the fusilli is especially enjoyable in this dish. If fusilli is unavailable, substitute rotini or fettuccine. If the delicate oyster mushrooms are unavailable, use another mushroom variety, but the oyster mushroom is really something special.

2 tablespoons olive oil
1 cup minced leek, white part only
½ cup minced scallion
2 cups oyster mushrooms, cut into ½-inch pieces (about ½ pound)
3 cups soy milk

¾ teaspoon salt
¼ teaspoon black pepper
¼ cup cornstarch
1 cup chopped watercress, leaves and tender stems
1 pound fusilli, cooked al dente and drained

Heat the oil in a large skillet over medium heat. Add the leek and scallion and cook for 2 minutes. Add the mushrooms and cook for 2 minutes, stirring constantly. Reduce the heat to low, add 2 ¾ cups of the soy milk and the salt and pepper. Bring to a simmer. In a small bowl, combine the remaining ¼ cup soy milk with the cornstarch, mixing until smooth. Add the cornstarch mixture to the skillet mixture, stirring, to achieve a smooth sauce. Stir in the watercress and cook over low heat for 2 minutes. Divide the hot cooked pasta among 4 serving plates, and spoon on the sauce. Serve immediately.

4 SERVINGS

Calories 542 Kc • Protein 18 Gm • Fat 10 Gm • Percent of calories from fat 17% • Cholesterol 0 mg • Dietary Fiber 4 Gm • Sodium mg 441 • Calcium 98 mg

Linguine and Asparagus with Orange-scented Pumpkin Sauce

Canned pumpkin works fine for this unusual and colorful pasta sauce. Substitute broccoli for the asparagus if you prefer.

2 cups cooked or canned pumpkin

1½ cups almond milk

¼ cup orange juice

2 tablespoons cornstarch

1 teaspoon sugar (or a natural sweetener)

¾ teaspoon salt

½ teaspoon allspice

⅛ teaspoon cayenne

2 tablespoons olive oil

1 cup minced onion

1 tablespoon minced garlic

1 tablespoon minced fresh basil, or 1 teaspoon dried

1 pound linguine, cooked al dente and drained

1 pound asparagus, cut on the diagonal, steamed 4 minutes

1 orange, peeled, segmented, and chopped

1 tablespoon snipped fresh chives, or 1 teaspoon dried

In a food processor, combine the pumpkin, almond milk, orange juice, cornstarch, sugar, salt, allspice, and cayenne, blending until smooth. Reserve. Heat the oil in a large skillet, add the onion, and cook for about 5 minutes. Add the garlic and basil, and cook 2 minutes longer. Add the pumpkin mixture and continue cooking, stirring constantly, for 5 minutes or until the sauce has thickened. Divide the hot cooked pasta among 6 serving plates, and spoon the sauce over the pasta. Divide the asparagus among the plates, and garnish with a sprinkling of chopped orange pieces and chives.

6 SERVINGS

Calories 434 Kc • Protein 14 Gm • Fat 9 Gm • Percent of calories from fat 19% • Cholesterol 0 mg • Dietary Fiber 6 Gm • Sodium 302 mg • Calcium 83 mg

Penne with Green Beans and Almonds

1½ pounds green beans, trimmed
2 tablespoons corn oil
2 tablespoons all-purpose flour
1 cup Vegetable Stock (see page 10)
2 tablespoons dry white wine

1½ cups almond milk
Salt and freshly ground pepper
1 pound penne, or other tubular pasta
1 cup toasted slivered almonds

Blanch the green beans in enough boiling salted water to cover, about 2 minutes. Drain and run under cold water. Drain again, cut diagonally into 2-inch pieces, and set aside. Heat the oil in a large skillet over low heat. Add the flour and cook, stirring for 1 minute. Whisk in the stock and wine and cook, stirring 1 minute longer. Stir in the almond milk and continue cooking, stirring constantly, until it thickens, about 5 minutes. Add the reserved green beans and salt and pepper to taste. Meanwhile, cook the pasta in a large pot of boiling salted water until tender but still firm to the bite. Drain and toss with the sauce mixture. Sprinkle with the toasted almonds and serve.

4 SERVINGS

Calories 683 Kc • Protein 22 Gm • Fat 28 Gm • Percent of calories from fat 36% • Cholesterol 0 mg • Dietary Fiber 11 Gm • Sodium 286 mg • Calcium 156 mg

Capellini with Wild Mushroom Sauce

Mix and match the amount and types of mushrooms according to taste and availability. Include some regular mushrooms for a more economical sauce.

3 tablespoons olive oil
1 cup chopped onions
2 tablespoons all-purpose flour
1 cup Vegetable Stock (see page 10)
1½ cups almond milk
1 cup chopped porcini mushrooms
1 cup chopped portobello mushrooms

½ cup chopped oyster mushrooms
½ cup shiitake mushrooms
Salt and freshly ground black pepper
1 pound capellini, cooked al dente and drained
2 tablespoons minced fresh parsley, or 2 teaspoons dried, for garnish

Heat 2 tablespoons of the oil in a large saucepan over medium-high heat. Add the onions and cook until softened, about 5 minutes. Add the flour and cook, stirring, for 2 minutes. Whisk in the stock, stirring until smooth, about 2 minutes. Slowly whisk in the almond milk and continue stirring to achieve a smooth sauce. Heat the remaining 1 tablespoon oil in a separate pan over medium heat. Add the mushrooms and cook, stirring frequently, for 3 minutes, until they begin to soften. Season with salt and pepper to taste. In a food processor, combine 1 cup of the cooked mushrooms with the sauce mixture and puree until well blended. Return the mixture to the saucepan and combine with the remaining mushrooms, cooking over low heat for 5 minutes or until hot. Toss the hot cooked pasta with the sauce and serve garnished with the fresh parsley.

4 SERVINGS

Calories 517 Kc • Protein 15 Gm • Fat 15 Gm • Percent of calories from fat 25% • Cholesterol 0 mg • Dietary Fiber 5 Gm • Sodium 61 mg • Calcium 62 mg

Ziti with Spicy Vegetable Sauce

1 tablespoon olive oil
1 red bell pepper, seeded and
  chopped
4 scallions, chopped
2 cloves garlic, crushed
2 tomatoes, chopped
1 cup tomato puree
1 cup soy milk

1 teaspoon Tabasco sauce
1 teaspoon minced fresh basil, or
  ¼ teaspoon dried
½ teaspoon salt
⅛ teaspoon cayenne
1 pound ziti, or other tubular
  pasta
Minced fresh parsley for garnish

Heat the oil in a large saucepan over medium heat. Add the bell pepper, scallions, and garlic and cook 5 minutes, or until softened. Add the tomatoes, puree, soy milk, and mix well. Stir in the Tabasco, basil, salt, and cayenne. Simmer over low heat for 10 minutes, being careful not to boil. Meanwhile, cook the ziti in a large pot of boiling salted water until tender. Drain and toss with the sauce. Sprinkle with minced parsley.

4 SERVINGS

Calories 529 Kc • Protein 18 Gm • Fat 7 Gm • Percent of calories from fat 11% • Cholesterol 0 mg • Dietary Fiber 5 Gm • Sodium 355 mg • Calcium 48 mg

5
Main Dishes

Many people who take the step of eliminating meat from their diets come to rely on dairy-based ingredients for their entrees. But once they discover that dairy products are not as beneficial as they had anticipated, it's often difficult for them to break the habit or to find appealing alternatives. That's where this chapter comes to the rescue.

Using vegetarian mainstays such as grains, beans, tempeh, and seitan, these recipes also incorporate tofu and soy cheese, as well as soy, almond, and rice milks to replace the dairy components of main dishes such as Creamy Chick-pea Stew, Artichoke Quiche, and Winter Vegetable Pie. From now on, you can dine on delicious main courses with no meat, no dairy—just wholesome goodness and lots of flavor.

Eggplant Parmesan

Add a sprinkling of soy Parmesan or mozzarella if you wish, but I find the layers of creamy tofu are satisfying enough without it.

¼ cup safflower oil
½ cup minced onion
1 teaspoon minced garlic
1 16-ounce can tomato puree
1 tablespoon minced fresh basil, or 1 teaspoon dried
Salt and freshly ground black pepper

1½ pounds eggplant
1 cup bread crumbs
2 cups firm tofu, drained and crumbled
2 tablespoons minced fresh parsley
¼ cup soy Parmesan or mozzarella (optional)

Preheat the broiler. Heat 1 tablespoon of the oil in a medium saucepan over medium heat. Add the onion and cook 5 minutes, or until softened. Add the garlic and cook 2 minutes longer. Add the tomato puree, basil, and salt and pepper to taste. Stir well and bring to a boil. Lower the heat and simmer for about 15 minutes. Slice the eggplant very thinly. Brush each slice with a little of the remaining oil on both sides, then dip into the bread crumbs. Put the slices on a baking sheet and broil until tender, about 2 minutes, turning once; remove the pan from the oven and set aside. Turn the oven down to 350 degrees. In a bowl, combine the tofu, parsley, and salt and pepper to taste, and mix well. Arrange half of the eggplant slices in a lightly oiled baking dish, top with half of the tofu mixture, and spread half of the tomato sauce on the tofu mixture. Repeat the layers. Bake 20 minutes. If using soy cheese, remove the casserole from the oven, sprinkle on the cheese, and bake 5 minutes longer.

6 SERVINGS

Calories 158 Kc • Protein 10 Gm • Fat 5 Gm • Percent of calories from fat 25% • Cholesterol 0 mg • Dietary Fiber 5 Gm • Sodium 112 mg • Calcium 66 mg

Spiced Lentil Gratin

3 tablespoons olive oil
1 cup chopped onion
1 clove garlic, minced
2 tablespoons fresh mint, or 2
    teaspoons dried
1 teaspoon ground cinnamon
2 cups Vegetable Stock (see
    page 10)
3 cups water
2 cups dried lentils, picked over
    and rinsed

1 tablespoon tomato paste
½ cup dry red wine
¼ cup minced fresh parsley, or 1
    tablespoon dried
Salt and freshly ground
    pepper
1 cup dried bread crumbs
½ cup firm tofu, drained and
    crumbled
½ cup grated soy mozzarella

Heat 1 tablespoon of the oil in a large saucepan over medium heat, add the onion and cook until softened, about 5 minutes, stirring occasionally. Add the garlic, mint, and cinnamon, and cook, stirring, for 2 minutes. Add the stock and water and bring the liquid to a boil. Add the lentils and simmer the mixture, covered, stirring occasionally, for 30 minutes. Add the tomato paste and the wine, simmer the mixture, uncovered, for 15 minutes, or until the lentils are tender. Remove from the heat, and stir in the parsley and salt and pepper to taste. Preheat the oven to 400 degrees. Transfer the mixture to a large gratin dish that has been lightly oiled or sprayed with nonstick vegetable spray. In a small bowl, toss together the bread crumbs, tofu, soy mozzarella, and the remaining 2 tablespoons oil. Sprinkle the crumb mixture evenly over the gratin, and bake for 15 minutes, or until heated through and lightly browned on top.

4 TO 6 SERVINGS

Calories 483 Kc • Protein 29 Gm • Fat 13 Gm • Percent of calories from fat 25% • Cholesterol 0 mg • Dietary Fiber 26 Gm • Sodium 199 mg • Calcium 151 mg

Fava Bean and Spinach Casserole

Meaty fava beans team up with tofu and spinach to make a hearty one-dish meal.

1 tablespoon olive oil
2 tablespoons minced shallot
1 teaspoon minced garlic
2 cups cooked fresh, frozen, or
   canned fava beans
Salt and freshly ground black
   pepper
2 cups soft tofu, drained

2 tablespoons lemon juice
1 tablespoon minced fresh dill, or
   1 teaspoon dried
1 10-ounce package frozen
   chopped spinach, thawed and
   squeezed dry
2 cups cooked rice
½ cup shredded soy mozzarella

Preheat the oven to 350 degrees. Heat the oil in a medium skillet over medium heat. Add the shallot and cook for 3 minutes. Add the garlic and cook 2 minutes longer, stirring occasionally. Add the cooked fava beans and season to taste with salt and pepper. Cook 1 minute to blend the flavors. Remove from the heat. In a small bowl combine the tofu with the lemon juice, dill, and salt and pepper to taste. Set aside. Squeeze all the liquid out of the spinach and chop well. Combine the spinach with the rice, season with salt and pepper to taste, and mix well. Lightly oil a casserole dish or coat with nonstick cooking spray and spoon a layer of the spinach-rice mixture evenly in the dish. Add a layer of fava beans, then a layer of the tofu mixture. Repeat until all ingredients are used, making the spinach-rice mixture the top layer. Sprinkle with the soy cheese. Cover and bake for 30 minutes or until hot.

6 SERVINGS

Calories 200 Kc • Protein 10 Gm • Fat 7 Gm • Percent of calories from fat 31% • Cholesterol 0 mg • Dietary Fiber 6 Gm • Sodium 85 mg • Calcium 81 mg

Mushroom Chick-pea Bake

2 tablespoons corn oil
1 small onion, minced
2 tablespoons all-purpose flour
1 cup Vegetable Stock (see page 10)
1 cup soy milk
2 tablespoons low-sodium tamari
1 pound mushrooms, sliced (about 4 cups)
2 cups cooked or canned chick-peas, drained
2 cups cooked brown rice
Salt and freshly ground pepper
½ cup dried bread crumbs
½ cup grated soy mozzarella cheese
½ teaspoon paprika

Preheat the oven to 350 degrees. Lightly oil a shallow baking dish or spray with nonstick cooking spray and set aside. Heat the oil in a small saucepan over medium heat. Add the onion and cook 5 minutes to soften. Whisk in the flour and cook 3 minutes, stirring constantly. Add the stock and bring to a boil. Reduce the heat, add the soy milk and tamari, and continue stirring for 2 minutes. In a bowl, combine the mushrooms, chick-peas, and rice. Add the sauce and mix well. Season with salt and pepper to taste. Spread the mixture in the prepared baking dish and sprinkle evenly with the bread crumbs, soy cheese, and paprika. Bake 30 minutes, or until heated through.

6 SERVINGS

Calories 314 Kc • Protein 12 Gm • Fat 10 Gm • Percent of calories from fat 28% • Cholesterol 0 mg • Dietary Fiber 5 Gm • Sodium 591 mg • Calcium 113 mg

Enchilada Bake

2 tablespoons corn oil
½ cup minced scallion
2 tablespoons all-purpose flour
1 cup Vegetable Stock (see page 10)
2 cups cooked or canned pinto beans, drained
¾ teaspoon salt

12 soft corn tortillas
2 cups chunky salsa
1½ cups firm silken tofu, drained
1 4-ounce can diced green chilies
2 tablespoons lime juice
½ cup grated soy Cheddar cheese

Preheat the oven to 350 degrees. Heat the oil in a medium skillet over medium heat. Add the scallion and cook about 3 minutes, or until softened. Stir in the flour and cook 1 minute. Add the stock and cook, stirring, to achieve a smooth consistency, about 1 minute longer. Add the pinto beans and ½ teaspoon of the salt, and set aside. Lightly oil a baking dish or coat with nonstick cooking spray. Line the bottom of the dish with a layer of 4 tortillas. Spread with half of the salsa and cover with half of the pinto bean mixture. Repeat the layers, ending with a layer of 4 tortillas, and set aside. In a small bowl, combine the tofu with the chilies and lime juice, and remaining ¼ teaspoon salt, whisking until smooth. Pour over the layered bean and tortilla mixture. Cover and bake for 25 minutes. Remove the cover; top with the soy cheese and bake, uncovered, 5 to 10 minutes longer to melt the cheese.

8 SERVINGS

Calories 334 Kc • Protein 17 Gm • Fat 8 Gm • Percent of calories from fat 19% • Cholesterol 0 mg • Dietary Fiber 4 Gm • Sodium 1119 mg • Calcium 178 mg

Tomato Chick-pea Casserole

This recipe is based on an old family recipe, one of my mom's variations of macaroni and cheese. I eliminate the dairy products and add chick-peas for texture, flavor, and nutrition.

4 cups cooked elbow macaroni

2 cups cooked or canned chick-peas, drained

1 28-ounce can tomatoes, drained and chopped

¼ cup flour

¼ cup soy milk

¾ teaspoon salt

1 teaspoon minced fresh basil, or ¼ teaspoon dried

½ cup dried bread crumbs

¼ cup shredded soy mozzarella

1 tablespoon olive oil

Preheat the oven to 375 degrees. Lightly oil a casserole dish or coat with nonstick cooking spray and set aside. In a large bowl, combine the pasta, chick-peas, and tomatoes. Stir in the flour, soy milk, salt, and basil and mix well. Transfer the mixture into the prepared casserole dish, and spread evenly. In a small bowl combine the bread crumbs, soy cheese, and oil with a fork until blended. Sprinkle on top of the casserole. Cover and bake for 30 minutes. Remove the cover and bake for 10 minutes longer to brown the crumbs.

4 SERVINGS

Calories 419 Kc • Protein 17 Gm • Fat 8 Gm • Percent of calories from fat 17% • Cholesterol 0 mg • Dietary Fiber 13 Gm • Sodium 929 mg • Calcium 128 mg

Creamy Cabbage and Apple Casserole

2 cups shredded cabbage
1 tablespoon corn oil
1 cup minced onion
1 Red Delicious apple, peeled,
  cored, and chopped
1 tablespoon lemon juice

Salt and freshly ground pepper
2 cups firm silken tofu, drained
1 cup soy milk (or more)
8 ounces rotini, cooked and
  drained
1 cup grated soy Cheddar cheese

Preheat the oven to 350 degrees. Cook the cabbage in a pot of boiling salted water for 5 to 6 minutes or until the cabbage is tender-crisp. Drain the cabbage and set aside. Heat the oil in a large skillet over medium heat, add the onion and cook for 5 minutes, stirring occasionally. Add the apple, lemon juice, and salt and pepper to taste, and cook 3 minutes longer. Add the reserved cabbage, combine well and set aside. In a small bowl, combine the tofu and soy milk until well blended. In a large bowl, combine the cabbage mixture with the tofu mixture, the cooked pasta, and 1/2 cup of the soy cheese. Taste and adjust the seasonings. If the mixture seems too dry, add some more soy milk. Lightly oil a casserole dish or coat it with nonstick cooking spray. Spread the mixture evenly in the pan and sprinkle the remaining 1/2 cup of grated soy cheese on top. Bake for 30 minutes, or until the casserole is bubbly and heated throughout.

6 SERVINGS

Calories 311 Kc • Protein 17 Gm • Fat 8 Gm • Percent of calories from fat 24% • Cholesterol 0 mg • Dietary Fiber 3 Gm • Sodium 124 mg • Calcium 132 mg

Creamy Tofu Pilaf

2 tablespoons corn oil
1 medium onion, chopped
1 carrot, diced
1 teaspoon minced fresh ginger,
    or ¼ teaspoon dried
1 cup basmati rice
½ teaspoon turmeric
¼ teaspoon cinnamon

2½ cups almond milk
½ cup frozen peas
½ pound firm tofu, drained and
    crumbled
1 cup silken tofu, drained
1 tablespoon low-sodium tamari
2 tablespoons minced fresh
    parsley, or 2 teaspoons dried

Heat the oil in a large saucepan over medium heat. Add the onion and carrot, cover, and cook 5 minutes. Add the ginger, rice, turmeric, and cinnamon and cook, stirring, for 1 minute. Add 2 cups of the almond milk, cover the pot, and bring just to a boil. Reduce the heat and simmer for 15 minutes. Remove the cover, add the peas and crumbled firm tofu, and stir to combine. In a small bowl, combine the remaining $1/2$ cup of almond milk with the silken tofu and the tamari, and slowly stir into the rice mixture. Cook over low heat for 3 minutes or until heated through. Serve sprinkled with the minced parsley.

4 SERVINGS

Calories 452 Kc • Protein 16 Gm • Fat 19 Gm • Percent of calories from fat 37% • Cholesterol 0 mg • Dietary Fiber 5 Gm • Sodium 224 mg • Calcium 110 mg

Thyme-scented Pot Pie

A warming and welcoming one-dish meal. Perfect for a cold winter's night.

Crust:
2 cups unbleached all-purpose flour
½ teaspoon salt
½ cup (1 stick) chilled margarine, cut into pieces
4 tablespoons cold water
Filling:
3 tablespoons corn oil
1 cup chopped onion
1 cup chopped celery
1 cup chopped carrots

2 cups firm tofu, cut into ½-inch cubes
1 cup frozen peas
3 tablespoons all-purpose flour
2 cups soy milk
Salt and freshly ground black pepper
1 tablespoon minced fresh parsley, or 1 teaspoon dried
½ teaspoon dried thyme
½ teaspoon paprika

To make the crust, combine the flour and salt in a food processor, then add the margarine using on/off pulses until the mixture becomes crumbly. Slowly add enough water, pulsing to form a soft, but not sticky dough. Transfer the dough to a lightly floured surface. Divide the dough into 2 balls and flatten them into discs. Wrap the dough in plastic wrap and refrigerate at least 30 minutes. Preheat the oven to 375 degrees. Roll the dough out on a lightly floured surface to fit a 9-inch pie pan. Fit one of the pastry rounds inside of the pan. Trim and flute the edges. Line the crust with aluminum foil, and fill with dried beans. Bake until the crust is set, about 10 minutes. Remove the crust from the oven, discard the foil and beans, and set the crust aside. Keep the oven on.

To make the filling, heat 1 tablespoon of the oil in a large skillet over medium heat. Add the onion, celery, and carrots and cook until softened, about 10 minutes. Remove the vegetables with a slotted spoon and reserve. In the same skillet, add the tofu cubes, and stir well over medium heat until browned. Add the peas and stir-fry for another minute or two. Remove the tofu and peas and add to the reserved vegetables. Add the remaining 2 tablespoons of oil to the same skillet over medium heat. Gradually stir in the flour, then the soy milk, stirring constantly to avoid lumps. When the milk mixture comes to a boil, add the salt and pepper to taste, parsley, thyme, and paprika. Combine the sauce with the reserved tofu and vegetable mixture and pour the filling into the baked pie shell. Put the top crust over it, seal the edges, prick the crust with a fork, and bake for 30 minutes, or until lightly browned.

6 TO 8 SERVINGS

Calories 415 Kc • Protein 15 Gm • Fat 16 Gm • Percent of calories from fat 35% • Cholesterol 0 mg • Dietary Fiber 4 Gm • Sodium 361 mg • Calcium 133 mg

Spinach and Pine Nut Pie

Crust:
1 cup unbleached all-purpose
  flour
¼ teaspoon salt
¼ cup (½ stick) chilled margarine,
  cut into pieces
2 tablespoons cold water
Filling:
2 10-ounce packages frozen
  spinach, thawed, squeezed dry,
  and finely chopped
1 tablespoon olive oil

1 onion, minced
2 cloves garlic, minced
Salt
1 cup silken firm tofu, well
  drained
¼ cup raisins
¼ cup ground walnuts
¼ cup oil-cured black olives,
  pitted and sliced thin
Freshly ground pepper
¼ cup shredded soy mozzarella
  cheese

To make the crust, combine the flour and the salt in a food processor, and then add the margarine and process using on/off pulses until the mixture is crumbly. Slowly add enough water, pulsing, to form a soft but not sticky dough. Form the dough into a ball and flatten the ball to a disc. Wrap the dough in plastic wrap and refrigerate 30 minutes. Preheat the oven to 375 degrees. Roll the dough out on a lightly floured surface and fit into a 9-inch tart pan or pie plate. Trim and flute the edges. Line the crust with aluminum foil, and fill with dried beans. Bake for 10 minutes, or until the crust is set. Discard the foil and beans. Continue baking until the crust is light brown, 8 to 10 minutes longer, and remove from the oven. Keep the oven on.

To make the filling, heat the oil in a large skillet, add the onion, cover, and cook for 5 minutes over medium heat. Remove the cover, add the garlic, and continue cooking, stirring, for 1 minute. Add the spinach, salt to taste, and cook the mixture, stirring, for 2 to 3 minutes, or until almost all the liquid is evaporated. Transfer the mixture to a bowl and let it cool. Add the tofu, raisins, walnuts, olives, and salt and pepper to taste and blend well. Spread the spinach mixture evenly in the shell, sprinkle with the soy cheese, and bake the pie for 30 minutes, or until the crust is golden and the filling is set. Cool several minutes before cutting.

4 TO 6 SERVINGS

Calories 314 Kc • Protein 11 Gm • Fat 15 Gm • Percent of calories from fat 41% • Cholesterol 0 mg • Dietary Fiber 6 Gm • Sodium 366 mg • Calcium 258 mg

Double Soy Cheese Pizza

Crust:
1¼ cups all-purpose flour
¼ cup whole wheat flour
½ teaspoon salt
1 teaspoon dry yeast
½ cup warm water (110 to 115 degrees)

1 tablespoon olive oil
Topping:
1 cup tomato sauce
1 cup grated soy mozzarella cheese
1 cup grated soy Cheddar cheese

In a food processor combine the flours and salt with on/off pulses. In a small bowl, dissolve the yeast in the water and add the olive oil. With the processor running, pour the yeast mixture through the feed tube and process to form a dough ball, about 1 minute. Turn out onto a lightly floured surface and knead about 1 minute. Transfer the dough to a large oiled bowl, coating the top of the dough with oil as well. Cover with plastic wrap and a dry cloth and allow to rise in a warm area until doubled, about 1½ hours. Preheat the oven to 425 degrees. Punch the dough down. On a floured surface, roll out the dough into a 12-inch circle. Place on a lightly floured pizza pan or baking sheet. Spread the tomato sauce on the dough, leaving a ½-inch border along the outside. Sprinkle the cheeses over the sauce. Bake 15 to 20 minutes or until crust is golden brown.

MAKES ONE 12-INCH PIZZA

Calories 358 Kc • Protein 18 Gm • Fat 12 Gm • Percent of calories from fat 31% • Cholesterol 0 mg • Dietary Fiber 5 Gm • Sodium 793 mg • Calcium 255 mg

Spring Vegetable Pie

Crust:
1 cup all-purpose flour
¼ teaspoon salt
¼ cup (½ stick) chilled margarine,
  cut into pieces
2 tablespoons cold water
Filling:
1 tablespoon corn oil
1 cup chopped onions
½ cup chopped carrot
½ cup chopped red bell pepper
1 cup chopped zucchini
2 tablespoons minced scallion
1 tablespoon minced garlic

1 cup sliced mushrooms (about ¼
  pound)
2 tablespoons minced fresh
  parsley, or 2 teaspoons dried
1 tablespoon minced fresh dill, or
  ¼ teaspoon dried
1 teaspoon salt
⅛ teaspoon cayenne
2½ cups extra-firm silken tofu,
  drained
½ cup soy milk
2 tablespoons cornstarch
  dissolved in 2 tablespoons soy
  milk

To make the crust, combine the flour and salt in a food processor, then add the margarine and process using on/off pulses until the mixture is crumbly. Slowly add enough water, pulsing the processor, to form a soft dough. Form the dough into a ball, and flatten to a disc. Wrap the dough in plastic wrap and refrigerate 30 minutes. Preheat the oven to 375 degrees. Roll the dough out on a lightly floured surface and fit into a 9-inch tart pan or pie plate. Trim and flute the edges. Line the crust with aluminum foil, and fill with dried beans. Bake for 10 minutes, or until the crust is set. Discard the foil and beans. Continue baking until the crust is light brown, 8 to 10 minutes longer, and remove from the oven. Keep the oven on.

To make the filling, heat the oil in a large saucepan over medium heat. Add the onions, carrot, and bell pepper. Cover and cook 5 minutes, stirring occasionally, until the vegetables begin to soften. Add the zucchini, scallion, garlic, and mushrooms and continue cooking 3 minutes, stirring occasionally. Add the parsley, dill, salt, cayenne, tofu, and soy milk and continue cooking 2 minutes to blend the flavors. Stir in the cornstarch mixture. Pour the filling into the crust and bake for 30 minutes.

6 SERVINGS

Calories 244 Kc • Protein 12 Gm • Fat 9 Gm • Percent of calories from fat 34%
• Cholesterol 0 mg • Dietary Fiber 2 Gm • Sodium 603 mg • Calcium 87 mg

Curried Tofu

The subtle flavor of almond milk is the perfect complement for this pungently spiced dish.

1 cup seedless raisins
2 tablespoons corn oil
1 medium onion, minced
1 teaspoon minced garlic
1 teaspoon minced fresh ginger,
  or ¼ teaspoon dried
1½ teaspoons curry powder
2 tablespoons flour

2¼ cups hot almond milk
1 small apple, peeled, cored, and
  chopped
2 tablespoons low-sodium tamari
1 tablespoon lemon juice
Salt and freshly ground pepper
1 pound extra-firm tofu, cut into
  ½-inch cubes

Soak the raisins in a bowl of hot water for 30 minutes to plump them up. Drain and reserve. Heat the oil in a large skillet over medium heat. Add the onion and cook, stirring, for 5 minutes. Add the garlic and ginger and continue cooking 2 minutes longer, or until fragrant. Stir in the curry powder and the flour. Slowly stir in the almond milk and simmer until thickened and smooth. Add the raisins, apple, tamari, and lemon juice. Simmer over low heat for 5 minutes. Season to taste with salt and pepper. Add the tofu to the curry sauce and cook gently for 5 minutes longer to heat through.

6 SERVINGS

Calories 259 Kc • Protein 10 Gm • Fat 12 Gm • Percent of calories from fat 38% • Cholesterol 0 mg • Dietary Fiber 3 Gm • Sodium 258 mg • Calcium 82 mg

Winter Vegetable Pie

Crust:
1½ cups all-purpose flour
2 teaspoons baking powder
1 teaspoon salt
½ cup (1 stick) chilled margarine,
   cut into small pieces
1 cup firm silken tofu, drained
   and pressed dry
1 teaspoon lemon juice
Filling:
2 tablespoons corn oil
4 cups finely chopped cabbage
2 cups grated carrot
1 cup grated parsnip

¼ cup minced scallion
1 teaspoon minced garlic
½ cup soy milk
½ cup silken tofu, drained and
   pressed dry
¼ cup tahini (sesame paste)
¼ cup minced fresh parsley, or 1
   tablespoon dried
1 teaspoon lemon juice
1 teaspoon salt
1 teaspoon dried marjoram
⅛ teaspoon cayenne
1 cup cooked or canned chick-
   peas, drained

To make the crust, combine the flour, baking powder, and salt in a food processor, then add the margarine and process with on/off pulses until the mixture resembles coarse meal. Add the tofu and lemon juice and process to form a stiff dough. Turn out and shape into a ball. Flatten to form a disc, wrap the dough in plastic wrap, and refrigerate 30 minutes.

To make the filling, heat the oil in a large skillet over medium heat. Add the cabbage, carrot, and parsnip, cover, and cook 5 minutes. Remove the cover, add the scallion and garlic, and cook 3 minutes longer. Transfer the mixture to a bowl and let it cool. In a food processor, combine the soy milk, tofu, tahini, parsley, lemon juice, salt, marjoram, and cayenne; stir into the vegetable mixture. Add the chick-peas, combine well, and set aside. Preheat the oven to 400 degrees. Lightly oil a 10-inch pie plate or coat with nonstick cooking spray and reserve. On a floured surface, roll out half the dough into a 12-inch circle and place into the prepared pan. Spoon in the vegetable mixture and spread evenly. Roll out the remaining dough into an 11-inch circle. Place on top of the pie and flute the edges. Trim the excess dough. Bake 45 minutes or until the crust browns.

6 TO 8 SERVINGS

Calories 381 Kc • Protein 13 Gm • Fat 19 Gm • Percent of calories from fat 44%
• Cholesterol 0 mg • Dietary Fiber 6 Gm • Sodium 1030 mg • Calcium 191 mg

Tofu with Chili Cream Sauce

2 tablespoons corn oil
1 red bell pepper, seeded and
  chopped
½ cup diced onions
2 small fresh red chilies, seeded
  and diced
1 clove garlic, minced

½ cup soy milk
2 tablespoons fresh lime juice
Salt
1 pound firm tofu, drained and
  cubed
6 cups freshly cooked rice
Minced fresh cilantro for garnish

Heat 1 tablespoon of the oil in a medium skillet over medium heat. Add the bell pepper, onions, chilies, and garlic. Cover and simmer until the bell pepper is tender, about 15 minutes. Transfer the mixture to a food processor and puree until smooth. Blend in the soy milk and lime juice and return to the skillet. Heat gently over low heat, stirring for about 2 minutes. Season to taste with salt. Heat the remaining 1 tablespoon of oil in a large skillet over high heat. Add the tofu and cook about 2 minutes, stirring to heat through. To serve, spoon a bed of rice on individual plates, spoon a portion of tofu on top of each, and spoon the sauce over the tofu. Garnish with a sprinkling of cilantro.

4 SERVINGS

Calories 165 Kc • Protein 11 Gm • Fat 10 Gm • Percent of calories from fat 53% • Cholesterol 0 mg • Dietary Fiber 1 Gm • Sodium 90 mg • Calcium 58 mg

Spanakopita

The classic spinach pie, but without the cholesterol. Usually the phyllo layers are brushed with melted butter, but I use olive oil which has health benefits as well as lots of flavor.

2 10-ounce packages frozen chopped spinach, thawed
1 cup minced scallion
½ cup chopped fresh parsley, or 2½ tablespoons dried
1 pound firm tofu, drained and crumbled
2 cups silken tofu, drained and pressed dry
½ cup freshly grated soy Parmesan cheese
1 teaspoon lemon juice
1 teaspoon salt
1 teaspoon dried oregano, crumbled
⅛ teaspoon cayenne
1 pound phyllo pastry
½ cup olive oil (approximately)

Squeeze the liquid out of the spinach and chop well. Combine the spinach, scallions, and parsley in a large bowl and set aside. In a medium bowl combine the firm tofu, silken tofu, soy Parmesan, lemon juice, salt, oregano, and cayenne and mix well. Stir the tofu mixture into the spinach mixture, and blend well. Taste and adjust the seasonings. Preheat the oven to 375 degrees. Lightly oil a 9 x 13-inch baking pan or coat with nonstick cooking spray and set aside. Brush 12 sheets of phyllo with olive oil and stack in the pan. Reserve an additional 8 phyllo sheets for the top layer and cover the sheets with wax paper and a damp towel to prevent drying. Pour the spinach mixture over the phyllo in the pan, spreading evenly. Lay the remaining phyllo sheets over the filling, 1 sheet at a time, brushing each with olive oil. Brush each of the 8 reserved sheets with olive oil and place over the top, folding the ends under to fit into the pan. Brush the top with olive oil. Make several slits in the top of the pastry with a sharp knife to allow steam to escape. Bake until golden and crisp, about 45 minutes. Serve hot.

8 TO 10 SERVINGS

Calories 414 Kc • Protein 15 Gm • Fat 25 Gm • Percent of calories from fat 54% • Cholesterol 4 mg • Dietary Fiber 2 Gm • Sodium 420 mg • Calcium 215 mg

Artichoke Quiche

Crust:
1 cup all-purpose flour
¼ cup (½ stick) chilled margarine,
   cut into pieces
⅛ teaspoon salt
1 to 2 tablespoons cold
   water
Filling:
1 tablespoon corn oil
1 small onion, minced

2 6-ounce jars marinated
   artichoke hearts, drained and
   chopped
2 cups firm silken tofu, drained
1 cup soy milk
1 tablespoon Dijon mustard
½ teaspoon salt
⅛ teaspoon cayenne
1 cup grated soy mozzarella
   cheese

To make the crust, combine the flour, margarine, and salt in a food processor and process with on/off pulses until the mixture is crumbly. Add just enough water, pulsing, to form a soft dough and roll into a ball. Flatten the dough, wrap the dough in plastic wrap, and refrigerate 1 hour. Preheat the oven to 350 degrees. Roll the dough out on a lightly floured surface to fit into a fluted 9-inch quiche pan or pie plate. Line the pastry with aluminum foil, and fill with dried beans. Bake 10 minutes. Discard the foil and beans. Continue baking until the bottom is lightly browned, about 5 minutes. Remove the crust from the oven and set aside.

To make the filling, Increase the oven temperature to 375 degrees. Heat the oil in a small skillet over medium-high heat. Add the onion and sauté until soft. Remove from the heat, add the artichokes, toss to combine, and set aside. In a food processor combine the tofu, soy milk, mustard, salt, and cayenne until well blended. Spoon the onion mixture into the crust and sprinkle with the soy cheese. Pour the tofu mixture over the cheese, making sure the mixture is evenly distributed. Bake until firm and lightly browned, 45 to 50 minutes. Let the quiche cool slightly before cutting.

6 SERVINGS

Calories 260 Kc • Protein 12 Gm • Fat 14 Gm • Percent of calories from fat 45%
• Cholesterol 0 mg • Dietary Fiber 3 Gm • Sodium 486 mg • Calcium 120 mg

Asparagus Quiche

Serve with a salad for an elegant lunch that can be prepared in advance and reheated. This quiche is also good served at room temperature.

Crust:
1 cup unbleached all-purpose flour
¼ teaspoon salt
¼ (½ stick) chilled margarine, cut into pieces
2 tablespoons cold water
Filling:
12 asparagus spears, trimmed

1 pound firm tofu, drained
½ cup soy milk
1 tablespoon corn oil
¼ teaspoon turmeric
2 medium onions, minced
2 tablespoons corn oil
Salt and freshly ground pepper
¼ teaspoon ground nutmeg

To make the crust, combine the flour and the salt in a food processor, then add the margarine and process in on/off pulses until the mixture is crumbly. Slowly add enough water, pulsing, to form a soft dough. Form the dough into a ball, and flatten to a disc. Wrap the dough in plastic wrap and refrigerate 30 minutes. Preheat the oven to 375 degrees. Roll out the dough on a lightly floured surface and fit into a 9-inch tart pan or pie plate. Trim and flute the edges. Line crust with aluminum foil, and fill with dried beans. Bake for 10 minutes or until the crust is set. Discard the foil and beans. Continue baking until the crust is light brown, 8 to 10 minutes longer, and remove the crust from the oven. Keep the oven on.

To make the filling, steam the asparagus until just tender but still firm. Reserve 6 spears; chop the remaining asparagus and set aside. Combine the tofu, soy milk, oil, and turmeric in a food processor and blend until smooth; pour into a large bowl. Sauté the onions in the oil until soft, then combine with the tofu mixture. Add the chopped asparagus. Season with salt and pepper to taste, and add the nutmeg. Pour the filling into the prepared crust, and arrange the reserved asparagus spears in a spoke design on top of the filling. Bake for 30 minutes or until the filling is firm. Let the quiche cool several minutes before cutting.

6 SERVINGS

Calories 254 Kc • Protein 10 Gm • Fat 13 Gm • Percent of calories from fat 46% • Cholesterol 0 mg • Dietary Fiber 2 Gm • Sodium 191 mg • Calcium 75 mg

Leek and Pear Quiche

Crust:
1 cup unbleached all-purpose flour
¼ teaspoon salt
¼ cup (½ stick) chilled margarine, cut into pieces
2 tablespoons cold water
Filling:
1 tablespoon corn oil
3 leeks, white part only, chopped
1 ripe pear, peeled, cored, and chopped

1 cup soy milk
½ cup firm tofu, drained and crumbled
1 teaspoon lemon juice
½ teaspoon salt
¼ teaspoon freshly ground black pepper
⅛ teaspoon ground nutmeg
2 tablespoons all-purpose flour

To make the crust, combine the flour and the salt in a food processor, then add the margarine and process in on/off pulses until the mixture is crumbly. Slowly add enough water, pulsing, to form a soft dough. Form the dough into a ball and flatten to a disc. Wrap the dough in plastic wrap and refrigerate 30 minutes. Preheat the oven to 375 degrees. Roll the dough out on a lightly floured surface and fit into a 9-inch tart pan or pie plate. Trim and flute the edges. Line the crust with aluminum foil, and fill with dried beans. Bake for 10 minutes, or until the crust is set. Discard the foil and beans. Continue baking until the crust is light brown, 8 to 10 minutes longer, and remove the crust from the oven. Keep the oven on.

To make the filling, heat the oil in a large skillet over medium heat. Add the leeks, cover, and cook until soft, about 5 minutes, stirring occasionally. Add the pear, cover, and cook 3 minutes longer. Set aside. In a food processor, combine the soy milk, tofu, lemon juice, salt, pepper, nutmeg, and flour, and process until smooth. Transfer to a large bowl and combine with the leek mixture. Pour into the prepared crust. Bake for 30 minutes, or until crust is browned and the filling is set.

6 SERVINGS

Calories 231 Kc • Protein 6 Gm • Fat 8 Gm • Percent of calories from fat 30%
• Cholesterol 0 mg • Dietary Fiber 3 Gm • Sodium 369 mg • Calcium 85 mg

Tomato and Pesto Tart

Use oil-packed sun-dried tomatoes instead of plum tomatoes for a more intense tomato flavor.

Pesto:
1½ cups packed fresh basil
2 cloves garlic
¼ cup pine nuts
½ teaspoon salt
¼ cup olive oil
Crust:
1 cup unbleached all-purpose
   flour
Pinch of salt
¼ cup (½ stick) chilled margarine,
   cut into small pieces
2 tablespoons ice water

Filling:
2 tablespoons olive oil
¼ cup minced shallot
1 pound firm tofu, drained and
   crumbled
1 cup canned Italian plum
   tomatoes, drained and
   chopped
1 teaspoon salt
¼ teaspoon freshly ground
   pepper

To make the pesto, puree the basil, garlic, pine nuts, and salt in a food processor. With the machine running, gradually add the oil through the feed tube. Transfer to a small bowl and set aside.

To make the crust, combine the flour and salt in a food processor, then add the margarine in on/off pulses until the mixture becomes crumbly. Slowly add enough water, pulsing, to form a soft dough. Transfer the dough to a lightly floured surface. Shape the dough into a ball and then flatten into a disc. Wrap the dough in plastic wrap and refrigerate at least 30 minutes. Preheat the oven to 375 degrees. Roll the dough out on a lightly floured surface. Fit the dough inside a lightly oiled 9-inch quiche pan or pie plate. Trim and flute the edges. Line the crust with aluminum foil, and fill with dried beans. Bake until the crust is set, about 10 minutes. Discard the foil and beans. Continue baking until the crust is light brown, 8 to 10 minutes longer, and remove from the oven. Keep the oven on.

To make the filling, heat the oil in a small skillet over low heat. Add the shallots and cook about 5 minutes, stirring frequently. Remove from the heat. Combine the tofu, tomatoes, salt, and pepper in a large bowl.

Add the shallots and stir until the mixture is smooth. Spoon the filling into the crust, and bake 30 minutes or until a knife inserted in the center comes out clean. Spread the reserved pesto evenly over the tart, and bake 5 minutes longer. Cool slightly before cutting.

6 SERVINGS

Calories 242 Kc • Protein 8 Gm • Fat 17 Gm • Percent of calories from fat 61% • Cholesterol 0 mg • Dietary Fiber 1 Gm • Sodium 553 mg • Calcium 60 mg

Spinach and Sun-dried Tomato Calzones

Crust:
1¼ cups all-purpose flour
¼ cup whole wheat flour
1 teaspoon salt
1 teaspoon dry yeast
½ cup warm water (110 to 115 degrees)
1 tablespoon olive oil
Cornmeal for dusting
Filling:
¾ cup tomato sauce

1 10-ounce package frozen chopped spinach, thawed
½ cup drained, chopped, oil-packed sun-dried tomatoes
½ cup firm tofu, drained and crumbled
Salt and freshly ground black pepper
½ cup grated soy mozzarella cheese

In a food processor, combine the flours and salt, pulsing to mix. Dissolve the yeast in the water in a small bowl, add the olive oil, and with the processor running, slowly pour the liquid through the feed tube. Process until the dough forms a ball, and continue processing for 1 minute. Turn the dough out onto a lightly floured surface, and knead about 1 minute. Transfer the dough to a large oiled bowl, lightly oil the top of the dough, and cover with plastic wrap and a dry cloth. Let the dough rest in a warm area until doubled in volume, about 1½ hours. Punch the dough down. Preheat the oven to 425 degrees. Sprinkle a baking sheet with cornmeal and set aside. Divide the dough into 4 pieces on a lightly floured surface. Roll each piece into a circle, about 7 inches in diameter. Spread 2 or 3 tablespoons of the tomato sauce onto the lower half of each circle, leaving a 1-inch edge.

Squeeze the excess liquid from the spinach. In a medium bowl, combine the spinach, tomatoes, tofu, and salt and pepper to taste. Spoon the spinach mixture evenly over the tomato sauce on each dough circle. Sprinkle the mixture with the cheese. Brush the edges of the dough with cold water and fold the top half of each circle over the filling. Fold the edges over and crimp with a fork to seal. Transfer the calzones to the prepared baking sheet. Bake for 15 minutes, or until golden.

MAKES 4 CALZONES

Calories 335 Kc • Protein 17 Gm • Fat 10 Gm • Percent of calories from fat 26% • Cholesterol 0 mg • Dietary Fiber 5 Gm • Sodium 1032 mg • Calcium 133 mg

Zucchini and Sun-dried Tomato Pizza

Crust:
1¼ cups all-purpose flour
¼ cup whole wheat flour
½ teaspoon salt
1 teaspoon dry yeast
½ cup warm water (110 to 115 degrees)
1 tablespoon olive oil
Topping:
¾ cup tomato sauce

2 tablespoons minced fresh basil, or 1 teaspoon dried
1 cup thinly sliced zucchini, blanched
½ cup chopped oil-packed sun-dried tomatoes
1 cup grated soy mozzarella cheese
Salt and freshly ground black pepper

In a food processor combine the flours and the salt with on/off pulses. In a small bowl, dissolve yeast in the water and add the olive oil. With the processor running, pour in the yeast mixture through the feed tube and process to form a dough ball, about 1 minute. Turn out onto a lightly floured surface and knead about 1 minute. Transfer the dough to a large oiled bowl, coating the top of the dough with oil as well. Cover with plastic wrap and a dry cloth and let it rise in a warm area until doubled, about 1½ hours. Preheat the oven to 425 degrees. Punch the dough down. On a floured surface, roll out the dough into a 12-inch circle. Place on a lightly floured pizza pan or baking sheet. Combine the tomato sauce and basil and spread on the dough, leaving a ½-inch border along the outside. Spread the zucchini slices over the tomato sauce. Sprinkle the sun-dried tomatoes over the zucchini, and top with the mozzarella, and salt and pepper to taste. Bake 15 to 20 minutes or until the crust is golden brown.

MAKES ONE 12-INCH PIZZA

Calories 318 Kc • Protein 13 Gm • Fat 10 Gm • Percent of calories from fat 28% • Cholesterol 0 mg • Dietary Fiber 4 Gm • Sodium 674 mg • Calcium 166 mg

Pizza Provençal

Crust:
1½ cups all-purpose flour
½ teaspoon salt
1 teaspoon dry yeast
½ cup warm water (110 to 115 degrees)
2 tablespoons olive oil
Topping:
1 small eggplant, cut into ¼-inch slices
Salt and freshly ground black pepper

1 teaspoon minced garlic
2 cups canned plum tomatoes, drained and chopped
¼ cup Niçoise olives, pitted and halved
1 teaspoon minced fresh basil, or ¼ teaspoon dried
¾ teaspoon minced fresh oregano, or ⅛ teaspoon dried
1 cup grated soy mozzarella cheese

In a food processor combine the flour and salt. In a small bowl, dissolve the yeast in the water, and add 1 tablespoon of the olive oil. With processor running, pour the yeast mixture through the feed tube and process to form a dough ball, about 1 minute. Turn out onto a lightly floured surface and knead about 1 minute. Transfer the dough to a large oiled bowl, coating the top of the dough with oil as well. Cover with plastic wrap and a dry cloth and let it rise in a warm area until doubled, about 1½ hours. Preheat the oven to 425 degrees.

Place the eggplant slices on a lightly oiled baking sheet, season with salt and pepper, and bake 6 to 8 minutes or until softened. Remove from the oven and set aside. Punch the dough down. On a floured surface, roll out the dough into a 12-inch circle. Place on a lightly floured pizza pan or baking sheet. Heat the remaining 1 tablespoon of olive oil in a large skillet over medium-high heat. Add the garlic, tomatoes, olives, basil, and oregano. Cook 3 minutes. Remove the sauce from the heat and let it cool to room temperature. Spread it on the prepared pizza dough and top with the eggplant slices. Sprinkle on the soy mozzarella and bake for 15 minutes, or until the crust turns light brown.

MAKES ONE 12-INCH PIZZA

Calories 354 Kc • Protein 13 Gm • Fat 13 Gm • Percent of calories from fat 33%
• Cholesterol 0 mg • Dietary Fiber 5 Gm • Sodium 484 mg • Calcium 179 mg

One-Pot Winter Stew

The meaty fava beans are especially good in this hearty and creamy stew, but feel free to substitute another type of bean, or some cubed seitan or tempeh, if you prefer.

1 tablespoon olive oil
1 cup chopped onion
1 cup sliced carrot
4 medium potatoes, peeled and cubed
½ pound fresh mushrooms, sliced (about 2 cups)
2 tablespoons snipped fresh chives, or 2 teaspoons dried
3 tablespoons minced fresh parsley, or 3 teaspoons dried

⅓ cup dry white wine
½ teaspoon paprika
¾ teaspoon salt
⅛ teaspoon freshly ground pepper
⅛ teaspoon ground nutmeg
3 cups cooked fresh, frozen, or canned fava beans
½ cup silken tofu, well drained
1 teaspoon Dijon mustard
1 teaspoon lemon juice

Heat the oil in a large skillet over medium-high heat. Add the onion, carrot, and potatoes, and cook 5 minutes. Reduce the heat to medium, add the mushrooms, chives, and 2 tablespoons of the parsley and cook 5 minutes longer. In a small bowl, combine the wine with the paprika, salt, pepper, and nutmeg. Add to the vegetable mixture and bring to a boil. Reduce the heat to low, cover, and simmer, stirring occasionally, 20 minutes, or until the vegetables are tender. If too much liquid evaporates, add more wine, some vegetable stock, or water. During the last 5 minutes of cooking, add the fava beans and mix well. In a small bowl, combine the tofu with the mustard and lemon juice. Remove the stew from the heat and stir in the tofu mixture. Adjust the seasonings. Transfer to a serving bowl and garnish with the remaining 1 tablespoon of parsley.

6 SERVINGS

Calories 229 Kc • Protein 7 Gm • Fat 4 Gm • Percent of calories from fat 16% • Cholesterol 0 mg • Dietary Fiber 11 Gm • Sodium 349 mg • Calcium 70 mg

Creamy Chick-pea Stew

This stew is especially good served over freshly cooked noodles.

1 tablespoon olive oil
2 cups chopped onion
2 green bell peppers, seeded
  and chopped
1 pound mushrooms, quartered
  (about 4 cups)
2 tablespoons paprika
1 tablespoon caraway seeds
⅛ teaspoon cayenne
2 cups Vegetable Stock (see
  page 10)

1 14-ounce can plum tomatoes,
  chopped, including the juice
3 cups cooked or canned chick-
  peas, drained
½ cup firm silken tofu, drained
1 tablespoon fresh lemon juice
Salt and freshly ground black
  pepper

Heat the oil in a large saucepan over medium heat. Add the onion and cook, stirring occasionally, until softened, about 5 minutes. Add the bell peppers and mushrooms, and cook, stirring occasionally, until most of the liquid is evaporated. Add the paprika, caraway, cayenne, and stock. Bring the liquid to a boil and simmer the mixture, covered, for 15 minutes. Add the tomatoes and chick-peas and simmer, stirring occasionally, for 10 minutes. In a food processor, puree 1 cup of the cooked vegetables from the stew together with the tofu and the lemon juice. Remove the stew from the heat and gently stir the puree into the stew. Season to taste with salt and pepper.

6 SERVINGS

Calories 225 Kc • Protein 10 Gm • Fat 7 Gm • Percent of calories from fat 26% • Cholesterol 0 mg • Dietary Fiber 9 Gm • Sodium 444 mg • Calcium 88 mg

Wheat Meat Goulash

Serve this hearty goulash over freshly cooked noodles and top with tofu sour cream for Old World goodness without the cholesterol.

2 tablespoons corn oil
1 pound seitan, cut into ½-inch cubes
1 cup chopped onion
½ cup sliced carrot
½ cup chopped celery
2 tablespoons paprika
3 tablespoons flour

1 tablespoon tomato paste
1½ cups Vegetable Stock (see page 10)
¼ cup dry white wine
¾ teaspoon salt
⅛ teaspoon cayenne
1½ cup silken tofu, well drained
1 tablespoon lemon juice

Heat 1 tablespoon of the oil in a large skillet over medium heat. Add the seitan and brown on all sides. Remove from the pan and reserve. Add the remaining 1 tablespoon of oil, onion, carrot, and celery. Cover and cook over medium heat for 5 minutes, or until the vegetables begin to soften. Stir in the paprika and cook 2 minutes. Add the flour and cook, stirring, for 2 minutes longer. Stir in the tomato paste until smooth. Add the stock and wine. Stir over low heat until the mixture comes to a boil. Season with ½ teaspoon of the salt and the cayenne. Simmer 5 minutes. Reduce the heat to very low. Slowly whisk in 1 cup of the tofu, a little at a time, blending after each addition. Add the reserved seitan, and cook gently to heat through, about 10 minutes. In a small bowl, combine the remaining ½ cup of tofu with the lemon juice and the remaining ¼ teaspoon of salt to make a quick tofu sour cream. Top each portion of goulash with a spoonful of tofu sour cream.

4 SERVINGS

Calories 656 Kc • Protein 67 Gm • Fat 15 Gm • Percent of calories from fat 20% • Cholesterol 0 mg • Dietary Fiber 10 Gm • Sodium 627 mg • Calcium 87 mg

Creamy Seitan Stew

2 tablespoons corn oil
1 pound seitan, cut into ½-inch cubes
1 cup chopped onions
1 cup diced carrots
½ cup diced celery
1 bay leaf
½ cup dry vermouth

1½ cups water
1 teaspoon salt
¼ teaspoon freshly ground pepper
¼ pound mushroom caps, quartered
1 cup almond milk combined with 2 tablespoons cornstarch

Heat 1 tablespoon of the oil in a large saucepan over medium-high heat. Add the seitan and brown on all sides. Remove the seitan from the pan and reserve. Add the remaining 1 tablespoon oil, the onions, carrots, and celery to the saucepan, cover, and cook 5 minutes, stirring occasionally. Remove the cover, add the bay leaf, vermouth, water, salt, and pepper. Simmer, covered, 15 minutes or until the vegetables are very tender. Add the mushroom caps and reserved seitan and cook uncovered 5 minutes longer. Slowly add the almond milk mixture, stirring constantly, and simmer until thickened, about 5 minutes, being careful not to boil. Remove the bay leaf before serving.

6 SERVINGS

Calories 400 Kc • Protein 42 Gm • Fat 9 Gm • Percent of calories from fat 20% • Cholesterol 0 mg • Dietary Fiber 6 Gm • Sodium 459 mg • Calcium 39 mg

Cloud Nine Tofu

1 pound extra-firm tofu, drained
Salt and freshly ground pepper
¼ cup grated soy mozzarella
2 tablespoons minced scallion

2 tablespoons Tofu Mayonnaise
   (see page 258)
1 tablespoon softened margarine
⅛ teaspoon Tabasco sauce

Preheat the broiler. Cut the tofu into ¼-inch slices. Lightly oil a shallow baking pan or coat with nonstick cooking spray and place tofu slices in a single layer in the pan. Sprinkle with salt and pepper to taste and set aside. In a small bowl, combine the soy mozzarella, scallion, Tofu Mayonnaise, margarine, and Tabasco, blending well. Spread the mixture on the tofu and broil about 6 inches from the heat source for 3 to 5 minutes, or until heated through and lightly browned on top.

4 SERVINGS

Calories 107 Kc • Protein 11 Gm • Fat 6 Gm • Percent of calories from fat 46% • Cholesterol 0 mg • Dietary Fiber 0 Gm • Sodium 140 mg • Calcium 72 mg

Tofu Cutlets with Creamy Olive Sauce

1 pound extra-firm tofu, drained
2 tablespoons corn oil
Salt and freshly ground pepper
1 teaspoon minced garlic
¼ cup minced scallion
½ cup sliced mushrooms
2 tablespoons dry sherry

1 cup sliced black olives
1 cup silken tofu, drained and
   pressed dry
1 teaspoon Dijon mustard
1 teaspoon Worcestershire sauce
1 teaspoon lemon juice

Cut the firm tofu into ½-inch slabs. Heat 1 tablespoon of the oil in a large skillet over medium-high heat. Add the tofu cutlets and cook 2 minutes on each side, seasoning to taste with salt and pepper. Remove the tofu cutlets from the skillet and keep warm. Heat the remaining 1 tablespoon of oil in a skillet over medium heat. Add the garlic, scallion, and mushrooms and cook for 2 to 3 minutes. Add the sherry and olives and remove from the heat. In a small bowl, combine the silken tofu with the mustard, Worcestershire sauce, and lemon juice. Slowly add to the mixture in the skillet, stirring, and heat gently until just hot. Taste and adjust the seasonings. Spoon the sauce over the tofu cutlets and serve.

4 SERVINGS

Calories 216 Kc • Protein 13 Gm • Fat 13 Gm • Percent of calories from fat 54%
• Cholesterol 0 mg • Dietary Fiber 0 Gm • Sodium 271 mg • Calcium 93 mg

Sautéed Tofu Cutlets with Tahini Sauce

1 tablespoon safflower oil
1 pound extra-firm tofu, cut into
  ½-inch-thick slices
4 tablespoons low-sodium
  tamari

3 tablespoons tahini (sesame
  paste)
1 cup hot soy milk
2 tablespoons minced fresh
  parsley, or 1 teaspoon dried

Preheat the oven to 250 degrees. Heat the oil in a large skillet over medium-high heat. Add the tofu slices and sauté until golden brown, about 2 minutes on each side. Add 2 tablespoons of the tamari, turning to coat. Place the tofu in the oven to keep warm. In a food processor, combine the tahini and the remaining 2 tablespoons of tamari. With the machine running, slowly stream in the hot soy milk. Transfer the mixture to a small saucepan and simmer over low heat for 2 minutes, stirring constantly. To serve, place the tofu slices on serving plates, and top with the sauce. Sprinkle with the minced parsley.

4 SERVINGS

Calories 231 Kc • Protein 16 Gm • Fat 14 Gm • Percent of calories from fat 56% • Cholesterol 0 mg • Dietary Fiber 0 Gm • Sodium 709 mg • Calcium 95 mg

Tofu and Mushrooms with Green Chili Cream Sauce

6 fresh mild green chilies
1½ cups firm silken tofu, drained
1 cup soy milk mixed with 2 tablespoons cornstarch
Salt and freshly ground white pepper
2 tablespoons olive oil

1 pound extra-firm tofu, cut into ½-inch slices
1½ cups sliced mushrooms (about ⅓ pound)
1 clove garlic, minced
½ cup grated soy Cheddar cheese

Preheat the broiler. Place the chilies on a broiler pan and broil 6 inches from the heat source, turning until blistered on all sides. Transfer the chilies to a paper or plastic bag and close tightly. Let the chilies stand for 10 minutes. Peel the chilies, discard the stems and seeds, cut into strips, and reserve. Whisk the silken tofu and soy milk mixture in a saucepan over medium heat. Stir in salt and pepper to taste. Increase the heat to medium-high and stir to thicken. Reduce the heat to low and simmer for 10 minutes, whisking occasionally. Heat 1 tablespoon of the oil in a large skillet over medium-high heat. Add the firm tofu and sauté until lightly browned, about 2 minutes per side. Remove from the heat. Heat the remaining 1 tablespoon oil in a medium skillet over medium-high heat. Add the chilies, mushrooms, and garlic, and cook, stirring frequently, 5 minutes. Drain well and combine with the sauce mixture.

Preheat the oven to 350 degrees. Arrange the tofu slices in a baking dish. Spoon the sauce mixture over the tofu, spreading evenly. Sprinkle with the cheese. Bake until heated through, about 10 minutes.

6 SERVINGS

Calories 200 Kc • Protein 17 Gm • Fat 10 Gm • Percent of calories from fat 45% • Cholesterol 0 mg • Dietary Fiber 1 Gm • Sodium 145 mg • Calcium 109 mg

Tempeh with Creole Mustard Sauce

Filé powder is a spice mixture used generously in Creole cooking and can be found among the spices in most grocery stores.

1 pound tempeh
1 tablespoon olive oil
2 shallots, minced
2 tomatoes, peeled, seeded, and chopped
½ cup dry white wine
½ cup silken tofu, drained

2 tablespoons Dijon mustard
¼ teaspoon filé powder
½ teaspoon Tabasco sauce
Salt and freshly ground pepper
2 tablespoons minced fresh parsley, or 2 teaspoons dried

Poach the tempeh in a shallow pan of boiling water for 10 minutes. Remove from the water and let the tempeh cool. Cut the tempeh in ¼-inch slices. Heat the oil in a large skillet over medium heat. Add the tempeh and cook until lightly browned, about 5 minutes. Remove from the skillet with a slotted spoon and set aside. In the same skillet, add the shallots and cook about 5 minutes. Add the tomatoes and cook until the liquid evaporates, 2 to 3 minutes. Add the wine and cook until reduced by half. Remove the pan from the heat, stir in the tofu, mustard, filé powder, Tabasco, and salt and pepper to taste. Heat through, being careful not to boil. Add the reserved tempeh and spoon the sauce over it to coat. Serve immediately, sprinkled with the minced parsley.

4 SERVINGS

Calories 299 Kc • Protein 21 Gm • Fat 11 Gm • Percent of calories from fat 32% • Cholesterol 0 mg • Dietary Fiber 7 Gm • Sodium 55 mg • Calcium 58 mg

Tempeh with Lemon Marsala Sauce

1 pound tempeh
1 tablespoon corn oil
2 tablespoons marsala wine
2 tablespoons lemon juice
1 tablespoon mirin (or dry white
  wine)

1 tablespoon lemon zest
½ teaspoon salt
¼ teaspoon pepper
1 cup silken tofu, drained
Snipped fresh chives for garnish

Cut the tempeh into 6 equal pieces. Poach the tempeh in boiling water to cover for 10 minutes. Remove from the water and pat dry. Heat the oil in a large skillet over medium heat. Add the tempeh and cook until golden brown, about 3 minutes per side. Remove the tempeh from the skillet and keep warm. Add the marsala, lemon juice, mirin, and lemon zest to the skillet. Stir and add the salt and pepper. Reduce the heat to low. Slowly add the tofu, whisking constantly. Add the tempeh and cook 5 minutes longer. Garnish with minced fresh chives.

4 TO 6 SERVINGS

Calories 233 Kc • Protein 17 Gm • Fat 9 Gm • Percent of calories from fat 34% • Cholesterol 0 mg • Dietary Fiber 5 Gm • Sodium 239 mg • Calcium 42 mg

Creamed Tempeh with Mushrooms and Bell Peppers

1 pound tempeh
1 tablespoon corn oil
1 green bell pepper, seeded and chopped
3 cups sliced mushrooms (about ¾ pound)
3 cups soy milk

2 tablespoons cornstarch combined with 2 tablespoons low-sodium tamari
½ teaspoon paprika
Salt and freshly ground black pepper
6 cups freshly cooked rice

Poach the tempeh for 10 minutes in a saucepan in boiling water to cover. Remove from the saucepan and let it cool. Cut into 1-inch cubes and set aside. Heat the oil in a saucepan, add the bell pepper, and cook 5 minutes or until softened. Add the mushrooms and continue cooking for about 3 minutes. Add the soy milk slowly, stirring constantly. Bring to a simmer, being careful not to boil. Whisk in the cornstarch mixture and continue stirring until thickened. Add the tempeh and the paprika and season to taste with salt and pepper. Serve over the rice.

4 SERVINGS

Calories 477 Kc • Protein 25 Gm • Fat 24 Gm • Percent of calories from fat 44% • Cholesterol 0 mg • Dietary Fiber 7 Gm • Sodium 115 mg • Calcium 80 mg

Five-Spice Tempeh

The almond milk mellows the pungent flavor of the five-spice powder.

1 pound tempeh
2 tablespoons safflower oil
2 tablespoons low-sodium tamari
2 tablespoons lemon juice
1 teaspoon five-spice powder
2 tablespoons brandy
1 cup almond milk

2 tablespoons cornstarch mixed
   with 2 tablespoons mirin (or
   dry white wine)
2 tablespoons chopped fresh
   parsley, or 1 teaspoon dried
½ cup lightly toasted slivered
   almonds

Place tempeh in a saucepan and poach for 10 minutes in boiling water to cover. Remove from the water, pat dry, and cut into 6 equal pieces. Heat the oil in a large skillet over medium heat. Add the tempeh and cook until golden brown on both sides, about 3 minutes per side. Remove the tempeh from the skillet and keep warm. In the same skillet, stir in the tamari, lemon juice, and five-spice powder and cook, stirring, about 1 minute to blend the flavors. Carefully add the brandy and ignite, shaking the skillet gently until the flame subsides. Slowly stir in the almond milk, and add the cornstarch mixture, stirring constantly to form a smooth sauce, about 2 minutes. Pour the sauce over the tempeh. Sprinkle with the parsley and almonds and serve.

4 TO 6 SERVINGS

Calories 405 Kc • Protein 23 Gm • Fat 22 Gm • Percent of calories from fat 48%
• Cholesterol 0 mg • Dietary Fiber 9 Gm • Sodium 359 mg • Calcium 82 mg

Curried Tempeh over Rice

1 pound tempeh
3 tablespoons corn oil
¾ cup finely chopped onion
2 cloves garlic, minced
2 tablespoons all-purpose flour
2 tablespoons curry powder (or to taste)

½ teaspoon ground ginger
2 cups almond milk
2 tablespoons fresh lemon juice
6 cups freshly cooked rice
Chopped peanuts for garnish
Chutney (as accompaniment)

Poach the tempeh in a shallow pan of boiling water for 10 minutes. Remove from the water and let it cool. Cut the tempeh in ½-inch cubes. Heat 1 tablespoon of the oil in a large skillet over medium heat. Add the tempeh and cook until lightly browned, about 5 minutes. Remove the tempeh from the skillet with a slotted spoon and set aside. In the same skillet, heat the remaining 2 tablespoons oil, add the onion and cook about 5 minutes, stirring occasionally. Add the garlic and cook 1 minute longer. Stir in the flour, curry powder, and ginger and cook 2 minutes. Slowly add the almond milk, stirring until thickened, about 5 minutes. Add the reserved tempeh and lemon juice and cook until heated through, about 2 minutes. Serve the tempeh over the rice, sprinkled with chopped peanuts. Pass the chutney separately.

4 SERVINGS

Calories 416 Kc • Protein 22 Gm • Fat 24 Gm • Percent of calories from fat 49% • Cholesterol 0 mg • Dietary Fiber 9 Gm • Sodium 7 mg • Calcium 94 mg

Cardamom-scented Tempeh and Pineapple with Rum Cream Sauce

1 pound tempeh, cut into 1-inch
   cubes
½ pineapple, peeled and cored
2 tablespoons corn oil
¼ teaspoon ground cardamom
½ teaspoon sugar (or a natural
   sweetener)
¼ teaspoon cinnamon

¼ cup dark rum
1 cup plus 2 tablespoons almond
   milk
2 tablespoons cornstarch
Salt and freshly ground pepper
Toasted slivered almonds for
   garnish (optional)

Simmer the tempeh in a saucepan in boiling water to cover for 10 minutes. Remove from the water and pat dry. Cut the pineapple into ¼-inch slices, and quarter each slice to make bite-size pieces. Set aside. Heat the oil in a large skillet over medium heat. Add the tempeh and cook until golden brown, about 3 minutes per side. Remove the tempeh from the skillet, set aside, and keep warm. Reheat the same skillet, add the pineapple, cardamom, sugar, and cinnamon and cook over medium heat, stirring occasionally, about 5 minutes. Return the tempeh to the skillet. Increase the heat to medium-high, carefully pour the rum into the pan and ignite, shaking the pan gently until the flame subsides. Reduce the heat to low, stir in 1 cup of the almond milk, stirring constantly. Combine the remaining 2 tablespoons of almond milk with the cornstarch and whisk into the mixture. Simmer until thickened, and season with salt and pepper to taste. Divide among 4 serving plates and sprinkle with the toasted almond slivers, if desired.

4 SERVINGS

Calories 395 Kc • Protein 20 Gm • Fat 17 Gm • Percent of calories from fat 36%
• Cholesterol 0 mg • Dietary Fiber 8 Gm • Sodium 3 mg • Calcium 55 mg

Tempeh in Apple Brandy Sauce

1 pound tempeh
1 tablespoon corn oil
1 cup chopped leek, white part only
1 cup thinly sliced carrot
½ cup applejack or brandy
½ cup dry white wine
1 cup Vegetable Stock (see page 10)

¼ cup minced shallot
1 bay leaf
1 teaspoon minced fresh thyme, or ¼ teaspoon dried
1 cup plus 2 tablespoons soy milk
2 tablespoons cornstarch
½ cup apple butter
Salt and freshly ground pepper

Poach the tempeh in a saucepan in boiling water to cover for 10 minutes. Remove the tempeh from the water, pat dry, and cut into 2-inch bars. Heat the oil in a large skillet over medium heat. Add the tempeh and cook over medium heat until golden brown, about 3 minutes per side. Remove from the skillet and keep warm. In the same skillet, add the leek and carrot and cook until softened, stirring frequently, about 10 minutes. Scoop the vegetables out of the skillet and set aside with the tempeh.

Carefully pour the applejack into the skillet over medium-high heat. Ignite, shaking the pan gently until the flame subsides. Add the wine and cook 3 minutes, stirring to loosen any browned bits. Add the stock, shallot, bay leaf, and thyme and boil until reduced by half, about 5 minutes. Reduce the heat to low. Combine 2 tablespoons of the soy milk with the cornstarch and reserve. Stir the remaining 1 cup soy milk into the skillet and simmer, being careful not to boil. Whisk in the cornstarch mixture and simmer, stirring to thicken. Stir in the apple butter and cook 2 minutes longer. Strain the sauce through a fine sieve into a medium saucepan. Season with salt and pepper, and reheat over low heat. To serve, divide the tempeh and vegetables among 4 serving plates and spoon the sauce over the tempeh. Pass the remaining sauce separately.

4 SERVINGS

Calories 516 Kc • Protein 21 Gm • Fat 12 Gm • Percent of calories from fat 21% • Cholesterol 0 mg • Dietary Fiber 8 Gm • Sodium 103 mg • Calcium 92 mg

Tempeh Poire William

A friend gave us a bottle of this exquisite pear brandy and, like most spirits, it found its way into my kitchen for experimentation. Regular brandy (or even pear or apple juice) can be used but with less sublime results.

1 pound tempeh
2 tablespoons corn oil
3 ripe pears, peeled, cored, and
   sliced
½ cup dry white wine
½ cup Poire William (pear brandy)
2 cups Vegetable Stock (see
   page 10)

1 cup almond milk
2 tablespoons cornstarch,
   combined with 2
   tablespoons low-sodium
   tamari
Salt and freshly ground white
   pepper

Poach the tempeh in boiling water to cover for 10 minutes. Remove from the pan, and quarter. Cut each piece diagonally to form triangles. Heat the oil in a large skillet over medium-high heat. Add the tempeh and brown on both sides. Remove the tempeh from the skillet and keep warm. In the same skillet, add the pears, place over medium-high heat, and toss briefly to coat with the oil in the pan. Add the wine to the skillet and bring to a boil, scraping up the brown bits. Carefully add the Poire William and ignite, shaking the skillet gently until the flame subsides. Stir in the stock and boil until reduced by half, 8 to 10 minutes. Reduce the heat to low. Add the almond milk and simmer until hot. Whisk in the cornstarch mixture and cook until the sauce thickens, about 5 minutes. Taste and adjust the seasoning with salt and white pepper. Divide the tempeh among 4 individual plates. Spoon the sauce over the tempeh and serve immediately.

4 SERVINGS

Calories 555 Kc • Protein 22 Gm • Fat 17 Gm • Percent of calories from fat 27%
• Cholesterol 0 mg • Dietary Fiber 11 Gm • Sodium 454 mg • Calcium 88 mg

Grand Marnier-laced Seitan with Oranges and Golden Raisins

The subtle flavor of almond milk is the perfect vehicle for the Grand Marnier. Serve this dish on special occasions.

½ cup golden raisins
1 cup water
¼ cup Grand Marnier
2 tablespoons olive oil
1 pound seitan, cut into ½-inch-wide strips
3 shallots, chopped
1 cup almond milk combined with 2 tablespoons cornstarch

1 teaspoon minced fresh thyme, or ¼ teaspoon dried
1 teaspoon minced fresh marjoram, or ½ teaspoon dried
Salt and freshly ground pepper
1 orange, peeled and segmented
1 tablespoon snipped fresh chives for garnish

Bring the raisins and water to a boil in a small saucepan over medium-high heat. Reduce the heat and simmer 3 minutes. Drain the raisins and place in a small bowl with the Grand Marnier and set aside. Heat the oil in a large skillet over medium-high heat. Add the seitan and brown lightly, about 5 minutes. Remove from the skillet using a slotted spoon. Add the shallots to the skillet and sauté until softened, 3 to 4 minutes. Remove the raisins from the Grand Marnier with a slotted spoon and reserve. Increase the heat to medium-high. Add the Grand Marnier to the skillet, scraping up the browned bits. Reduce the heat to medium, add the almond milk mixture and cook, stirring constantly, until thickened, about 2 minutes. Stir in the raisins, thyme, marjoram, and salt and pepper to taste. Stir in the seitan and orange pieces and heat until warmed through. Garnish with the chives.

4 TO 6 SERVINGS

Calories 504 Kc • Protein 49 Gm • Fat 11 Gm • Percent of calories from fat 18% • Cholesterol 0 mg • Dietary Fiber 6 Gm • Sodium 50 mg • Calcium 35 mg

Seitan in Shiitake Cream Sauce

3 tablespoons corn oil
½ pound seitan, cut in ¼-inch-
    thick slices
¼ cup minced shallots
2 cups fresh shiitake mushrooms,
    cleaned, stemmed, and sliced
    (about ½ pound)

1 teaspoon minced garlic
2 tablespoons all-purpose flour
½ teaspoon minced fresh thyme
    or ¼ teaspoon dried
¼ teaspoon salt
⅛ teaspoon black pepper
1½ cups soy milk

Heat 1 tablespoon of the oil in a large skillet over medium-high heat. Add the seitan and cook 2 minutes. Turn the seitan pieces and cook on the other side for 2 minutes more or until lightly browned. Remove the seitan from the skillet and keep warm. Heat the remaining 2 tablespoons of oil in the skillet over medium heat, add the shallots, mushrooms, and garlic, and cook for 5 minutes, or until tender. Stir in the flour, thyme, salt, and pepper, and cook 1 minute. Reduce the heat and slowly add the soy milk, whisking to achieve a smooth sauce. Cook and stir until thickened, about 3 minutes. Return the seitan to the skillet, and heat through, about 3 minutes, spooning the sauce over the seitan.

4 SERVINGS

Calories 416 Kc • Protein 34 Gm • Fat 14 Gm • Percent of calories from fat 29% • Cholesterol 0 mg • Dietary Fiber 5 Gm • Sodium 220 mg • Calcium 33 mg

6
Sides

Side dishes can add variety to meals, complement the main course, or provide a special touch to formal or informal dining. They can even stand alone as light meals, combined with a salad.

Some of my favorite comfort foods, formerly made with dairy products, include creamy vegetable side dishes such as Scalloped Potatoes and Creamed Spinach. You'll find recipes for all these tasty traditions in this chapter, as well as dairy-free recipes for Corn Pudding and Tomato Zucchini Gratin.

Although classified as side dishes in this book, some of these recipes, such as Mushroom Almond Gratin or Vegetable Loaf, are hearty enough to serve as entrees for a lunch or light supper.

Zucchini Pecan Pancakes

Make mini-pancakes to serve as hors d'oeuvres by using less batter to form smaller pancakes.

¾ cup almond milk
½ cup grated zucchini
¼ cup grated onion
2 tablespoons corn oil
1 cup all-purpose flour

1 teaspoon baking powder
1 teaspoon baking soda
½ teaspoon salt
½ cup chopped pecans
Oil for sautéing

Combine all the ingredients except sautéing oil in the order given and mix well. Heat a large skillet with 1 tablespoon of oil over medium-high heat. Spoon about ¼ cup of batter onto the skillet and cook until bubbly and the underside is golden brown. Turn and cook on the second side until golden brown. Remove and keep warm. Repeat with the remaining batter, using more oil as necessary.

4 SERVINGS

Calories 299 Kc • Protein 6 Gm • Fat 19 Gm • Percent of calories from fat 55% • Cholesterol 0 mg • Dietary Fiber 3 Gm • Sodium 709 mg • Calcium 97 mg

Root Vegetables in "Sour Cream" Sauce

1 pound parsnips, cut into ¼-inch
slices
1 pound carrots, cut into ¼-inch
slices
¼ cup soy milk
1 teaspoon salt

¼ teaspoon cayenne
1 cup silken tofu, well drained
1 tablespoon lemon juice
1 teaspoon minced fresh dill, or ¼
teaspoon dried

Cook the parsnips and carrots in boiling salted water to cover until soft,
6 to 8 minutes, and drain. Puree the carrots and parsnips in a food
processor with the soy milk, salt, and cayenne. Mix in the tofu, lemon
juice, and dill. Taste and adjust the seasonings. Transfer the mixture to a
saucepan and heat gently before serving.

4 TO 6 SERVINGS

Calories 151 Kc • Protein 5 Gm • Fat 2 Gm • Percent of calories from fat 12%
• Cholesterol 0 mg • Dietary Fiber 7 Gm • Sodium 515 mg • Calcium 78 mg

Cucumber Raita

The addition of asafetida adds an authentic Indian flavor to this side dish, but the raita is also good without it. Try the raita as a cooling contrast to hot or spicy food.

1 teaspoon corn oil
½ teaspoon mustard seeds
½ teaspoon asafetida (available in Indian markets)
1 large cucumber, peeled and grated

1 cup firm silken tofu, drained
1 tablespoon lemon juice
¼ teaspoon salt
2 tablespoons minced fresh cilantro

Heat the oil in a small skillet over medium heat. Add the mustard seeds and asafetida and cook briefly until fragrant. Remove from the heat and set aside. Squeeze the excess liquid from the cucumber. In a small bowl, combine the cucumber with the tofu, lemon juice, and salt. Add the asafetida mixture and the cilantro and mix well.

4 SERVINGS

Calories 61 Kc • Protein 6 Gm • Fat 3 Gm • Percent of calories from fat 38% • Cholesterol 0 mg • Dietary Fiber 1 Gm • Sodium 188 mg • Calcium 37 mg

Mashed Potatoes

Everyone's favorite and every bit as delicious made with rice milk and margarine instead of cream and butter. The chives add a special, fragrant touch.

5 medium (about 2 pounds) white potatoes, peeled and cut into 1-inch chunks
1 cup rice milk

1 tablespoon margarine
1 tablespoon snipped fresh chives, or 1 teaspoon dried
Salt and freshly ground pepper

Cook the potatoes in a pot of boiling salted water for 15 to 20 minutes or until tender. Drain. Return to the saucepan and add the rice milk and margarine. Mash with a rotary mixer or a potato masher until smooth. Add the chives and season with salt and pepper to taste.

4 TO 6 SERVINGS

Calories 166 Kc • Protein 5 Gm • Fat 2 Gm • Percent of calories from fat 10% • Cholesterol 0 mg • Dietary Fiber 3 Gm • Sodium 31 mg • Calcium 22 mg

Mashed Sweet Potatoes

2 pounds sweet potatoes
¼ cup soft silken tofu, drained
¼ cup rice milk
¼ cup apple juice

¼ teaspoon cinnamon
¼ teaspoon salt
⅛ teaspoon freshly ground black
   pepper

Peel the potatoes and cut into ¼-inch-thick slices. Place in a saucepan and add water to cover. Bring to a boil, reduce the heat to medium, cover, and cook for 15 minutes, or until tender. Drain the potatoes and puree in a food processor or beat with an electric mixer along with the tofu, rice milk, and apple juice. Season with the cinnamon, salt, and pepper.

4 SERVINGS

Calories 337 Kc • Protein 5 Gm • Fat 2 Gm • Percent of calories from fat 5%
• Cholesterol 0 mg • Dietary Fiber 1 Gm • Sodium 234 mg • Calcium 46 mg

Curried Cauliflower Puree

1 medium cauliflower, trimmed
   (about 4 cups)
2 tablespoons corn oil
1 teaspoon curry powder

¼ cup almond milk
Salt
2 tablespoons snipped fresh
   chives for garnish

Cut the cauliflower into small pieces and place in a saucepan with lightly salted boiling water to cover. Cook until tender, about 5 minutes; drain. Place the cooked cauliflower in a food processor and puree until smooth. Heat the oil in a saucepan over low heat. Add the curry powder and cook 1 minute, stirring to release its flavor. Add the cauliflower puree to the saucepan and stir to combine. Slowly stir in the almond milk to achieve a smooth consistency, and season with salt to taste. Garnish with the chives.

4 SERVINGS

Calories 100 Kc • Protein 3 Gm • Fat 8 Gm • Percent of calories from fat 69%
• Cholesterol 0 mg • Dietary Fiber 4 Gm • Sodium 19 mg • Calcium 28 mg

Root Vegetable Puree

2 tablespoons corn oil
2 leeks, white part only, chopped
3 carrots, chopped
3 parsnips, chopped
2 sweet potatoes, peeled and cut
into 1-inch chunks
1½ cups Vegetable Stock (see
page 10)

½ cup almond milk
Salt and freshly ground pepper
2 tablespoons minced fresh
parsley for garnish, or 2
teaspoons dried

Heat the oil in a large skillet over low heat. Add the leeks, carrots, and parsnips, cover and cook until softened, about 5 minutes. Add the sweet potatoes and stock. Increase the heat to high and bring to a boil. Reduce the heat to low, cover and simmer until the vegetables are tender, about 25 minutes. Transfer the vegetable mixture to a food processor in batches and puree. Return the puree to the skillet. Blend in the almond milk and salt and pepper to taste. Stir over medium-high heat until heated through. To serve, spoon the puree into a serving bowl and garnish with the minced parsley.

6 TO 8 SERVINGS

Calories 186 Kc • Protein 3 Gm • Fat 6 Gm • Percent of calories from fat 30% • Cholesterol 0 mg • Dietary Fiber 4 Gm • Sodium 87 mg • Calcium 68 mg

Spiced Sweet Potato Gratin

¼ cup brown sugar (or a natural
   sweetener)
½ teaspoon cinnamon
⅛ teaspoon allspice

⅛ teaspoon nutmeg
1 pound sweet potatoes, peeled
1½ cups soy milk

Preheat the oven to 400 degrees. Lightly oil a 1½-quart gratin dish or spray with nonstick cooking spray. In a small bowl combine the brown sugar, cinnamon, allspice, and nutmeg. Cut the sweet potatoes into ¼-inch slices, and arrange half of them in the prepared dish. Sprinkle the slices with half of the sugar mixture. Arrange the remaining half of the potatoes on top and sprinkle with the remaining sugar mixture. Heat the soy milk in a saucepan until hot, being careful not to boil. Pour the soy milk slowly over the potatoes. Bake, covered, for 1 hour, or until the liquid is absorbed.

4 SERVINGS

Calories 266 Kc • Protein 5 Gm • Fat 2 Gm • Percent of calories from fat 8%
• Cholesterol 0 mg • Dietary Fiber 1 Gm • Sodium 89 mg • Calcium 56 mg

Potato and Onion Casserole

Try to find the sweet Vidalia onion and buttery Yukon Gold potato to give this casserole an incomparable natural richness.

4 tablespoons corn oil
1 large Vidalia onion, thinly sliced
2 pounds Yukon Gold potatoes, peeled and cut into ¼-inch slices

2 tablespoons chopped capers
Salt and freshly ground white pepper
1 cup soy milk
½ cup fresh bread crumbs

Heat 2 tablespoons of the oil in a large skillet over medium-low heat. Add the onion, cover and cook until tender, stirring occasionally, about 5 minutes. Preheat the oven to 375 degrees. Lightly oil a large baking dish, or spray it with nonstick cooking spray. Layer ⅓ of the potatoes in the prepared dish. Top with half of the capers and half of the onion. Season with salt and pepper to taste. Layer on another ⅓ of the potatoes, the remaining capers, onion, and salt and pepper to taste. Top with the remaining potatoes. Heat the soy milk until hot, being careful not to boil, and pour over the potatoes. In a small bowl, combine the bread crumbs with the remaining 2 tablespoons oil, mixing with a fork, and sprinkle on top of casserole. Bake until the top is golden brown and the potatoes are tender, about 1 hour. Serve hot.

6 TO 8 SERVINGS

Calories 202 Kc • Protein 5 Gm • Fat 9 Gm • Percent of calories from fat 39% • Cholesterol 0 mg • Dietary Fiber 3 Gm • Sodium 128 mg • Calcium 29 mg

Scalloped Potatoes

5 medium potatoes, peeled and
   cut into ¼-inch slices
1 large onion, minced
1¼ cups soy milk

2 tablespoons all-purpose flour
½ teaspoon salt
⅛ teaspoon freshly ground
   pepper to taste

Preheat the oven to 375 degrees. Lightly oil a shallow baking dish or spray with vegetable cooking spray. Cover the bottom with a layer of the potatoes, overlapping them slightly, then sprinkle a layer of onion on top. Repeat with alternating layers, ending with a layer of potatoes. In a small bowl combine the soy milk, flour, salt, and pepper, whisking until smooth. Pour the soy milk mixture over the potatoes and onion. Cover loosely with foil and bake 30 minutes. Remove the foil and bake 15 minutes longer, or until the vegetables are tender and the top is lightly browned.

4 SERVINGS

Calories 200 Kc • Protein 7 Gm • Fat 2 Gm • Percent of calories from fat 9% • Cholesterol 0 mg • Dietary Fiber 4 Gm • Sodium 333 mg • Calcium 47 mg

Garlicky Scalloped Potatoes

Like no scalloped potatoes you've ever had. The flavor of the garlic, enhanced by the olive oil, permeates the entire dish as it bakes.

2 pounds boiling potatoes,
   peeled and sliced ⅛-inch thick
4 cloves garlic, mashed
⅓ cup olive oil
2 tablespoons corn oil

2 tablespoons all-purpose flour
4 cups hot soy milk
1 teaspoon salt
⅛ teaspoon cayenne
⅛ teaspoon ground nutmeg

Place the sliced potatoes in a bowl of cold water to prevent discoloration. Preheat the oven to 400 degrees. Combine the garlic with 2 tablespoons of the olive oil to form a paste and spread in the bottom of a shallow baking dish. In a medium saucepan, heat the corn oil, whisk in the flour and cook 1 minute, stirring constantly. Whisk in the hot soy milk, salt, cayenne, and nutmeg. Do not boil. Drain the potatoes and pat them dry. Ladle some of the sauce over the garlic mixture in the baking dish. Top with a layer of potatoes. Layer the remaining sauce and potatoes, adding a dash of salt to each layer of potatoes and a teaspoon of the remaining olive oil, if desired, until all the sauce and potatoes are used up. Bake for 25 to 30 minutes, or until the potatoes are tender and browned lightly. Allow the dish to set for 5 to 10 minutes before serving.

8 SERVINGS

Calories 276 Kc • Protein 7 Gm • Fat 15 Gm • Percent of calories from fat 49% • Cholesterol 0 mg • Dietary Fiber 2 Gm • Sodium 352 mg • Calcium 46 mg

Corn Pudding

2 tablespoons corn oil
2 tablespoons all-purpose
   flour
1½ cups soy milk
½ cup soft silken tofu,
   drained

4 cups corn kernels, fresh or
   frozen (about 8 ears)
1 tablespoon minced fresh
   parsley, or 1 teaspoon dried
1 teaspoon salt
¼ teaspoon cayenne

Preheat the oven to 350 degrees. Lightly oil a baking dish or spray with nonstick cooking spray. Heat the oil in a small skillet over medium-high heat. Add the flour and stir until smooth. Cook 1 minute, stirring constantly. Gradually add the soy milk, stirring constantly until the sauce is thickened. Remove from the heat. Whisk the tofu in a large bowl to a smooth consistency. Gradually add the sauce, blending well after each addition. Add the corn, parsley, salt, and cayenne and mix thoroughly. Turn into the prepared baking dish. Bake until the top is golden and the center is set, about 30 minutes.

4 TO 6 SERVINGS

Calories 218 Kc • Protein 7 Gm • Fat 7 Gm • Percent of calories from fat 28% • Cholesterol 0 mg • Dietary Fiber 3 Gm • Sodium 507 mg • Calcium 29 mg

Vegetable Pudding

2 tablespoons corn oil
½ cup minced onion
2 cups sliced mushrooms (about
 ½ pound)
1 cup chopped cooked broccoli
1 cup chopped cooked
 cauliflower
1 cup sliced cooked carrots
1 cup cooked peas

1 tablespoon margarine,
 softened
1 tablespoon flour
1 cup soy milk
1 cup silken tofu, drained
¾ teaspoon salt
¼ teaspoon pepper
1 cup fresh bread crumbs

Preheat the oven to 350 degrees. Lightly oil a baking dish or coat with nonstick cooking spray. Heat the oil in a large skillet over medium heat. Add the onion and cook 5 minutes, or until softened. Add the mushrooms and continue cooking for 5 minutes longer. Transfer the onion and mushrooms to a large bowl and add the broccoli, cauliflower, carrots, and peas. In a separate bowl combine the margarine and flour to form a paste. Whisk in the soy milk and tofu, blending, and season with the salt and pepper. Fold the mixture into the vegetables and combine well. Taste and adjust the seasonings, and pour the mixture into the prepared baking dish. Spread the mixture evenly in the baking dish, sprinkle the bread crumbs on top, and bake for 1 hour, or until a knife inserted in the center comes out clean.

6 SERVINGS

Calories 177 Kc • Protein 7 Gm • Fat 8 Gm • Percent of calories from fat 40% • Cholesterol 0 mg • Dietary Fiber 4 Gm • Sodium 403 mg • Calcium 64 mg

Creamed Spinach

2 10-ounce packages frozen
  chopped spinach
2 tablespoons corn oil
½ cup minced onion

2 tablespoons flour
1 cup soy milk
Salt and freshly ground pepper
⅛ teaspoon ground nutmeg

Cook the spinach in boiling salted water for 5 minutes. Drain thoroughly and squeeze out any excess liquid. Reserve the spinach. Heat the oil in a medium saucepan over medium heat. Add the onion, cover, and cook 5 minutes, or until soft. Remove the lid, add the flour and cook, stirring, about 2 minutes. Heat the soy milk until hot, being careful not to boil. Slowly whisk the hot soy milk into the onion mixture, whisking constantly to achieve a smooth consistency. Cook over low heat for 2 minutes. Add the reserved spinach to the sauce. Season to taste with salt, pepper, and nutmeg; combine well, and serve.

4 TO 6 SERVINGS

Calories 128 Kc • Protein 5 Gm • Fat 7 Gm • Percent of calories from fat 45% • Cholesterol 0 mg • Dietary Fiber 4 Gm • Sodium 354 mg • Calcium 185 mg

Baked Spinach with Raisins

A tasty way to make a spinach lover out of anyone.

2 tablespoons golden raisins
½ cup silken tofu, well drained
1 tablespoon lemon juice
¼ teaspoon salt
⅛ teaspoon ground nutmeg
⅛ teaspoon ground cinnamon

1 10-ounce package frozen
  chopped spinach, thawed and
  squeezed dry
¾ cup almond milk
½ cup grated soy mozzarella
  cheese

Soak the raisins in a small bowl of hot water for 20 minutes, or until plump, and drain them. Preheat the oven to 375 degrees. In a large bowl combine the tofu, lemon juice, salt, nutmeg, and cinnamon and blend well. Stir in the spinach, raisins, almond milk, and soy cheese. Transfer the mixture to a quiche pan or 9-inch glass pie plate which has been lightly oiled or coated with nonstick cooking spray. Bake for 30 minutes, or until set and slightly puffed.

6 SERVINGS

Calories 90 Kc • Protein 7 Gm • Fat 4 Gm • Percent of calories from fat 35% • Cholesterol 0 mg • Dietary Fiber 4 Gm • Sodium 203 mg • Calcium 190 mg

Creamed Rice and Kale

I often make this dish when I have leftover kale or other greens. By stretching the kale with rice and tofu, you can serve four as a hearty side or make this a complete meal for two.

1 tablespoon olive oil
1 tablespoon minced shallot
2 cups cooked brown rice
1½ cup chopped cooked kale

½ cup silken tofu, drained
1 tablespoon lemon juice
Salt and freshly ground pepper

Heat the oil in a medium saucepan over medium heat. Add the shallot and cook 5 minutes, or until softened. Reduce the heat to low, add the rice and kale, and cook 2 minutes. In a small bowl, combine the tofu and lemon juice. Stir the tofu mixture into the rice and kale mixture. Stir to combine. Season with salt and pepper to taste, and cook another 2 to 3 minutes to heat through.

4 SERVINGS

Calories 171 Kc • Protein 5 Gm • Fat 5 Gm • Percent of calories from fat 28% • Cholesterol 0 mg • Dietary Fiber 3 Gm • Sodium 18 mg • Calcium 55 mg

Vegetable Mornay Casserole

2 cups coarsely chopped broccoli
  florets
1½ cups coarsely chopped
  cauliflower
2 carrots, thinly sliced
1 small zucchini, thinly sliced
3 tablespoons corn oil
2 tablespoons minced scallion
Salt and freshly ground pepper

2 tablespoons cornstarch
2 cups almond milk
2 tablespoons white miso paste
2 tablespoons dry white wine
⅛ teaspoon cayenne
⅛ teaspoon nutmeg
1 cup dried bread crumbs
¼ cup grated soy Parmesan
  (optional)

Combine the broccoli, cauliflower, and carrots in a saucepan with salted water to cover and bring to a boil over high heat. Reduce the heat to medium and simmer 2 minutes. Add the zucchini and simmer until the vegetables are crisp-tender, about 2 minutes. Drain well, and reserve the vegetables in a bowl. In a small skillet, heat 1 tablespoon of the oil over medium heat, add the scallion and cook 2 minutes until softened. Stir the scallion into the vegetables, and season with salt and pepper to taste.

Dissolve the cornstarch in the almond milk and heat in a saucepan over medium heat, stirring to thicken, about 2 minutes. Reduce the heat to low. Stir in the miso, wine, cayenne, nutmeg, and salt to taste and simmer, stirring, 5 minutes. Reserve.

Preheat the oven to 350 degrees. Lightly oil a baking dish or coat with nonstick cooking spray and spread the vegetables evenly in the prepared dish. Pour the sauce over the vegetables. In a small bowl, combine the bread crumbs with the remaining 2 tablespoons oil and toss to combine with a fork. Sprinkle the bread crumb mixture over the casserole. Bake the casserole 30 minutes or until heated through. Sprinkle with soy Parmesan, if using. Serve immediately.

8 SERVINGS

Calories 178 Kc • Protein 5 Gm • Fat 10 Gm • Percent of calories from fat 47%
• Cholesterol 0 mg • Dietary Fiber 4 Gm • Sodium 292 mg • Calcium 75 mg

Tomato Zucchini Gratin

1 tablespoon corn oil
4 small zucchini, cut into ¼-inch
  slices
1 cup chopped peeled tomato
1 cup soy milk
½ cup soft silken tofu, drained
½ cup grated soy mozzarella
  cheese
1 tablespoon minced fresh basil,
  or 1 teaspoon dried

½ teaspoon salt
¼ teaspoon freshly ground
  pepper
¼ cup fresh bread crumbs
1 tablespoon olive oil
2 tablespoons minced fresh
  parsley
1 clove garlic, minced
1 tablespoon minced shallot

Preheat the oven to 350 degrees. In a large skillet, heat the corn oil over medium heat. Add the zucchini and sauté, tossing, until lightly browned, 3 to 5 minutes. Remove the zucchini with a slotted spoon, and drain on paper towels. Add the tomato to the same skillet and cook over medium heat stirring until all the liquid is absorbed. Set aside.

In a large bowl, combine the soy milk, tofu, ¼ cup of the soy cheese, the basil, salt, and pepper. Whisk to blend well. Add the zucchini and tomatoes and stir to mix.

Lightly oil a 2-quart gratin dish or spray with nonstick cooking spray. Sprinkle with 2 tablespoons of the bread crumbs. Transfer the zucchini mixture to the prepared dish and bake for about 20 minutes or until almost set.

Meanwhile, heat the olive oil in a small skillet over medium heat. Add the remaining 2 tablespoons bread crumbs, the parsley, garlic, and shallot and sauté over low heat for about 1 minute. Set aside. When the gratin has baked for 20 minutes, remove it from the oven, sprinkle the bread crumb mixture on top of the gratin, and sprinkle the remaining ¼ cup soy cheese on top of bread crumbs. Return the gratin to the oven for another 5 minutes to lightly brown. Let it stand 5 minutes before serving.

6 SERVINGS

Calories 144 Kc • Protein 5 Gm • Fat 10 Gm • Percent of calories from fat 61%
• Cholesterol 0 mg • Dietary Fiber 2 Gm • Sodium 251 mg • Calcium 65 mg

Cauliflower au Gratin

2 tablespoons corn oil
½ cup minced onion
1 teaspoon minced garlic
2 tablespoons all-purpose flour
1½ cups hot soy milk
Salt and freshly ground pepper
Pinch ground nutmeg

1 medium head cauliflower
  (about 4 cups), cut into 1-inch
  pieces
2 tablespoons dried bread
  crumbs
½ teaspoon paprika

Heat the oil in a medium saucepan over medium heat. Add the onion, cover, and cook 5 minutes, or until soft. Uncover, stir in the garlic and cook 1 minute. Add the flour and cook, stirring, about 2 minutes longer. Slowly whisk the hot soy milk into the onion mixture, whisking constantly to achieve a smooth consistency. Cook over low heat for 2 minutes. Season to taste with salt, pepper, and nutmeg, and set aside.

Steam the cauliflower lightly until almost tender but still firm, about 5 minutes. Rinse under cold water and drain very well. Place the cauliflower in a bowl and gently add the reserved sauce. Preheat the oven to 350 degrees. Lightly oil a gratin dish or spray with nonstick cooking spray. Pour the vegetable mixture into the dish and spread evenly. Sprinkle the bread crumbs and paprika over the vegetables and bake for 30 minutes.

6 SERVINGS

Calories 121 Kc • Protein 4 Gm • Fat 6 Gm • Percent of calories from fat 46% • Cholesterol 0 mg • Dietary Fiber 3 Gm • Sodium 61 mg • Calcium 40 mg

Mushroom Almond Gratin

A sublime almond-derived cheese alternative is available in many natural food stores. If unavailable, soy mozzarella works just fine.

2 tablespoons olive oil
5 cups sliced white mushrooms (about 1¼ pounds)
1 clove garlic, minced
½ cup dry white wine
½ teaspoon minced fresh thyme, or ⅛ teaspoon dried
Salt and freshly ground pepper

2 tablespoons all-purpose flour
1 cup hot almond milk
½ cup dried bread crumbs
¼ cup slivered almonds
1 tablespoon minced fresh parsley
½ cup grated almond milk cheese

Heat the oil in a large saucepan over medium heat. Add the mushrooms and garlic and cook 5 minutes, stirring occasionally. Add the wine and cook until the liquid is nearly evaporated. Add the thyme, and salt and pepper to taste. Whisk in the flour and cook, stirring, for 2 minutes. Slowly whisk the hot almond milk into the mushroom mixture, whisking constantly to achieve a smooth consistency. Cook over low heat for 2 minutes.

Preheat the oven to 350 degrees. Lightly oil a gratin dish or coat with nonstick cooking spray. Pour the mushroom mixture into the dish and spread evenly. In a small bowl, combine the bread crumbs, almonds, parsley, and almond cheese. Spread the crumb mixture evenly on top of the mushroom mixture. Bake for 30 minutes.

4 SERVINGS

Calories 323 Kc • Protein 10 Gm • Fat 21 Gm • Percent of calories from fat 56% • Cholesterol 0 mg • Dietary Fiber 5 Gm • Sodium 129 mg • Calcium 125 mg

Green Bean Casserole

Each year at holiday time, my husband's family used to serve a rich green bean casserole loaded with sour cream. To satisfy his yearly craving for this tradition, I've adapted it to our nondairy lifestyle.

1½ pounds green beans
2 tablespoons corn oil
2 tablespoons minced shallot
¼ cup dried bread crumbs
2 tablespoons minced fresh
  parsley, or 2 teaspoons
  dried

Salt and freshly ground black
  pepper
1 cup soft silken tofu, drained
2 tablespoons lemon juice
2 teaspoons minced fresh dill, or
  ½ teaspoon dried
⅛ teaspoon cayenne

Trim the green beans and cut into 2-inch lengths. Place the beans in a pot with salted water to cover, bring to a boil, and simmer, uncovered, until just tender, about 6 minutes. Drain well and set aside. Heat the oil in a medium skillet, add the shallot, and cook over medium heat for 5 minutes or until soft. Add the bread crumbs and brown lightly. Add the parsley, and salt and pepper to taste and remove from the heat. Preheat the oven to 350 degrees. Lightly oil a casserole dish or coat with non-stick cooking spray, and set aside. In a small bowl combine the tofu, lemon juice, dill, and cayenne. Combine the tofu mixture with the green beans and place in the prepared casserole. Sprinkle with the bread crumb mixture and bake 20 minutes.

6 SERVINGS

Calories 122 Kc • Protein 5 Gm • Fat 6 Gm • Percent of calories from fat 43% • Cholesterol 0 mg • Dietary Fiber 4 Gm • Sodium 46 mg • Calcium 77 mg

Vegetable Loaf

Serve this light and savory loaf with the delicate "Hollandaise" Sauce on page 291.

1 cup green beans, trimmed and cut into 1-inch lengths

1 cup asparagus, trimmed and cut into 1-inch lengths

2 tablespoons corn oil

½ cup minced onion

½ cup grated carrot

½ cup chopped zucchini

1 cup cracker crumbs

2 tablespoons minced fresh parsley, or 2 teaspoons dried

1 teaspoon minced fresh dill, or ¼ teaspoon dried

¾ teaspoon salt

¼ teaspoon white pepper

2 cups soy milk

¼ cup soft tofu, drained

1 tablespoon Dijon mustard

1 teaspoon Worcestershire sauce

2 tablespoons cornstarch combined with 2 tablespoons mirin (or dry white wine)

Preheat the oven to 375 degrees. Lightly oil a loaf pan. Lightly steam the green beans and asparagus until just tender, and set aside. Heat the oil in a large skillet over medium heat. Add the onion, carrot, and zucchini and sauté for 5 minutes, or until softened. Add the green beans and asparagus, the cracker crumbs, parsley, dill, salt, and pepper and combine well. Cook 5 minutes longer to blend the flavors. In a small saucepan combine the soy milk, tofu, mustard, and Worcestershire sauce, blending well. Heat to a simmer over medium heat, being careful not to boil. Whisk in the cornstarch mixture and continue whisking to thicken. Combine the sauce and the vegetable mixture and blend well. Transfer to the prepared pan and spread the mixture evenly. Bake for 30 minutes or until set.

6 SERVINGS

Calories 169 Kc • Protein 5 Gm • Fat 7 Gm • Percent of calories from fat 39% • Cholesterol 0 mg • Dietary Fiber 2 Gm • Sodium 391 mg • Calcium 54 mg

Country Cabbage

1 small head cabbage, quartered
   and cored
2 tablespoons corn oil
1 cup minced onion
½ cup chopped celery
½ cup chopped green bell
   pepper

1 cup soft tofu, drained
1 cup soy milk
1 cup grated soy Cheddar cheese
2 cups fresh bread crumbs
1 teaspoon salt
¼ teaspoon freshly ground
   pepper

Preheat the oven to 375 degrees. Lightly oil a baking dish. Shred the cabbage and set aside. Heat the oil in a large skillet over medium heat. Add the onion and celery. Cover and cook 5 minutes, then add the bell pepper and the reserved cabbage, cover, and cook 5 minutes longer, or until the vegetables are tender. In a large bowl combine the tofu, soy milk, and soy cheese. Stir in the bread crumbs, salt, and pepper. Add the cooked vegetables and mix well. Transfer the mixture to the prepared dish and bake for 30 minutes or until set.

4 TO 6 SERVINGS

Calories 358 Kc • Protein 15 Gm • Fat 14 Gm • Percent of calories from fat 35% • Cholesterol 0 mg • Dietary Fiber 4 Gm • Sodium 940 mg • Calcium 235 mg

Creamy Sautéed Cucumbers

Cucumbers are usually used raw in salads, but they can also be served hot as in this recipe.

2 large cucumbers
1½ teaspoons salt
2 tablespoons corn oil
1 tablespoon all-purpose flour

1 cup rice milk
2 tablespoons minced fresh dill,
  or 2 teaspoons dried
Pinch of cayenne

Peel the cucumbers, halve lengthwise, and remove the seeds. Cut into ¼-inch slices, and toss with the salt in a colander, and let them drain for 15 minutes. Rinse under cold running water and let them drain again. Pat them dry and reserve. Meanwhile, heat 1 tablespoon of the oil in a small saucepan over low heat. Whisk in the flour and stir for 1 minute. Whisk in the rice milk and continue cooking for 2 minutes. Add the dill and cayenne and keep warm. Heat the remaining 1 tablespoon oil in a large skillet over medium-high heat. Add the cucumber slices and sauté until crisp-tender, 3 to 5 minutes. Reduce the heat to low, stir in the rice milk mixture, and simmer about 2 minutes to blend the flavors. Serve immediately.

4 SERVINGS

Calories 117 Kc • Protein 2 Gm • Fat 8 Gm • Percent of calories from fat 54%
• Cholesterol 0 mg • Dietary Fiber 1 Gm • Sodium 895 mg • Calcium 29 mg

Cauliflower with Broccoli Sauce

1 medium head cauliflower
1 small bunch broccoli, trimmed
(about 2 cups)
¼ cup almond milk (or more)

1 teaspoon corn oil
Pinch nutmeg
Salt and freshly ground pepper
¼ cup toasted slivered almonds

Trim the cauliflower and place the entire head in a pot with salted water to cover. Bring to a boil, lower heat, cover and simmer until tender, about 15 minutes. Meanwhile, steam the broccoli until tender, about 5 minutes. Transfer the cooked broccoli to a food processor and puree with the almond milk, corn oil, nutmeg, and salt and pepper to taste. Transfer to a small saucepan and heat gently. If the sauce is too thick, gently stir in more almond milk. Adjust the seasonings. Drain the cauliflower well and place on a serving plate. Spoon the broccoli sauce over the cauliflower, sprinkle with the toasted almonds, and serve.

4 SERVINGS

Calories 121 Kc • Protein 6 Gm • Fat 8 Gm • Percent of calories from fat 55% • Cholesterol 0 mg • Dietary Fiber 6 Gm • Sodium 108 mg • Calcium 68 mg

Asparagus with Pecan Sauce

¼ cup dry white wine
2 tablespoons lemon juice
1½ teaspoons minced shallot
½ cup almond milk combined
   with 1 tablespoon cornstarch

¾ cup chopped toasted pecans
Salt and freshly ground white
   pepper
1½ pounds asparagus, stalks
   trimmed and peeled

Combine the wine, lemon juice, and shallot in a small saucepan over medium-high heat and boil until reduced by half. Reduce the heat to low and whisk in the almond milk mixture. Stir 1 minute to thicken. Stir in the pecans, and season with salt and pepper to taste. Keep warm. Bring a pot of salted water to a boil over high heat. Add the asparagus and cook until crisp-tender, about 4 minutes. Drain well. To serve, place the asparagus in a serving dish and spoon the sauce over the asparagus.

4 SERVINGS

Calories 212 Kc • Protein 7 Gm • Fat 16 Gm • Percent of calories from fat 64% • Cholesterol 0 mg • Dietary Fiber 4 Gm • Sodium 182 mg • Calcium 39 mg

Cabbage in "Yogurt" Sauce

2 tablespoons corn oil
1 medium onion, thinly sliced
1 yellow bell pepper, seeded and thinly sliced
1 medium cabbage, quartered, cored, and shredded (about 6 cups)
1 cup Vegetable Stock (see page 10)

1½ teaspoons sugar (or a natural sweetener)
1 teaspoon salt
¼ teaspoon caraway seeds
1 cup silken tofu, drained
1 tablespoon lemon juice
1 tablespoon minced fresh parsley

Heat the oil in a large saucepan. Add the onion and bell pepper slices, and cook until limp, stirring occasionally. Add the cabbage, stock, sugar, salt, and caraway seeds, and bring to a boil. Cover and cook over medium heat until the cabbage is tender, 8 to 10 minutes. Meanwhile, in a small bowl, combine the tofu, lemon juice, and parsley. When the cabbage is cooked, remove from the heat, and gently stir in the tofu "yogurt," blending well. Transfer to a bowl and serve.

6 SERVINGS

Calories 118 Kc • Protein 4 Gm • Fat 7 Gm • Percent of calories from fat 50% • Cholesterol 0 mg • Dietary Fiber 2 Gm • Sodium 440 mg • Calcium 53 mg

New Potato and Walnut Salad

While the walnut oil intensifies the walnut flavor of this salad, a good quality olive oil may be used, if desired.

2 pounds small red new potatoes
1½ cups soft silken tofu, drained
2 tablespoons walnut oil
2 tablespoons lemon juice

½ teaspoon salt
⅛ teaspoon cayenne
¼ cup minced scallion
¾ cup walnut pieces

Cook the potatoes in salted boiling water to cover until tender, and drain well. Halve or quarter the potatoes, depending on their size, and place in a large bowl. In a food processor combine the tofu, walnut oil, lemon juice, salt, and cayenne, mixing until thoroughly blended. Gently fold the dressing into the potatoes, and add the scallion and walnut pieces. Taste and adjust the seasonings. Chill at least 1 hour before serving.

6 SERVINGS

Calories 284 Kc • Protein 9 Gm • Fat 16 Gm • Percent of calories from fat 49%
• Cholesterol 0 mg • Dietary Fiber 4 Gm • Sodium 205 mg • Calcium 53 mg

7
Sauces

A flavorful sauce can turn a simple meal of vegetables and grains into something simply delicious. Unfortunately, many of our favorites are made with a base of cream or mayonnaise. Not to worry, for this chapter is filled with recipes for wonderful dairy-free sauces, both hot and cold, that are so rich and creamy you will swear they are loaded with dairy products. Beginning with a basic Tofu Mayonnaise, there are also recipes for chilled mayonnaise-based sauces such as Lime Jalapeño Sauce and a tangy Remoulade. Most of the cold sauces make wonderful party dips for vegetables, pita crisps, or your favorite chips. The warm sauces range from creamy classics such as Béchamel and Soubise, to zesty offerings like Green Peppercorn Sauce and Tarragon Caper Sauce.

For best results, remember to squeeze or press excess water from the tofu before using in sauces.

Tofu Mayonnaise

A basic mayonnaise recipe that can be used in the same ways as commercial mayonnaise, at a fraction of the cost and with the added health benefits of soy.

1½ cups firm silken tofu, well
   drained
2 tablespoons safflower oil
2 tablespoon cider vinegar
1 tablespoon lemon juice

1 tablespoon Dijon mustard
1 teaspoon salt
¼ teaspoon white pepper
¼ teaspoon cayenne

Place all of the ingredients in a food processor and mix until smooth and creamy. Refrigerate covered until chilled. Refrigerated and tightly covered, this mayonnaise will keep for up to 2 weeks.

MAKES ABOUT 2 CUPS

Calories 29 Kc • Protein 1Gm • Fat 2 Gm • Percent of calories from fat 73% • Cholesterol 0 mg • Dietary Fiber 0 Gm • Sodium 152 mg • Calcium 9 mg

Tofu Sour Cream

This sour cream alternative couldn't be easier. Blend in some snipped chives and try it on baked potatoes.

¾ cup firm tofu, well drained
¼ cup soy milk

1 tablespoon lemon juice
¼ teaspoon salt

In a food processor combine the tofu and soy milk until smooth and creamy. Add the lemon juice and salt. Refrigerate, covered, until ready to use. Refrigerated and tightly covered, this sour cream will keep for up to 2 weeks.

MAKES ABOUT 1 CUP

Calories 17 Kc • Protein 1Gm • Fat 1 Gm • Percent of calories from fat 42% • Cholesterol 0 mg • Dietary Fiber 0 Gm • Sodium 77 mg • Calcium 9 mg

Ginger Mayonnaise

The spicy bite of the ginger is mellowed by the tofu and enhanced by the sesame oil. Combine this mayonnaise with poached, grated tempeh for an intriguing sandwich filling.

1 large clove garlic
2 teaspoons chopped fresh
 ginger, or ¼ teaspoon dried
1 scallion, chopped
1 cup silken tofu, drained
2 tablespoons lemon juice

½ teaspoon Tabasco sauce
½ teaspoon salt
⅛ teaspoon freshly ground
 pepper
1 tablespoon toasted sesame oil

Place the garlic, ginger, and scallion in a food processor and mince well. Add the remaining ingredients to the processor and blend until smooth. Transfer to a small bowl. Refrigerate, covered, until serving. Refrigerated and tightly covered, this mayonnaise will keep for up to 2 weeks.

MAKES ABOUT 1½ CUPS

Calories 23 Kc • Protein 1Gm • Fat 2 Gm • Percent of calories from fat 66% • Cholesterol 0 mg • Dietary Fiber 0 Gm • Sodium 99 mg • Calcium 7 mg

Creamy Dijon Mayonnaise

This is great on a sandwich or as a base for a Dijon potato salad.

1½ cups firm silken tofu,
  drained
2 tablespoons safflower oil
2 tablespoons cider vinegar

3 tablespoons Dijon mustard
½ teaspoon salt
Pinch cayenne

Place all of the ingredients in a food processor and blend until smooth and well combined. Refrigerate, covered, until ready to use. Refrigerated and tightly covered, this mayonnaise will keep for up to 2 weeks.

MAKES 1³/₄ CUPS

Calories 36 Kc • Protein 1Gm • Fat 3 Gm • Percent of calories from fat 72% • Cholesterol 0 mg • Dietary Fiber 0 Gm • Sodium 103 mg • Calcium 12 mg

Tartar Sauce

1 scallion, trimmed
1 medium dill pickle
1 tablespoon capers, drained
1 cup silken tofu, drained
1 tablespoon Dijon mustard
2 teaspoons cider vinegar

⅛ teaspoon dried tarragon,
  crumbled
½ teaspoon salt
⅛ teaspoon freshly ground
  pepper

Combine the scallion, pickle, and capers in a food processor and pulse until minced. Add the tofu, mustard, vinegar, tarragon, salt, and pepper and mix until well blended. Transfer to a small bowl and refrigerate, covered, until serving. Refrigerated and tightly covered, this sauce will keep for up to 2 weeks.

MAKES ABOUT 1¹/₂ CUPS

Calories 13 Kc • Protein 1Gm • Fat 1 Gm • Percent of calories from fat 46% • Cholesterol 0 mg • Dietary Fiber 0 Gm • Sodium 209 mg • Calcium 10 mg

Sassy Tartar Sauce

A more full-bodied sauce than the previous entry, owing to the addition of onion, fresh tarragon, and a bit of cayenne, this is marvelous on broiled or grilled food.

1½ cups Tofu Mayonnaise (see page 258)
3 medium sweet pickles, minced
¼ cup minced onion
1 tablespoon minced capers
1 tablespoon minced fresh parsley, or 1 teaspoon dried

1 tablespoon minced fresh tarragon, or 1 teaspoon dried
1 teaspoon Dijon mustard
1 teaspoon lemon juice
1 teaspoon sugar (or a natural sweetener)
½ teaspoon salt
⅛ teaspoon cayenne

Combine all of the ingredients in a small bowl. Adjust the seasonings. Refrigerate, covered, for 2 hours before serving. Refrigerated and tightly covered, this sauce will keep for up to 2 weeks.

MAKES ABOUT 2 CUPS

Calories 27 Kc • Protein 1Gm • Fat 2 Gm • Percent of calories from fat 60% • Cholesterol 0 mg • Dietary Fiber 0 Gm • Sodium 220 mg • Calcium 11 mg

Sesame Mayonnaise

1 cup firm silken tofu, drained
2 tablespoons toasted sesame oil
1 tablespoon tahini (sesame paste)

2½ tablespoons cider vinegar
1 tablespoon low-sodium tamari
⅛ teaspoon cayenne

Place all of the ingredients in a food processor and mix until smooth and well combined. Refrigerate, covered, until ready to use. Refrigerated and tightly covered, this mayonnaise will keep for up to 2 weeks.

MAKES ABOUT 1½ CUPS

Calories 44 Kc • Protein 2Gm • Fat 3 Gm • Percent of calories from fat 72% • Cholesterol 0 mg • Dietary Fiber 0 Gm • Sodium 64 mg • Calcium 12 mg

Lemon-Horseradish Mayonnaise

A terrific spread for seitan sandwiches, this also makes a zippy condiment for baked potatoes.

1 cup Tofu Mayonnaise (see page 258)
3 tablespoons freshly grated horseradish

1 tablespoon grated lemon rind
1 teaspoon lemon juice
¼ teaspoon salt

Combine all of the ingredients in a small bowl. Serve at room temperature, or refrigerate, covered, for 2 hours to chill. Refrigerated and tightly covered, this mayonnaise will keep for up to 2 weeks.

MAKES ABOUT 1¼ CUPS

Calories 28 Kc • Protein 1Gm • Fat 2 Gm • Percent of calories from fat 61% • Cholesterol 0 mg • Dietary Fiber 0 Gm • Sodium 180 mg • Calcium 14 mg

Provençal Mayonnaise

1 tablespoon olive oil
1 green bell pepper, minced
1 clove garlic, minced
1 teaspoon minced shallot
½ cup canned tomato puree
¼ teaspoon salt
⅛ teaspoon freshly ground
   pepper

1 teaspoon minced fresh
   tarragon, or ¼ teaspoon
   dried
½ teaspoon snipped fresh
   chives
2 cups Tofu Mayonnaise (see
   page 258)

Heat the oil in a medium saucepan over medium heat. Add the bell pepper, garlic, and shallot, and cook, covered, for 5 minutes. Remove the cover, add the tomato puree, salt, and pepper, and cook, stirring, about 5 minutes longer. Remove from the heat, transfer to a small bowl, and let it cool in the refrigerator. When the puree is cool, remove it from the refrigerator and fold in the tarragon, chives, and Tofu Mayonnaise. Refrigerated and tightly covered, this mayonnaise will keep for up to 2 weeks.

MAKES ABOUT 2³/₄ CUPS

Calories 30 Kc • Protein 1Gm • Fat 2 Gm • Percent of calories from fat 70% • Cholesterol 0 mg • Dietary Fiber 0 Gm • Sodium 138 mg • Calcium 7 mg

Chili Lime Mayonnaise

Try this combined with crumbled firm tofu, to make a refreshingly different sandwich spread.

2 tablespoons chopped green chili (hot or mild)

1 tablespoon chopped onion

1 tablespoon chopped fresh parsley, or 1 teaspoon dried

1 cup silken tofu, drained

1 tablespoon lime juice

½ teaspoon salt

⅛ teaspoon cayenne

Place the chili, onion, and parsley in a food processor and mince well. Add the remaining ingredients and process until smooth. Transfer to a bowl and refrigerate until serving. Refrigerated and tightly covered, this mayonnaise will keep for up to 2 weeks.

MAKES ABOUT 1¼ CUPS

Calories 15 Kc • Protein 1Gm • Fat 1 Gm • Percent of calories from fat 43% • Cholesterol 0 mg • Dietary Fiber 0 Gm • Sodium 129 mg • Calcium 12 mg

Remoulade Sauce

The dairy version is traditionally served with chilled seafood. Try this new version to start your own tradition.

1½ cups Tofu Mayonnaise
  (see page 258)
1 medium sweet pickle, minced
1½ teaspoons minced capers
1 tablespoon Dijon mustard
1 teaspoon tomato paste
1 tablespoon minced fresh parsley,
  or 1 teaspoon dried

1 teaspoon minced fresh
  tarragon, or ¼ teaspoon dried
½ teaspoon salt
⅛ teaspoon freshly ground
  pepper

Combine all of the ingredients in a small bowl until well blended. Adjust the seasonings. Refrigerate until serving. Refrigerated and tightly covered, this sauce will keep for up to 2 weeks.

MAKES ABOUT 1³/₄ CUPS

Calories 29 Kc • Protein 1Gm • Fat 2 Gm • Percent of calories from fat 67% • Cholesterol 0 mg • Dietary Fiber 0 Gm • Sodium 240 mg • Calcium 10 mg

Rouille

A cholesterol-free version of the garlicky red mayonnaise from France.

3 cloves garlic, halved
¼ cup pimientos, drained
2 tablespoons minced fresh
  basil, or 1 tablespoon dried
  and crumbled
1 cup silken tofu, drained and
  pressed

1 tablespoon olive oil
1 tablespoon lemon juice
½ teaspoon salt
Pinch cayenne

Combine the garlic, pimientos, and basil in a food processor and blend until smooth. Add the tofu, olive oil, lemon juice, salt, and cayenne and mix until thoroughly blended. Transfer to a small bowl and refrigerate until ready to use. Refrigerated and tightly covered, this sauce will keep for up to 2 weeks.

MAKES ABOUT 1¼ CUPS

Calories 29 Kc • Protein 1Gm • Fat 2 Gm • Percent of calories from fat 62% • Cholesterol 0 mg • Dietary Fiber 0 Gm • Sodium 119 mg • Calcium 18 mg

Lime "Yogurt" Sauce

Terrific drizzled on vegetables or grains cooked with Indian spices.

1½ cups silken tofu, drained
3 tablespoons finely minced
   scallion
2 tablespoons lime juice
1 tablespoon lemon juice

1 teaspoon grated lime zest
½ teaspoon salt
⅛ teaspoon freshly ground white
   pepper

Combine all of the ingredients in a bowl and mix well until thoroughly blended. Refrigerate, covered, for several hours before serving. Refrigerated and tightly covered, this sauce will keep for up to 2 weeks.

MAKES ABOUT 1³/₄ CUPS

Calories 16 Kc • Protein 1Gm • Fat 1 Gm • Percent of calories from fat 43% • Cholesterol 0 mg • Dietary Fiber 0 Gm • Sodium 85 mg • Calcium 9 mg

Watercress Sauce

A light but flavorful sauce that is delightful served with composed salads or as a dip for crudités.

¾ cup fresh watercress leaves
   and tender stems, blanched
¼ cup fresh parsley leaves and
   tender stems, blanched
1½ tablespoons chopped
   shallot
½ teaspoon minced garlic
¼ cup silken tofu, drained

¼ cup olive oil
1 tablespoon fresh lemon
   juice
1 tablespoon Dijon mustard
¼ teaspoon salt
⅛ teaspoon freshly ground
   pepper

Combine the watercress, parsley, shallot, and garlic in a food processor and process until fine. Add remaining ingredients and process until smooth. Adjust the seasonings. Refrigerate, covered, until ready to use. Refrigerated and tightly covered, this sauce will keep for up to 1 week.

MAKES ABOUT 1 CUP

Calories 68 Kc • Protein 1Gm • Fat 7 Gm • Percent of calories from fat 91% • Cholesterol 0 mg • Dietary Fiber 0 Gm • Sodium 86 mg • Calcium 12 mg

Spicy Walnut Sauce

Use less soy milk for a thicker mixture that can be used as a spread or to fill croustades.

1 cup walnut pieces
1 teaspoon minced garlic
2 tablespoons olive oil
1 tablespoon balsamic vinegar
¼ cup silken tofu, drained

4 tablespoons soy milk
¼ teaspoon hot red pepper flakes
¼ teaspoon salt
⅛ teaspoon paprika

Grind the walnuts in a food processor with short on/off bursts. Add the remaining ingredients and process until smooth. Adjust the seasonings, and refrigerate, covered, until ready to use. Refrigerated and tightly covered, this sauce will keep for up to 2 weeks.

MAKES ABOUT 1½ CUPS

Calories 92 Kc • Protein 2Gm • Fat 9 Gm • Percent of calories from fat 81% • Cholesterol 0 mg • Dietary Fiber 0 Gm • Sodium 52 mg • Calcium 13 mg

Creamy Chutney Sauce

This is a perfect complement to a composed salad, or can be combined with chopped tempeh for a delicious sandwich filling.

1 tablespoon chopped fresh
   parsley, or 1 teaspoon dried
1 tablespoon chopped fresh
   cilantro
¼ cup chutney
1 cup silken tofu, drained

¼ cup soy milk
1 teaspoon curry powder
1 teaspoon fresh lemon juice
½ teaspoon salt
Pinch cayenne

In a food processor, combine the parsley, cilantro, chutney, and tofu, until well blended. Add the remaining ingredients, blending until smooth. Serve at room temperature, or refrigerate to chill. Refrigerated and tightly covered, this sauce will keep for up to 1 week.

MAKES ABOUT 1½ CUPS

Calories 28 Kc • Protein 1Gm • Fat 1 Gm • Percent of calories from fat 23% • Cholesterol 0 mg • Dietary Fiber 0 Gm • Sodium 102 mg • Calcium 10 mg

Mustard-Caper Sauce

1 cup silken tofu, drained
1 large tomato, seeded and
   chopped
¼ cup Dijon mustard
3 tablespoons capers, drained

1 tablespoon lemon juice
½ teaspoon salt
⅛ teaspoon freshly ground
   pepper

Combine all of the ingredients in a medium bowl. Mix together until thoroughly blended. Refrigerate, covered, until ready to serve. Refrigerated and tightly covered, this sauce will keep for up to 1 week.

MAKES ABOUT 1½ CUPS

Calories 20 Kc • Protein 1Gm • Fat 1 Gm • Percent of calories from fat 43% • Cholesterol 0 mg • Dietary Fiber 0 Gm • Sodium 206 mg • Calcium 14 mg

Honey Lime Sauce

This bright and tasty sauce makes a great accompaniment to a fresh fruit salad.

1 cup silken tofu, drained
1 cup honey (or a natural
  sweetener)
½ cup fresh lime juice

1 teaspoon grated lime zest
¼ teaspoon paprika
Pinch turmeric

Combine all of the ingredients in a food processor and mix until well blended. Cover and refrigerate until ready to use. Refrigerated and tightly covered, this sauce will keep for up to 2 weeks.

MAKES 2 CUPS

Calories 74 Kc • Protein 1Gm • Fat 0 Gm • Percent of calories from fat 5% • Cholesterol 0 mg • Dietary Fiber 0 Gm • Sodium 2 mg • Calcium 7 mg

Creamy Pesto

Use this dairy-free pesto as you would the cheese-rich dairy version: on pasta, baked potatoes, or on top of ripe tomato slices.

2 cups packed fresh basil leaves
3 cloves garlic
½ cup pine nuts

1 cup extra-virgin olive oil
¼ cup firm tofu, drained
¾ teaspoon salt

Place the basil, garlic, and pine nuts in a food processor and process until they form a paste. Add the remaining ingredients and blend until well combined. Refrigerate, covered, in a jar with a coating of olive oil on top of the sauce. Refrigerated and tightly covered, this pesto will keep for up to 2 weeks.

MAKES 2 CUPS

Calories 151 Kc • Protein 2Gm • Fat 16 Gm • Percent of calories from fat 92% • Cholesterol 0 mg • Dietary Fiber 0 Gm • Sodium 114 mg • Calcium 13 mg

Parsley Sauce

This fresh green sauce is a wonderful accompaniment to raw or steamed vegetables, and makes a stunning pasta sauce.

3 cups packed chopped fresh
   parsley
½ cup blanched almonds
2 cloves garlic
2 tablespoons drained capers
1 cup soft tofu, drained

¼ cup lemon juice
1 teaspoon salt
½ teaspoon freshly ground
   white pepper
1 cup safflower oil

In a food processor, combine the parsley, almonds, garlic, and capers, until finely minced. Add the tofu, lemon juice, salt, and pepper and mix well. Slowly stream in the oil, and process to achieve a smooth consistency. Refrigerated and tightly covered, this sauce will keep for up to 2 weeks.

MAKES ABOUT 2 CUPS

Calories 158 Kc • Protein 2Gm • Fat 16 Gm • Percent of calories from fat 89% • Cholesterol 0 mg • Dietary Fiber 1 Gm • Sodium 192 mg • Calcium 32 mg

Horseradish Dill Sauce

1½ cups silken tofu, drained
¼ cup prepared horseradish
1 tablespoon lemon juice
1 tablespoon minced fresh dill,
   or 1 teaspoon dried

1 teaspoon salt
⅛ teaspoon freshly ground
   pepper

Combine all of the ingredients in a small bowl and stir until well blended. Refrigerate, covered, until ready to use. Refrigerated and tightly covered, this sauce will keep for up to 1 week.

MAKES ABOUT 1³/₄ CUPS

Calories 16 Kc • Protein 1Gm • Fat 1 Gm • Percent of calories from fat 42% • Cholesterol 0 mg • Dietary Fiber 0 Gm • Sodium 172 mg • Calcium 11 mg

Cucumber Dill Sauce

1 medium cucumber
1½ cups silken tofu, well
   drained
1 tablespoon chopped onion
1 scallion, minced

1 teaspoon minced fresh dill,
   or ¼ teaspoon dried
½ teaspoon salt
¼ teaspoon freshly ground white
   pepper

Peel, seed, and chop the cucumber. Place in a small bowl, and add the remaining ingredients, stirring until well blended. Refrigerate, covered, for at least 2 hours before serving. Refrigerated and tightly covered, this sauce will keep for up to 1 week.

MAKES ABOUT 2 CUPS

Calories 15 Kc • Protein 1 Gm • Fat 1 Gm • Percent of calories from fat 40% • Cholesterol 0 mg • Dietary Fiber 0 Gm • Sodium 74 mg • Calcium 10 mg

Tarragon-Caper Dipping Sauce

1 cup silken tofu, drained
¼ cup capers, drained
1 scallion, chopped
2 tablespoons Dijon mustard
1½ tablespoons lemon juice
1 tablespoon tarragon vinegar

1 tablespoon fresh minced
   tarragon, or 1 teaspoon dried
½ teaspoon salt
⅛ teaspoon freshly ground
   black pepper
¼ cup soy milk (optional)

Place all of the ingredients in a food processor, and mix until well blended. Transfer to a small bowl and refrigerate, covered, for 2 hours before serving. If a thinner consistency is desired, add the soy milk. Refrigerated and tightly covered, this sauce will keep for up to 2 weeks.

MAKES ABOUT 2 CUPS

Calories 14 Kc • Protein 1 Gm • Fat 1 Gm • Percent of calories from fat 42% • Cholesterol 0 mg • Dietary Fiber 0 Gm • Sodium 165 mg • Calcium 10 mg

Ginger-Lime Dipping Sauce

Perfect as an accompaniment to a fresh fruit salad or as a dipping sauce for chunks of fresh ripe fruit.

1 cup firm silken tofu, drained
2 tablespoons lime juice
1 tablespoon grated lime zest

1 tablespoon sugar (or a natural
    sweetener)
½ teaspoon ground ginger

Combine all of the ingredients in a medium bowl, stirring until well mixed. Refrigerate, covered, until ready to use. Best served chilled. Refrigerated and tightly covered, this sauce will keep for up to 2 weeks.

MAKES ABOUT 1 CUP

Calories 25 Kc • Protein 1 Gm • Fat 1 Gm • Percent of calories from fat 32% • Cholesterol 0 mg • Dietary Fiber 0 Gm • Sodium 2 mg • Calcium 11 mg

Walnut Dill Dipping Sauce

1½ cups silken tofu, drained
1 cucumber, peeled, seeded, and
    minced
¾ cup chopped walnuts
⅓ cup minced fresh dill,
    or 1½ tablespoons dried

1 tablespoon minced shallot
½ teaspoon paprika
½ teaspoon salt
⅛ teaspoon Tabasco sauce

In a food processor, combine all of the ingredients until well blended. Refrigerate, covered, for 2 hours. Refrigerated and tightly covered, this sauce will keep for up to 1 week.

MAKES ABOUT 2½ CUPS

Calories 41 Kc • Protein 1 Gm • Fat 3 Gm • Percent of calories from fat 69% • Cholesterol 0 mg • Dietary Fiber 0 Gm • Sodium 60 mg • Calcium 12 mg

White Sauce

A versatile white sauce that is both quick and easy to prepare.

2 cups almond milk	¾ teaspoon salt
3 tablespoons margarine	⅛ teaspoon cayenne
3 tablespoons all-purpose flour	⅛ teaspoon nutmeg
1 teaspoon Dijon mustard	

Heat the almond milk in a small saucepan, being careful not to boil; keep warm. Melt the margarine in a medium saucepan over medium-high heat. Add the flour and cook, stirring, about 1 minute. Add the heated almond milk slowly, whisking constantly. Continue whisking until the sauce is smooth. Reduce the heat to medium, add the mustard, salt, cayenne, and nutmeg, and continue cooking 1 minute longer. Adjust the seasonings.

MAKES ABOUT 2 CUPS

Calories 34 Kc • Protein 1 Gm • Fat 3 Gm • Percent of calories from fat 71% • Cholesterol 0 mg • Dietary Fiber 0 Gm • Sodium 121 mg • Calcium 12 mg

Peanut Sauce

This pungent Thai-inspired sauce makes a great dipping sauce for egg rolls or tempura. It is also good tossed with hot pasta or vegetables.

1 teaspoon safflower oil
¼ cup minced scallion
1 teaspoon minced garlic
1 cup silken tofu, drained
6 tablespoons creamy peanut
   butter

2 tablespoons low-sodium tamari
2 teaspoons chopped fresh
   cilantro
1 tablespoon toasted sesame oil
½ teaspoon hot red pepper oil

In a medium skillet, heat the safflower oil over medium heat. Add the scallion and garlic and sauté lightly until softened, about 3 minutes. Meanwhile, place the remaining ingredients in a food processor and process until well blended. Add the tofu mixture to the skillet and stir over medium heat until well combined and warm. The sauce may be served warm or at room temperature.

MAKES ABOUT 1³/₄ CUPS

Calories 66 Kc • Protein 3 Gm • Fat 5 Gm • Percent of calories from fat 70% • Cholesterol 0 mg • Dietary Fiber 0 Gm • Sodium 121 mg • Calcium 11 mg

Chive Mustard Sauce

An elegant alternative to regular mustard for veggie burgers, or seitan or tempeh cutlets.

½ cup Vegetable Stock (see page 10)
2 tablespoons snipped fresh chives
1 tablespoon minced scallion
¼ teaspoon minced garlic
2 tablespoons coarse-grained mustard

1 tablespoon Dijon mustard
¾ cup silken tofu, drained
¼ cup soy milk
¼ teaspoon salt
⅛ teaspoon freshly ground black pepper

Combine the stock, chives, scallion, and garlic in a medium skillet and bring to a boil over medium-high heat. Continue boiling until reduced by half. Reduce the heat to low, and whisk in the remaining ingredients. Adjust the seasonings and serve immediately.

MAKES 1½ CUPS

Calories 20 Kc • Protein 1 Gm • Fat 1 Gm • Percent of calories from fat 41% • Cholesterol 0 mg • Dietary Fiber 0 Gm • Sodium 101 mg • Calcium 13 mg

Green Peppercorn Sauce

½ cup Vegetable Stock (see
    page 10)
¼ cup dry white wine
1 cup soy milk
2 tablespoons cornstarch
    dissolved in 2 tablespoons
    water

2 teaspoons green peppercorns,
    drained and rinsed
½ teaspoon salt

In a small saucepan, combine the stock and white wine. Boil over high heat until reduced by half, about 5 minutes. Reserve. Meanwhile, in a medium saucepan, heat the soy milk to almost boiling. Whisk in the cornstarch mixture, and stir to thicken, about 2 to 3 minutes. Add the reserved stock mixture, peppercorns, and salt. Heat briefly to warm through, and serve hot.

MAKES ABOUT 1$^1/_2$ CUPS

Calories 26 Kc • Protein 1 Gm • Fat 1 Gm • Percent of calories from fat 22% • Cholesterol 0 mg • Dietary Fiber 0 Gm • Sodium 117 mg • Calcium 8 mg

Béchamel Sauce

The onions add a flavorful dimension to this creamy sauce, but are strained out to achieve a smooth consistency.

2 cups almond milk

3 tablespoons corn oil

⅓ cup chopped onion

3 tablespoons all-purpose flour

½ teaspoon salt

¼ teaspoon freshly ground white pepper

Pinch of nutmeg

Heat the almond milk in a small saucepan, being careful not to boil. Keep warm. Heat the oil in a medium saucepan over medium heat. Add the onion, cover, and cook 5 minutes or until softened. Remove the lid, reduce the heat to low, add the flour and cook for 2 minutes, stirring constantly. Slowly whisk in the almond milk, whisking constantly. Add the salt, pepper, and nutmeg. Continue to cook for 2 to 3 minutes, stirring frequently. Strain through a sieve.

MAKES ABOUT 2 CUPS

Calories 48 Kc • Protein 1 Gm • Fat 4 Gm • Percent of calories from fat 76% • Cholesterol 0 mg • Dietary Fiber 0 Gm • Sodium 74 mg • Calcium 11 mg

Tarragon Caper Sauce

This flavorful sauce is especially good on grilled seitan or tempeh. It also works well on fresh steamed asparagus.

2 teaspoons olive oil
2 teaspoons drained capers
½ teaspoon dried tarragon
1 tablespoon lemon juice or
  white wine

1 cup Tofu Mayonnaise (see
  page 258)
Salt and freshly ground
  pepper

Heat the oil in a small skillet over medium-high heat. Add the capers, tarragon, and lemon juice and bring to a boil until the liquid is reduced by half. Remove from the heat and let it cool. Place the mixture in a small bowl, add the Tofu Mayonnaise, and combine well. Season with salt and pepper to taste.

MAKES ABOUT 1 CUP

Calories 40 Kc • Protein 1 Gm • Fat 3 Gm • Percent of calories from fat 78% • Cholesterol 0 mg • Dietary Fiber 0 Gm • Sodium 178 mg • Calcium 10 mg

Mushroom Wine Sauce

1 tablespoon olive oil
1 large shallot, finely minced
4 ounces fresh mushrooms,
   chopped (about 1½ cups)
⅓ cup dry white wine
1 cup Vegetable Stock (see page
   10)
1 teaspoon minced fresh
   parsley, or ¼ teaspoon dried

1 teaspoon minced fresh thyme,
   or ½ teaspoon dried
½ teaspoon salt
⅛ teaspoon freshly ground
   pepper
1 tablespoon cornstarch
   dissolved in 1 tablespoon
   water
½ cup soy milk

Heat the oil in a medium skillet over medium heat. Add the shallot and cook, stirring, for 5 minutes or until softened. Add the mushrooms, and stir over medium-low heat for about 5 minutes longer. Add the wine to the skillet, increase the heat to medium-high, and bring to a boil. Lower the heat to medium, stir in the stock, parsley, thyme, salt, and pepper. Simmer 10 minutes, stirring occasionally. Whisk in the cornstarch mixture and stir until the mixture is thickened and well blended. Whisk in the soy milk and adjust the seasonings.

MAKES ABOUT 1³/₄ CUP

Calories 30 Kc • Protein 1 Gm • Fat 1 Gm • Percent of calories from fat 44% • Cholesterol 0 mg • Dietary Fiber 0 Gm • Sodium 105 mg • Calcium 8 mg

Curry Sauce

2 tablespoons safflower oil
1 small onion, minced
1 clove garlic, minced
2 tablespoons all-purpose flour
1 tablespoon curry powder (or to taste)

1½ cups Vegetable Stock (see page 10)
½ cup soy milk
1 teaspoon lemon juice
Salt and freshly ground pepper

Heat the oil in a medium skillet over medium heat. Add the onion and cook, covered, until softened, about 5 minutes. Remove the cover, add the garlic, and continue cooking for 1 minute, stirring. Add the flour and cook, stirring, for 2 minutes. Add the curry powder and cook, stirring, for 1 minute. Slowly add the stock, stirring, and bring the mixture to a boil. Reduce the heat and simmer for 5 minutes, stirring. Strain the mixture through a fine sieve into a medium saucepan, stir in the soy milk, and simmer for 2 minutes. Add the lemon juice and salt and pepper to taste.

MAKES ABOUT 2 CUPS

Calories 39 Kc • Protein 1 Gm • Fat 2 Gm • Percent of calories from fat 53% • Cholesterol 0 mg • Dietary Fiber 0 Gm • Sodium 26 mg • Calcium 11 mg

Three Mushroom Sauce

A flavorful and versatile sauce. Equally good over sautéed cutlets or tossed with pasta.

⅓ cup cloud ears (dried black mushrooms)
1 cup boiling water
1 cup Vegetable Stock (see page 10)
½ cup dry white wine
2 tablespoons minced scallion
½ teaspoon minced garlic
½ cup sliced shiitake mushrooms
½ cup sliced button or white mushrooms

2 cups soy milk
1 tablespoon low-sodium tamari
½ teaspoon minced fresh thyme, or ⅛ teaspoon dried
2 tablespoons cornstarch dissolved in two tablespoons water
½ teaspoon salt
⅛ teaspoon freshly ground pepper

Place the cloud ear mushrooms in a medium bowl, add the boiling water, and set aside for 30 minutes to soften. Meanwhile, combine the stock, white wine, scallion, and garlic in large skillet and bring to a boil over medium-high heat. Boil until reduced by half. Drain the cloud ears, rinse under cold water, and chop coarsely. Place the cloud ears in the skillet with the sauce. Add the shiitake and button mushrooms, soy milk, tamari, and thyme to the sauce and bring to a boil over medium-high heat. Whisk in the cornstarch mixture, stirring constantly. Season with the salt and pepper. Serve hot.

MAKES 2 CUPS

Calories 40 Kc • Protein 1 Gm • Fat 1 Gm • Percent of calories from fat 22% • Cholesterol 0 mg • Dietary Fiber 0 Gm • Sodium 141 mg • Calcium 13 mg

Mustard Peppercorn Sauce

This assertive sauce gives a lift to veggie burgers or grilled seitan. Vegetarian Worcestershire sauce is made without anchovies and is available in natural food stores.

½ cup dry white wine
½ tablespoon green peppercorns,
    drained
1 teaspoon vegetarian
    Worcestershire sauce

2 tablespoons Dijon mustard
1 cup silken tofu, drained
Salt and freshly ground
    pepper

Bring the wine to a boil over medium-high heat in a small skillet. Add the peppercorns, Worcestershire sauce, and whisk in the mustard until smooth. Cook 1 minute to reduce the liquid by half. Remove from the heat, whisk in the tofu, and combine well. Season with salt and pepper to taste. Return to low heat and heat through before serving.

MAKES ABOUT 1¼ CUPS

Calories 26 Kc • Protein 1 Gm • Fat 1 Gm • Percent of calories from fat 32% • Cholesterol 0 mg • Dietary Fiber 0 Gm • Sodium 24 mg • Calcium 14 mg

Spicy Almond Sauce

A rich and flavorful sauce, wonderful spooned over seitan satés, tossed with pasta, or used as a dipping sauce. If a thinner sauce is desired, add more almond milk.

½ cup dry white wine
½ cup rice vinegar
¼ teaspoon hot red pepper flakes
1 small green chili, seeded and finely chopped (hot or mild)
2 tablespoons minced scallion

5 tablespoons almond butter
⅓ cup almond milk
1 tablespoon brown sugar (or a natural sweetener)
1 tablespoon low-sodium tamari

Combine the wine, vinegar, and red pepper flakes in a medium saucepan and bring to a boil over medium-high heat. Continue boiling until reduced to ¹/₄ cup. Remove from the heat, and allow to cool. Meanwhile, in a food processor, combine the remaining ingredients until well blended. Add the wine mixture and process again until smooth.

MAKES 1 CUP

Calories 85 Kc • Protein 2 Gm • Fat 6 Gm • Percent of calories from fat 58% • Cholesterol 0 mg • Dietary Fiber 0 Gm • Sodium 85 mg • Calcium 29 mg

Brandy Peppercorn Sauce

A quick sauce with a sophisticated taste. Serve over sautéed seitan cutlets for an elegant dinner entree.

2 tablespoons safflower oil
2 shallots, minced
⅓ cup brandy
1½ cups Vegetable Stock (see page 10)
2 tablespoons cornstarch dissolved in 2 tablespoons water

2 tablespoons green peppercorns, drained
½ cup soy milk
Salt and freshly ground pepper

Heat the oil in a medium skillet over medium heat. Add the shallots and cook until softened, about 5 minutes. Increase the heat to medium-high, add the brandy and deglaze the pan, scraping up the brown bits. Add the stock, bring it to a boil, stirring, and reduce to about 1 cup. Strain the mixture through a fine sieve into a medium saucepan, bring it to a boil, and continue cooking for 1 minute, stirring. Add the cornstarch mixture and cook, stirring, for 2 minutes. Crush half of the peppercorns with the flat side of a large knife, add them along with remaining peppercorns to the sauce. Stir in the soy milk, salt and pepper to taste, and simmer for 2 minutes longer.

MAKES ABOUT 2 CUPS

Calories 48 Kc • Protein 0 Gm • Fat 2 Gm • Percent of calories from fat 42% • Cholesterol 0 mg • Dietary Fiber 0 Gm • Sodium 26 mg • Calcium 8 mg

Red Pepper Sauce

1 tablespoon olive oil
¼ cup chopped onion
1 teaspoon chopped garlic
4 cups chopped red bell pepper
1 cup Vegetable Stock (see page 10)
⅓ cup dry white wine

2 tablespoons cornstarch dissolved in 2 tablespoons water
1 cup soy milk
¼ teaspoons salt
⅛ teaspoon cayenne

Heat the oil in a large saucepan over medium-high heat. Add the onion and garlic, stirring. Cook for 1 minute. Add the red pepper, stir to combine, and cook 1 minute longer. Add the stock and wine; heat to boiling. Reduce the heat to low; simmer, covered, until the peppers are tender, about 20 minutes. Place the contents of the saucepan in a food processor, working in batches, and process until the peppers are finely minced. Press the mixture through a fine sieve into the saucepan, discarding the skins left in sieve. Place the saucepan over medium-high heat, and bring to a boil. When the sauce reaches the boiling point, reduce the heat to low, and whisk in the cornstarch mixture, stirring for 1 minute. Slowly stir in the soy milk, salt, and cayenne and heat through before serving.

MAKES ABOUT 3 CUPS

Calories 32 Kc • Protein 1 Gm • Fat 1 Gm • Percent of calories from fat 28% • Cholesterol 0 mg • Dietary Fiber 1 Gm • Sodium 40 mg • Calcium 9 mg

Creamy Mustard Sauce

2 tablespoons safflower oil
2 tablespoons all-purpose flour
½ cup dry white wine
2 cups Vegetable Stock (see
 page 10)

½ cup soy milk
3 tablespoons Dijon mustard
½ teaspoon vegetarian
 Worcestershire sauce
Salt and freshly ground pepper

Heat the oil in a medium skillet over medium-low heat, add the flour, and cook, stirring, for 3 minutes. Whisk in the wine and the stock, bring the liquid to a boil and stir constantly for 2 minutes. Reduce the heat to low, stir in the soy milk, mustard, Worcestershire sauce, and salt and pepper to taste. For a more silky sauce, strain the sauce through a fine sieve before serving.

MAKES ABOUT 3 CUPS

Calories 31 Kc • Protein 0 Gm • Fat 2 Gm • Percent of calories from fat 51% • Cholesterol 0 mg • Dietary Fiber 0 Gm • Sodium 34 mg • Calcium 9 mg

Minted Orange Sauce

Use this refreshing full-flavored sauce as you would a hollandaise or béarnaise on fresh, steamed vegetables.

½ cup dry white wine
¼ cup lemon juice
¼ cup minced shallot
1 clove garlic, minced
¼ cup minced fresh mint, or
   1 tablespoon dried
⅛ teaspoon freshly ground
   black pepper

1 cup Tofu Mayonnaise (see
   page 258)
2 tablespoons orange
   juice
1 teaspoon minced orange
   zest

Place the wine, lemon juice, shallot, garlic, mint, and pepper in a small saucepan over medium heat and cook, stirring occasionally, until reduced by half. Strain through a fine sieve into a food processor. Add the Tofu Mayonnaise, orange juice, and orange zest, process until blended, and serve immediately.

MAKES 1¼ CUPS

Calories 36 Kc • Protein 1 Gm • Fat 2 Gm • Percent of calories from fat 48% • Cholesterol 0 mg • Dietary Fiber 0 Gm • Sodium 122 mg • Calcium 13 mg

Lime Jalapeño Sauce

1 tablespoon olive oil
2 jalapeño chilies, seeded and chopped
¾ cup silken tofu, drained
2 tablespoons fresh lime juice
1 teaspoon grated lime zest

1 tablespoon snipped fresh chives, or 1 teaspoon dried
½ teaspoon salt
⅛ teaspoon freshly ground white pepper

Heat the oil in a small saucepan over medium-low heat. Add the chilies and cook until tender, stirring occasionally, about 3 minutes. Place the tofu, lime juice and zest, chives, salt, and pepper in a food processor, add the chili mixture, and process until combined. Adjust the seasonings and serve at room temperature, or return to the saucepan and heat, stirring, over low heat, until heated through. Do not boil.

MAKES ABOUT 1 CUP

Calories 34 Kc • Protein 1 Gm • Fat 2 Gm • Percent of calories from fat 68% • Cholesterol 0 mg • Dietary Fiber 0 Gm • Sodium 164 mg • Calcium 14 mg

"Hollandaise" Sauce

A quick and cholesterol-free alternative to hollandaise sauce. Brightens up fresh steamed broccoli or asparagus.

1 cup Tofu Mayonnaise (see page 258)
3 tablespoons lemon juice
1 teaspoon Dijon mustard

½ teaspoon salt
Pinch cayenne
Pinch turmeric

Combine all of the ingredients in a food processor and mix until well combined. Serve at room temperature or heat slowly in a saucepan over low heat (do not boil), stirring until heated through.

MAKES ABOUT 1¹/₄ CUPS

Calories 25 Kc • Protein 1 Gm • Fat 2 Gm • Percent of calories from fat 68% • Cholesterol 0 mg • Dietary Fiber 0 Gm • Sodium 241 mg • Calcium 8 mg

Brown Sauce

A full-flavored brown sauce that can be used over grains, stuffed squash, or sautéed seitan.

1 tablespoon safflower oil
1 cup minced onion
½ cup minced celery
½ cup minced carrots
2 ripe tomatoes, chopped
½ cup sliced mushrooms
2 cloves garlic, chopped
½ cup dry red wine
3 tablespoons low-sodium
   tamari

½ teaspoon minced fresh
   thyme, or pinch dried
3 cups Vegetable Stock (see
   page 10)
4 tablespoons margarine
4 tablespoons flour
Salt and freshly ground pepper

Heat the oil in a large saucepan over medium heat, add the onion, celery, and carrots and cook, covered, until tender, about 5 minutes. Remove the cover, add the tomatoes, mushrooms, garlic, wine, tamari, and thyme and bring to a boil. Add the stock. Bring to a boil, lower the heat, cover, and simmer for about 45 minutes. Pour the mixture though a colander into a bowl, pressing on the vegetables to strain out the liquid. Discard the vegetables. Meanwhile, melt the margarine in the same saucepan over medium heat, add the flour, and cook for 2 minutes, stirring with a wire whisk. Add the hot stock, whisking, and cook over low heat until thickened, about 3 minutes. Season with salt and pepper to taste.

MAKES ABOUT 3 CUPS

Calories 46 Kc • Protein 1 Gm • Fat 2 Gm • Percent of calories from fat 42% • Cholesterol 0 mg • Dietary Fiber 1 Gm • Sodium 121 mg • Calcium 15 mg

White Wine Sauce

This delicately flavored sauce adds an elegant touch to sautéed tofu cutlets, or to grain or pasta dishes.

2 tablespoons safflower oil
¼ cup minced onions
2 tablespoons all-purpose flour
½ cup dry white wine
1 cup almond milk

½ teaspoon salt
⅛ teaspoon freshly ground
  pepper
Pinch nutmeg

Heat the oil in a medium skillet over medium heat. Add the onions and cook, covered, for 5 minutes or until softened. Add the flour and cook 1 minute, stirring with a wire whisk. Add the wine, stirring, and cook 5 minutes. Reduce the heat to low, slowly add the almond milk, whisking constantly, until smooth. Add the salt, pepper, and nutmeg and simmer 2 to 3 minutes longer, being careful not to boil.

MAKES ABOUT 1³/₄ CUPS

Calories 39 Kc • Protein 0 Gm • Fat 3 Gm • Percent of calories from fat 66% • Cholesterol 0 mg • Dietary Fiber 0 Gm • Sodium 84 mg • Calcium 8 mg

Soubise Sauce

The classic creamy onion sauce, with all the flavor of its dairy counterpart.

3 tablespoons safflower oil
3 medium onions, chopped
¾ teaspoon salt
3 tablespoons all-purpose flour

3 cups soy milk
¼ teaspoon freshly ground white
 pepper
Pinch nutmeg

Heat the oil in a large skillet over low heat. Add the onions, sprinkle with ¼ teaspoon of the salt, and cook, covered, for about 20 minutes, stirring occasionally, being careful not to brown. Add the flour and cook for 1 minute, stirring constantly. Slowly add the soy milk, remaining ½ teaspoon salt, pepper, and nutmeg, and whisk continuously until smooth and thick. Continue cooking for another 5 minutes over low heat, stirring occasionally. Transfer the mixture to a food processor and puree until smooth. Adjust the seasonings.

MAKES 4 CUPS

Calories 34 Kc • Protein 1 Gm • Fat 2 Gm • Percent of calories from fat 47% • Cholesterol 0 mg • Dietary Fiber 0 Gm • Sodium 66 mg • Calcium 9 mg

Tastes Like Béarnaise Sauce

This cholesterol-free version of béarnaise sauce is a good choice for sautéed seitan cutlets or steamed green vegetables.

½ cup white wine
¼ cup cider vinegar
¼ cup minced shallots
2 tablespoons minced fresh
    tarragon, or 1 teaspoon
    dried

1¾ cups firm silken tofu, drained
1 tablespoon corn oil
2 tablespoons lemon juice
½ teaspoon salt
⅛ teaspoon turmeric
⅛ teaspoon cayenne

Combine the wine, vinegar, shallots, and tarragon in a small saucepan over medium-high heat and bring to a boil. Reduce the heat to low and simmer until reduced by half. Transfer the mixture to a food processor, add the tofu, oil, lemon juice, salt, turmeric, and cayenne and process until smooth. Adjust the seasonings.

MAKES ABOUT 2 CUPS

Calories 29 Kc • Protein 1 Gm • Fat 1 Gm • Percent of calories from fat 49% • Cholesterol 0 mg • Dietary Fiber 0 Gm • Sodium 75 mg • Calcium 12 mg

Tahini Lemon Sauce

This creamy sauce does wonders to perk up steamed vegetables. It's also fabulous tossed with hot pasta.

½ cup tahini (sesame paste)
½ cup firm silken tofu, drained
¼ cup minced scallion
¼ cup minced fresh parsley, or 1 tablespoon dried
½ teaspoon minced garlic

⅓ cup lemon juice
½ teaspoon salt
⅛ teaspoon cayenne
⅛ teaspoon turmeric
Water

Place all of the ingredients in a food processor and process until well blended. Slowly add up to $1/2$ cup water until a smooth consistency is reached. Transfer to a saucepan and bring to a simmer over low heat, stirring occasionally. Be careful not to boil. Adjust the seasonings.

MAKES ABOUT 2 CUPS

Calories 59 Kc • Protein 2 Gm • Fat 5 Gm • Percent of calories from fat 76% • Cholesterol 0 mg • Dietary Fiber 0 Gm • Sodium 74 mg • Calcium 25 mg

Vermouth Cream Sauce

1 tablespoon minced fresh
   tarragon, or 1 teaspoon dried
½ cup dry white vermouth
1 teaspoon minced fresh parsley
¾ cup Vegetable Stock (see page
   10)

1 teaspoon cornstarch dissolved
   in 1 teaspoon water
¾ cup soy milk
Salt and freshly ground white
   pepper

Combine the tarragon and vermouth in a saucepan and boil down rapidly until reduced by half. Add the parsley and the stock and reduce again to half the volume. Whisk in the cornstarch mixture, stirring. Cook for 1 minute. Reduce the heat to low, add the soy milk, and cook over very low heat, stirring to thicken. Be careful not to boil. Add salt and pepper to taste.

MAKES ABOUT 1¼ CUPS

Calories 29 Kc • Protein 1 Gm • Fat 1 Gm • Percent of calories from fat 23% • Cholesterol 0 mg • Dietary Fiber 0 Gm • Sodium 27 mg • Calcium 11 mg

8

Desserts

Eliminating dairy products from your diet is most challenging in the area of desserts. Fortunately, however, healthful dairy alternatives such as soy milk, almond milk, tofu, and tofu chocolate can be used to create many classic favorites.

In this chapter, luscious recipes for Chocolate Mousse Fantasy, Three-Nut Butter Pie, and Pumpkin Cheesecake will convince you that giving up dairy products doesn't mean you have to feel deprived. You can even bake cakes without eggs or dairy products! A tempting selection of puddings, cookies, cakes, and pies are sure to turn you into a believer. There are recipes for whipped creams, frostings, and ice cream cakes that will satisfy your most decadent cravings.

Pumpkin Cheesecake

2 cups graham cracker
  crumbs
2 tablespoons sugar
2 tablespoons margarine,
  melted
1½ cups firm silken tofu, well
  drained
1½ cups canned pumpkin

½ cup sugar (or a natural
  sweetener)
2 tablespoons corn oil
1 tablespoon cornstarch
1 teaspoon ground cinnamon
½ teaspoon ground allspice
¼ teaspoon ground nutmeg
¼ teaspoon ground ginger

Preheat the oven to 350 degrees. Lightly oil a 9-inch springform pan, or coat with nonstick cooking spray. Place the crumbs, sugar, and margerine in the bottom of the pan and toss with a fork until blended. Press the crust into the bottom and sides of the pan, and bake for 5 minutes. Set aside. Combine the tofu and pumpkin in a food processor and process until smooth. Add the sugar, oil, cornstarch, cinnamon, allspice, nutmeg, and ginger and process until thoroughly blended. Spoon the filling into the crust and bake for 1 hour or until firm, and a toothpick inserted in the center comes out clean. Remove the cake from the oven and let it set a few minutes before removing the sides of pan. Let the cheesecake cool to room temperature and chill at least 2 hours before serving. Refrigerate any leftovers.

8 SERVINGS

Calories 164 Kc • Protein 4 Gm • Fat 6 Gm • Percent of calories from fat 33% • Cholesterol 0 mg • Dietary Fiber 1 Gm • Sodium 61 mg • Calcium 35 mg

Tofu Cheesecake

This basic cheesecake is smooth and creamy and just waiting to be crowned with your favorite fruit topping.

2 cups graham cracker crumbs
2 tablespoons sugar
2 tablespoons margarine, melted
2½ cups firm silken tofu, well drained

¾ cup soy milk
¼ cup corn oil
1 tablespoon cornstarch
1 teaspoon vanilla extract
Fruit topping (optional)

Preheat the oven to 350 degrees. Lightly oil a 9-inch springform pan, or coat with nonstick cooking spray. Place the crumbs, sugar, and margarine in the bottom of the pan, and toss with a fork until blended. Press the crust into the bottom and sides of pan and bake for 5 minutes. Set aside. Combine the tofu, soy milk, oil, cornstarch, and vanilla in a food processor and blend until smooth. Pour the filling into the prepared crust and bake for 30 minutes, or until firm. Remove from the oven and let the cake come to room temperature. Leave it plain or top with a fruit topping of your choice, such as whole fresh strawberries or sliced fresh strawberries combined with fruit-sweetened strawberry jam. Chill at least 2 hours before serving.

8 SERVINGS

Calories 175 Kc • Protein 7 Gm • Fat 11 Gm • Percent of calories from fat 56%
• Cholesterol 0 mg • Dietary Fiber 0 Gm • Sodium 105 mg • Calcium 37 mg

Chocolate Banana Pie

Crust:
1 cup unbleached all-purpose flour
2 tablespoons sugar
Pinch of salt
¼ cup (½ stick) chilled margarine,
    cut into small pieces
1 tablespoon water
Filling:
1½ cup firm silken tofu, well
    drained

2 ripe bananas
¼ cup sugar (or a natural
    sweetener)
2 tablespoons margarine,
    softened at room temperature
2 tablespoons lemon juice
1 teaspoon vanilla extract
2 ounces tofu chocolate
    (available in natural food
    stores)

Preheat the oven to 350 degrees. Lightly oil a 9-inch pie plate or coat with nonstick spray and set aside. To make the crust, combine the flour, sugar, and salt in a food processor. Add the margarine with short pulses until the mixture resembles coarse crumbs. Add the water and mix until a dough ball begins to form. Transfer the dough to the prepared plate and press gently into the bottom and sides. Line the crust with aluminum foil, and fill with dried beans. Bake for 10 minutes, or until the crust is set. Discard the foil and beans. Continue baking until the crust is light brown, 8 to 10 minutes longer. Remove the crust from the oven, and set aside.

To make the filling, put the silken tofu, bananas, sugar, softened margarine, lemon juice, and vanilla into a food processor and mix until well combined. Spoon the filling into the crust. Melt the tofu chocolate in a double boiler over simmering water. Pour the melted chocolate over the filling and swirl with a thin spatula or knife to create a light and dark swirled pattern in the batter. Bake for 30 minutes, or until firm. Cool to room temperature before refrigerating. Chill at least 2 hours before serving.

8 SERVINGS

Calories 225 Kc • Protein 6 Gm • Fat 10 Gm • Percent of calories from fat 36%
• Cholesterol 0 mg • Dietary Fiber 2 Gm • Sodium 69 mg • Calcium 44 mg

Strawberry "Cream" Pie

For a more spectacular presentation, cover the pie with whole strawberries. Choose whole berries of uniform size, and glaze as directed for sliced berries.

Crust:
1 cup unbleached all-purpose flour
⅛ teaspoon salt
½ cup (1 stick) chilled margarine, cut into small pieces
Filling:
2½ tablespoons cold water
1½ cups firm silken tofu, well drained

½ cup sugar (or a natural sweetener)
1 tablespoon safflower oil
1 teaspoon vanilla extract
2 cups sliced fresh strawberries (about 1 pint)
1 cup fruit-sweetened strawberry preserves

Preheat the oven to 375 degrees. Place the flour and salt in a food processor and blend. Add the margarine and process until crumbly. Processing, slowly add the water until a dough ball forms. On a lightly floured surface, roll out the dough to fit a 9-inch pie plate, and arrange in the pie plate, trimming the dough and fluting the edges. Prick holes in the bottom of the dough with a fork. Line the crust with aluminum foil, and fill with dried beans. Bake for 10 minutes, or until the crust is set. Discard the foil and beans. Continue baking until the crust is light brown, 8 to 10 minutes longer. Remove the crust from the oven, and set aside. Turn the oven temperature down to 350 degrees.

In a food processor, combine the tofu, sugar, oil, and vanilla and blend thoroughly. Pour into the prepared crust, and bake for 30 minutes. Remove the pie from the oven and let it cool. Beginning at the outer edge, arrange the strawberry slices on top of the pie in a circular pattern until the entire surface is covered. Puree the preserves in a blender or food processor and spoon the strawberry glaze over the pie. Refrigerate at least 1 hour to set the glaze before serving. Refrigerate any leftovers.

8 SERVINGS

**Calories 251 Kc • Protein 6 Gm • Fat 9 Gm • Percent of calories from fat 30%
• Cholesterol 0 mg • Dietary Fiber 1 Gm • Sodium 147 mg • Calcium 42 mg**

Apple Custard Pie

2 cups graham cracker
crumbs
2 tablespoons margarine,
melted
1½ teaspoons cinnamon
1½ cups extra-firm silken tofu,
well drained
1 cup applesauce

½ cup sugar (or a natural
sweetener)
¼ cup tahini (sesame paste)
2 tablespoons corn oil
1 teaspoon vanilla extract
¼ teaspoon nutmeg
¼ teaspoon allspice
⅛ teaspoon salt

Preheat the oven to 350 degrees. Lightly oil a 9-inch pie plate. Place the graham cracker crumbs, margarine, and $1/2$ teaspoon of the cinnamon into the pie plate and toss lightly with a fork to combine. Press the crumbs evenly into the bottom and sides of the plate. Bake 10 minutes, and set aside. In a food processor, combine the tofu, applesauce, sugar, tahini, oil, and vanilla, and blend thoroughly. Add the remaining 1 teaspoon of cinnamon, the nutmeg, allspice, and salt and blend well. Pour the mixture into the prepared crust and bake for 25 to 30 minutes, or until set. Remove from the oven and cool to room temperature. Refrigerate several hours to chill before serving. Refrigerate any leftovers.

8 SERVINGS

Calories 222 Kc • Protein 6 Gm • Fat 11 Gm • Percent of calories from fat 45%
• Cholesterol 0 mg • Dietary Fiber 1 Gm • Sodium 111 mg • Calcium 47 mg

Chocolate Rum Pie

For more chocolate flavor, substitute a pie crust made from carob cookie crumbs.

Crust:
1 cup unbleached all-purpose
   flour
⅛ teaspoon salt
½ cup (1 stick) chilled margarine,
   cut into small pieces
3 tablespoons cold water
Filling:
5 ounces tofu chocolate,
   chopped (available in natural
   food stores)

¼ cup carob soy milk, heated
¼ cup dark rum
1 teaspoon instant coffee
   granules
1 teaspoon vanilla extract
⅛ teaspoon salt
1 cup Tofu Whipped Cream (see
   page 341)
Tofu chocolate curls for garnish

Preheat the oven to 375 degrees. Place the flour and salt in a food processor and combine. Add the margarine and process until crumbly. Processing slowly, add the water until a dough ball forms. On a lightly floured surface, roll out the dough to fit a 9-inch pie plate, and arrange in the pie plate, trimming the dough and fluting the edges. Prick holes in the bottom of the dough with a fork. Line the crust with aluminum foil, and fill with dried beans. Bake for 10 minutes, or until the crust is set. Discard the foil and beans. Continue baking until the crust is light brown, 8 to 10 minutes longer. Remove the crust from the oven, and set aside.

Melt the chopped chocolate in the top of a double boiler set over gently simmering water. Stir in the soy milk, rum, coffee, vanilla, and salt. Remove from the heat and cool to room temperature. Fold the whipped cream into the chocolate mixture. Spoon the filling into the prepared crust, and smooth the top evenly. Refrigerate at least 2 hours to firm up. Just prior to serving, sprinkle the top of the pie with the chocolate curls. Refrigerate any leftovers.

6 TO 8 SERVINGS

Calories 325 Kc • Protein 6 Gm • Fat 17 Gm • Percent of calories from fat 46%
• Cholesterol 0 mg • Dietary Fiber 1 Gm • Sodium 170 mg • Calcium 73 mg

Three-Nut Butter Pie

Allow at least 1 day in the freezer for this pie before serving—if you can manage to wait that long.

2 cups chocolate or carob cookie crumbs

½ cup ground walnuts

¼ cup (½ stick) margarine, melted

½ gallon vanilla frozen nondairy dessert, softened

2 cups creamy peanut butter

½ cup honey or brown rice syrup

1 cup ground toasted almonds

Preheat the oven to 350 degrees. Lightly oil a 9-inch springform pan, or coat with nonstick cooking spray. Blend the cookie crumbs, ground walnuts, and melted margarine in a medium bowl. Transfer to the prepared pan and press the crumb mixture onto the bottom and up the sides of the pan. Bake 5 minutes. Cool.

In a large bowl combine the frozen dessert, peanut butter, and honey, mixing until well blended. Spoon into the prepared crust. Freeze several hours or overnight.

Before serving, put the pie out at room temperature for 5 minutes, carefully remove the sides of the pan, and spread the ground almonds evenly over the top of the pie.

12 SERVINGS

Calories 582 Kc • Protein 16 Gm • Fat 35 Gm • Percent of calories from fat 52% • Cholesterol 6 mg • Dietary Fiber 4 Gm • Sodium 459 mg • Calcium 56 mg

Sweet Potato Pie

Crust:
1 cup unbleached all-purpose flour
Pinch of salt
½ cup (1 stick) chilled margarine,
cut into 1-inch pieces
2½ tablespoons cold water
Filling:
1 cup cooked mashed sweet
potatoes
1 tablespoon margarine,
softened to room temperature
½ cup soft silken tofu, drained (or
2 eggs)

1 cup vanilla soy milk
1¼ cup firmly packed light
brown sugar (or a natural
sweetener)
1 teaspoon vanilla extract
1 teaspoon cinnamon
½ teaspoon salt
¼ teaspoon ground ginger
¼ teaspoon ground nutmeg
1 cup chilled Tofu Whipped
Cream (see page 341) for
garnish

To make the crust, combine the flour and salt in a food processor. Blend in the margarine with short pulses, until the mixture resembles coarse crumbs. With the machine running, add the water through the feed tube and blend until the dough just starts to hold together. Transfer the dough to a work surface and flatten to form a disc. Wrap the dough in plastic wrap and refrigerate at least 1 hour.

To make the filling, in a large mixing bowl, combine the sweet potatoes and margarine with an electric mixer. Blend in the tofu. Add the soy milk, sugar, vanilla, cinnamon, salt, ginger, and nutmeg, mixing until well blended. Preheat the oven to 350 degrees. Roll out the dough on a lightly floured surface to fit a 9-inch pie plate. Fit the dough into the pie plate and trim and flute the edges. Pour the filling into the crust and bake for 45 to 50 minutes, or until firm. Serve garnished with a dollop of Tofu Whipped Cream on each slice.

8 SERVINGS

Calories 337 Kc • Protein 5 Gm • Fat 10 Gm • Percent of calories from fat 25%
• Cholesterol 0 mg • Dietary Fiber 1 Gm • Sodium 244 mg • Calcium 74 mg

Peanut Butter Pie

1 cup graham cracker crumbs
¼ cup sugar (or a natural
   sweetener)
¼ cup margarine, melted
2 cups creamy peanut butter
1 cup sugar
1 pound extra-firm silken tofu,
   drained

2 tablespoons margarine,
   softened
2 teaspoons vanilla extract
1½ cups Tofu Whipped Cream
   (see page 341)
Tofu chocolate curls or ground
   peanuts for garnish

Combine the crumbs, sugar, and the melted margarine. Press into the
bottom and halfway up the sides of a 9-inch springform pan. Combine
the peanut butter, sugar, tofu, the softened margarine, and vanilla in
large mixing bowl, and beat with an electric mixer until smooth and
creamy. Fold the whipped cream into the peanut butter mixture. Spoon
into the prepared crust. Refrigerate several hours or overnight. When
ready to serve, garnish with tofu chocolate curls or ground peanuts.
Refrigerate any leftovers.

10 TO 12 SERVINGS

Calories 554 Kc • Protein 17 Gm • Fat 30 Gm • Percent of calories from fat 46%
• Cholesterol 0 mg • Dietary Fiber 3 Gm • Sodium 306 mg • Calcium 44 mg

Pumpkin Pie

Crust:
1 cup unbleached all-purpose flour
Pinch of salt
½ cup (1 stick) chilled margarine,
    cut into pieces
2½ tablespoons ice water
Filling:
2 cups canned or cooked
    pumpkin puree
2 cups extra-firm silken tofu, well
    drained

½ cup sugar (or a natural
    sweetener)
1½ teaspoons cinnamon
½ teaspoon ginger
¼ teaspoon allspice
¼ teaspoon nutmeg
⅛ teaspoon salt
1 tablespoon cornstarch
Tofu Whipped Cream (see page
    341) (optional)

To make the crust, combine the flour and salt in a food processor. Blend in the margarine with short pulses, until the mixture resembles coarse crumbs. With the machine running, add the water through the feed tube and blend until the dough just starts to hold together. Transfer the dough to a work surface and flatten to form a disc. Wrap the dough in plastic wrap and refrigerate at least 1 hour.

To make the filling, combine the pumpkin and tofu in a food processor until well blended. Add the sugar, cinnamon, ginger, allspice, nutmeg, salt, and cornstarch, mixing until smooth and well combined.

Preheat the oven to 375 degrees. Roll out the dough on a lightly floured surface to fit a 9-inch pie plate. Fit the dough into the pie plate and trim and flute the edges. Pour the filling into the crust, and bake for 50 minutes or until firm. Serve plain or with a dollop of Tofu Whipped Cream on each slice.

8 SERVINGS

Calories 220 Kc • Protein 7 Gm • Fat 8 Gm • Percent of calories from fat 30% • Cholesterol 0 mg • Dietary Fiber 2 Gm • Sodium 131 mg • Calcium 65 mg

Fresh Berry Tart

Pastry:
½ cup (1 stick) margarine, room temperature
2 tablespoons sugar (or a natural sweetener)
½ cup finely chopped almonds
1 teaspoon vanilla extract
1 teaspoon almond extract
1¼ cups unbleached all-purpose flour
Custard:
⅓ cup firm silken tofu, drained

2 tablespoons sugar
2 tablespoons cornstarch
½ teaspoon vanilla extract
1 cup almond milk
4 tablespoons (½ stick) margarine, room temperature
2 cups fresh raspberries (about 1 pint)
2 cups fresh blueberries (about 1 pint)
½ cup apple jelly

To make the pastry, lightly oil a 10-inch tart pan with a removable bottom or spray with nonstick vegetable spray. In a large bowl, blend the margarine and sugar until well combined. Add the almonds. Blend in the vanilla and almond extracts. Stir in the flour until completely incorporated. Press the dough into the prepared pan. Refrigerate for 30 minutes. Preheat the oven to 350 degrees. Prick the bottom of the crust with a fork and bake the pie shell until golden brown, about 15 minutes. Cool the pie crust to room temperature.

To make the custard, blend the tofu, sugar, cornstarch, and vanilla in a blender or food processor until thoroughly blended. Heat the almond milk in a medium saucepan. Add the almond milk to the tofu mixture and blend until smooth. Stir the mixture back into the saucepan and whisk over medium heat until very thick, about 5 minutes. Return the mixture to the bowl and beat until cool. Beat in the softened margarine 1 tablespoon at a time. Refrigerate until chilled.

To assemble, spread the custard evenly over the bottom of the crust. Starting from the outside edge, arrange the raspberries in concentric circles over the custard, placing the berries as close together as possible. Then complete the circle with circular rows of blueberries until the entire surface of the custard is covered. Refrigerate 30 minutes. Melt the jelly in a small saucepan over low heat, stirring occasionally. Brush gently over the berries. Refrigerate at least 2 hours before serving.

6 TO 8 SERVINGS

Calories 429 Kc • Protein 9 Gm • Fat 18 Gm • Percent of calories from fat 30% • Cholesterol 0 mg • Dietary Fiber 6 Gm • Sodium 93 mg • Calcium 99 mg

Blueberry Cobbler

Serve this delightfully nostalgic cobbler while still warm with a scoop of nondairy vanilla "ice cream."

Filling:
5 cups blueberries, picked over and washed (2½ pints)
3 tablespoons sugar (or a natural sweetener)

Biscuit Topping:
1 cup flour
1½ teaspoons baking powder
2 teaspoons sugar (or a natural sweetener)
⅓ cup rice milk
3 tablespoons margarine, melted

Preheat the oven to 400 degrees. Place the berries and sugar in a saucepan and heat gently. Place the hot fruit into a shallow baking dish and set aside. In a mixing bowl, combine the flour, baking powder, and sugar. Slowly add the milk and melted margarine, stirring until it forms a smooth dough. Pat the dough into small round biscuits about ¼-inch thick and place over the hot fruit. Overlap the biscuits to cover the entire surface of the filling. Bake about 15 minutes or until the biscuits are lightly browned and cooked through.

6 SERVINGS

Calories 205 Kc • Protein 3 Gm • Fat 4 Gm • Percent of calories from fat 15% • Cholesterol 0 mg • Dietary Fiber 4 Gm • Sodium 137 mg • Calcium 73 mg

Vanilla-scented Fresh Pear Tart

Pastry:
1 cup unbleached all-purpose
  flour
Pinch of salt
½ cup (1 stick) chilled margarine,
  cut into pieces
2½ tablespoons cold water
Custard:
¼ cup cornstarch
3 cups vanilla soy milk

5 tablespoons sugar (or a natural
  sweetener)
1½ teaspoons vanilla extract
⅓ cup firm silken tofu, well drained
3 ripe pears, peeled, cored, and
  halved
1 tablespoon lemon juice
2 tablespoons apple jelly
  (optional)
Mint sprig for garnish

To make the pastry, combine the flour and salt in a food processor. Blend in the margarine with short pulses, until the mixture resembles coarse crumbs. With the machine running, add the water through the feed tube and blend until the dough just starts to hold together. Transfer the dough to a work surface and flatten to form a disc. Wrap the dough in plastic wrap and refrigerate at least 1 hour. Preheat the oven to 350 degrees. Roll out the dough on a lightly floured surface to fit a 9-inch pie plate. Fit the dough into the pie plate and trim and flute the edges. Prick the bottom of the crust with a fork, and bake for 15 minutes, or until lightly browned. Remove from the oven and set aside to cool.

To make the custard, combine the cornstarch, soy milk, 2 tablespoons of the sugar, and ³/₄ teaspoon of the vanilla in a large saucepan and whisk until smooth. Place the saucepan over medium heat and cook, stirring constantly, until the mixture thickens and just begins to boil, about 5 minutes. Remove from the heat. Place the tofu in a small bowl and stir in 2 tablespoons of the hot custard mixture. Stir the tofu mixture into the custard in the saucepan and mix well. Transfer the custard to a bowl and let it cool to room temperature, stirring several times. Refrigerate until ready to assemble. Place the pears in a saucepan with the lemon juice, remaining 3 tablespoons sugar, and remaining ³/₄ teaspoon vanilla, with enough water to cover. Poach gently until just tender, about 10 minutes. Remove the pears from the water and let them cool.

To assemble the tart, cut the pears lengthwise into ¹/₄-inch-thick slices. Whisk the custard smooth and spoon into the baked tart crust.

Starting from the outside edge of the crust, cover the custard with slightly overlapping rows of pear slices, to cover entire surface. If a glossy sheen is desired, melt the apple jelly in a small saucepan and brush over the pears with a pastry brush. Place a sprig of mint in the center of the tart and serve. Refrigerate the tart if made ahead of time, and refrigerate any leftovers.

8 SERVINGS

Calories 233 Kc • Protein 4 Gm • Fat 7 Gm • Percent of calories from fat 28% • Cholesterol 0 mg • Dietary Fiber 2 Gm • Sodium 87 mg • Calcium 38 mg

Peach Clafouti

A clafouti is part custard and part fruit pie. It is crustless, and is traditionally made with eggs and heavy cream.

2 cups peeled peach slices (about 4 peaches)
²⁄₃ cup almond milk
¼ cup soft silken tofu (or 1 egg or egg replacer)
2 tablespoons unbleached all-purpose flour
2 tablespoons sugar (or a natural sweetener)

½ teaspoon vanilla extract
¼ teaspoon ground nutmeg
Pinch of salt
Confectioners' sugar (optional)
1 pint vanilla nondairy frozen dessert

Preheat the oven to 375 degrees. Lightly oil a 9-inch pie plate and arrange the peaches in the pie plate in a single layer. In a medium bowl, mix the almond milk, tofu, flour, sugar, vanilla, nutmeg, and salt until smooth. Pour the mixture over the peaches. Bake the clafouti until puffed and golden, about 30 minutes. Sprinkle with confectioners' sugar, if using. Cut into wedges and serve with a scoop of the frozen dessert.

6 SERVINGS

Calories 46 Kc • Protein 1 Gm • Fat 1 Gm • Percent of calories from fat 27% • Cholesterol 0 mg • Dietary Fiber 1 Gm • Sodium 1 mg • Calcium 11 mg

Fresh Cherry Clafouti

Enhance this luscious dessert by nestling a scoop of vanilla "ice cream" alongside each serving. Serve clafouti warm or at room temperature.

3 cups fresh dark cherries
½ cup sugar (or a natural
   sweetener)
1½ cups soy milk
½ cup soft silken tofu (or 2 eggs
   or egg replacer)

1 tablespoon corn oil
6 tablespoons unbleached all-
   purpose flour
Confectioners' sugar (optional)

Preheat the oven to 375 degrees. Wash, stem, and pit the cherries. Lightly oil a 9-inch glass pie plate or quiche pan, or coat with nonstick cooking spray. Sprinkle the cherries with 1/4 cup of the sugar and spread in the pie plate. In a blender or food processor, combine the soy milk, tofu, oil, flour, and remaining 1/4 cup sugar, mixing until well blended. Pour the batter over the cherries and bake for 30 minutes, or until firm and lightly browned and puffed. Serve warm, sprinkled with confectioners' sugar.

6 SERVINGS

Calories 188Kc • Protein 4 Gm • Fat 4 Gm • Percent of calories from fat 20% • Cholesterol 0 mg • Dietary Fiber 1 Gm • Sodium 31 mg • Calcium 35 mg

Apple Crisp with Apple Cream

Filling:
8 Granny Smith apples, peeled,
   cored and sliced
1 tablespoon fresh lemon juice
1 teaspoon cinnamon
¾ cup quick-cooking oats
¾ cup unbleached all-purpose
   flour
¾ cup firmly packed brown sugar
   (or a natural sweetener)

2 tablespoons corn oil
Topping:
¾ cup soft silken tofu, well
   drained
¾ cup applesauce
1 teaspoon vanilla extract
1 tablespoon sugar (or a natural
   sweetener)

Preheat the oven to 350 degrees. In a large bowl combine the apples
with the lemon juice and the cinnamon and arrange them in a lightly
oiled shallow baking dish. In a bowl combine the oats, flour, brown
sugar, and oil. Sprinkle the mixture over the apples, and bake for 45
minutes, or until the top is lightly browned. To make the topping, combine the tofu, applesauce, vanilla, and sugar in a small bowl and mix
well. Transfer the topping to a small serving bowl, and pass separately
with the warm apple crisp.

8 SERVINGS

Calories 284 Kc • Protein 4 Gm • Fat 5 Gm • Percent of calories from fat 16%
• Cholesterol 0 mg • Dietary Fiber 4 Gm • Sodium 11 mg • Calcium 51 mg

Fresh Fruit with Grand Marnier Sauce

Feel free to use whatever fruits are at their peak. To serve a crowd, increase the amounts of fruit and arrange on one large serving platter.

¼ cup sugar (or a natural sweetener)
1 tablespoon minced orange zest
¾ cup silken tofu, drained
2 tablespoons Grand Marnier
1 tablespoon frozen orange juice concentrate
1 tablespoon lemon juice

½ cantaloupe, peeled and seeded
2 kiwi fruit, peeled and sliced
3 plums, halved and pitted
1 orange, peeled and segmented
1 cup seedless red grapes
1 cup sliced hulled strawberries

In a food processor, combine the sugar and orange zest. Add the tofu, liqueur, orange juice concentrate, and lemon juice and blend well. Transfer to a small serving bowl and set aside. Slice the cantaloupe into ¼-inch crescent-shaped slices, and arrange in a circular pattern on individual serving plates. Arrange the kiwi slices in a circular pattern in the center of each plate. Quarter each plum half into wedges and arrange in a circular pattern along the outer edge of the kiwi circle, on top of the cantaloupe. Arrange the orange segments, grapes, and strawberries attractively on each plate, either by scattering on top of the other fruit, or maintaining a consistent pattern. Pass the sauce separately.

4 SERVINGS

Calories 258 Kc • Protein 5 Gm • Fat 2 Gm • Percent of calories from fat 7% • Cholesterol 0 mg • Dietary Fiber 6 Gm • Sodium 38 mg • Calcium 72 mg

Bread Pudding with Bourbon Sauce

Use French or Italian bread or mix in some whole grain bread if you prefer. Day-old bread works best for this pudding.

1 large loaf bread, cut into 1-inch cubes (about 12 cups)

1½ cups sugar (or a natural sweetener)

¼ cup (½ stick) margarine, melted

¼ teaspoon salt

4 cups almond milk

¾ cup soft silken tofu, drained (or 3 eggs or egg replacer)

2 tablespoons vanilla extract

1 cup golden raisins

Bourbon Sauce (see page 343)

Preheat the oven to 350 degrees. Lightly oil a shallow baking dish and set aside. In a large bowl, combine the bread cubes, sugar, margarine, and salt. Stir in the almond milk. Combine the tofu and vanilla in a food processor or blender until well blended. Add the tofu mixture to the bread mixture, and stir in the raisins, mixing well. Spoon into the prepared baking dish. Bake until golden brown, 45 to 50 minutes. Serve with Bourbon Sauce.

8 SERVINGS

Calories 417 Kc • Protein 8 Gm • Fat 11 Gm • Percent of calories from fat 23% • Cholesterol 0 mg • Dietary Fiber 2 Gm • Sodium 337 mg • Calcium 53 mg

Winter Fruit Bread Pudding

The variety of dried fruits and spices in this tasty bread pudding reminds me of a delicious fruitcake.

½ cup dried apricots
½ cup dried apple slices
½ cup golden raisins
1 loaf day-old home-style white
    bread, cubed (about 12 cups)
4 cups soy milk
¼ cup soft silken tofu, drained

½ cup applesauce
¼ cup corn oil
½ cup sugar
¼ cup bourbon (or apple juice)
1 teaspoon vanilla extract
1 teaspoon cinnamon
½ teaspoon allspice

Preheat the oven to 350 degrees. Lightly oil a shallow baking dish and set aside. With a scissors, snip the apricots and dried apples into 1/2-inch pieces. Place the apricots, apples, and raisins in a heatproof bowl and pour on boiling water to cover. Allow the fruit to soak for 15 minutes to plump up slightly. Drain. Place the bread cubes and fruit in the prepared baking dish, stirring to combine. In a small saucepan, heat the soy milk until hot, but not boiling. In a medium bowl, whisk together the tofu, applesauce, oil, and sugar until well blended. Stir in the hot soy milk, whisking constantly. Whisk in the bourbon, vanilla, cinnamon, and allspice. Pour over the bread and fruit mixture, and bake for 40 minutes, or until puffy and lightly browned. Remove from the oven and cool 10 minutes before serving.

12 SERVINGS

Calories 242 Kc • Protein 5 Gm • Fat 7 Gm • Percent of calories from fat 25% • Cholesterol 0 mg • Dietary Fiber 1 Gm • Sodium 200 mg • Calcium 29 mg

Apple Raisin Bread Pudding

1 pound loaf French or Italian
bread
1 quart vanilla soy milk
1½ cups sugar (or a natural
sweetener)
½ cup soft silken tofu, drained
¼ cup apple butter

¼ cup corn oil
2 tablespoons vanilla extract
1 teaspoon ground cinnamon
½ teaspoon allspice
2 cups chopped peeled apple
1 cup golden raisins

Lightly oil a 9 × 13-inch baking pan and set aside. Preheat the oven to
350 degrees. Break the bread into small pieces and place in a large
bowl. Add the soy milk and let the bread soak for 10 minutes, stirring
occasionally to mix well. Blend in the sugar, tofu, apple butter, oil,
vanilla, cinnamon, and allspice. Fold in the apples and raisins, and pour
the mixture into the prepared pan. Bake until firm, 40 to 50 minutes. Let
the pudding cool slightly. Serve warm.

12 SERVINGS

Calories 330 Kc • Protein 6 Gm • Fat 7 Gm • Percent of calories from fat 19%
• Cholesterol 0 mg • Dietary Fiber 1 Gm • Sodium 195 mg • Calcium 34 mg

Peach Almond Bread Pudding

½ cup soft silken tofu, drained
4 cups almond milk (or more)
1 loaf French or Italian bread, cubed (about 8 cups)
¾ cup sugar (or a natural sweetener)

1 teaspoon ground ginger
4 peaches, peeled, pitted, and sliced
1 cup chopped almonds

In a small bowl, combine the tofu with ½ cup of the almond milk until well blended. Reserve. Place the bread cubes in a large bowl and pour the remaining 3½ cups almond milk and sugar over them, tossing to coat. Let the bread stand for 1 hour to soak up the liquid. Add more almond milk as needed to soften the bread cubes. Preheat the oven to 350 degrees. Lightly oil a shallow baking pan and set aside. Mix into the reserved tofu mixture, the ginger, peaches, and almonds. Pour the mixture into the prepared baking pan and bake for 45 minutes or until firm.

8 SERVINGS

Calories 372 Kc • Protein 10 Gm • Fat 17 Gm • Percent of calories from fat 39% • Cholesterol 0 mg • Dietary Fiber 4 Gm • Sodium 371 mg • Calcium 92 mg

Pumpkin Rum Bread Pudding

A comforting bread pudding that tastes like pumpkin pie. The rum adds a touch of sophistication. Serve it with the Rum Cream Sauce on page 344 at your next holiday brunch.

1 loaf French or Italian bread, cut into 1-inch cubes (about 8 cups)
4 cups vanilla soy milk
¼ cup dark rum
¼ cup golden raisins
2 cups pumpkin puree
1 cup soft silken tofu, drained
½ cup sugar (or a natural sweetener)

1 teaspoon vanilla extract
1 tablespoon unbleached all-purpose flour
1 teaspoon ground cinnamon
¼ teaspoon ground nutmeg
⅛ teaspoon allspice
⅛ teaspoon ground cardamom

Lightly oil a 9 × 13-inch baking pan and set aside. Preheat the oven to 350 degrees. Place the bread cubes in a large bowl. Add 3 cups of the soy milk and let the bread soak for 10 minutes, stirring occasionally to mix well. Heat the rum, being careful not to boil. Pour the rum over the raisins in a small heatproof bowl and reserve. In a mixing bowl, combine the remaining 1 cup soy milk with the pumpkin, tofu, sugar, and vanilla and blend well. Mix in the flour, cinnamon, nutmeg, allspice, and cardamom. Fold in the rum–raisin mixture. Combine the bread mixture with the pumpkin mixture and pour into the prepared pan. Bake 45 to 50 minutes, or until firm. Serve warm.

12 SERVINGS

Calories 172 Kc • Protein 5 Gm • Fat 2 Gm • Percent of calories from fat 9% • Cholesterol 0 mg • Dietary Fiber 1 Gm • Sodium 183 mg • Calcium 21 mg

Mom's Rice Pudding

One of my all-time favorite comfort foods. No need to do without it, thanks to dairy alternatives.

1½ cups golden raisins
6 cups vanilla rice milk
1 cup sugar (or a natural
    sweetener)
¼ cup (½ stick) margarine

1 cup short-grain brown rice
1 teaspoon cinnamon
1 teaspoon vanilla extract
½ cup soft silken tofu, drained
Cinnamon for garnish

Place the raisins in a saucepan with enough water to cover and bring to a simmer. Cook 3 minutes, drain, and set aside. In a large saucepan, combine the rice milk, sugar, and margarine and bring to boil, stirring to dissolve the sugar. Add the rice, cinnamon, and vanilla and bring to a boil. Reduce the heat to medium-low, cover, and cook 30 minutes, or until the rice is tender, stirring occasionally. Stir in the tofu and raisins, and simmer 5 minutes longer. Cool, cover, and refrigerate until well chilled, stirring occasionally, several hours or overnight. Serve the rice pudding in bowls, and sprinkle with cinnamon.

6 TO 8 SERVINGS

Calories 450 Kc • Protein 5 Gm • Fat 6 Gm • Percent of calories from fat 11% • Cholesterol 0 mg • Dietary Fiber 2 Gm • Sodium 103 mg • Calcium 44 mg

Apple Vanilla Rice Pudding

A flavorful interpretation of a favorite comfort food.

2 cups vanilla rice milk
½ cup short-grain brown rice
½ cup apple juice
2 tablespoons sugar (or a natural sweetener)
¼ cup soft silken tofu, drained

¼ cup applesauce
2 tablespoons tahini (sesame paste)
2 teaspoons vanilla extract
1 teaspoon cinnamon

Combine the rice milk, rice, 1/4 cup of the apple juice, and the sugar in a saucepan and heat until the mixture comes to a boil. Reduce the heat to low, cover, and cook for 45 minutes or until the rice is tender. Combine the tofu, applesauce, tahini, vanilla, and cinnamon in a blender or food processor until smooth. Stir the tofu mixture into the rice, and cook over low heat for 2 minutes, stirring to blend well. Spoon into individual serving dishes and refrigerate for several hours or until the rice is set.

4 SERVINGS

Calories 246 Kc • Protein 5 Gm • Fat 7 Gm • Percent of calories from fat 24% • Cholesterol 0 mg • Dietary Fiber 1 Gm • Sodium 33 mg • Calcium 50 mg

Fresh Peach Pudding

A cool and creamy dessert that's easy to prepare. A great way to use up an overabundance of ripe peaches.

1 pound peaches (4 medium)
2 tablespoons sugar (or a natural sweetener)
3 tablespoons water
¾ cup firm silken tofu, well drained

2 teaspoons corn oil
½ teaspoon lemon juice
½ teaspoon vanilla extract
Pinch salt
Mint sprigs for garnish

Peel the peaches. Halve and remove the pits. Chop the peaches into ½-inch dice, and place in a saucepan with the sugar and water, bring to a boil, then lower the heat and simmer until tender, about 10 minutes. Remove from the heat and let cool. In a food processor, combine the tofu, oil, lemon juice, vanilla, and salt and blend well. Add the cooked peaches and process until thoroughly mixed. Transfer to dessert dishes and serve chilled, garnished with fresh mint sprigs.

4 TO 6 SERVINGS

Calories 101 Kc • Protein 4 Gm • Fat 3 Gm • Percent of calories from fat 24% • Cholesterol 0 mg • Dietary Fiber 2 Gm • Sodium 27 mg • Calcium 20 mg

Chocolate Mousse Fantasy

Substitute a splash of almond or rum extract for the amaretto for a non-alcoholic version of this easy dessert that will satisfy any chocolate lover's craving.

2 8-ounce tofu chocolate candy bars (available in natural food stores)

⅓ cup coarsely chopped almonds

2 tablespoons amaretto or other liqueur

4 cups Tofu Whipped Cream (see page 341)

Grated tofu chocolate or chopped almonds for garnish

Melt the candy bars in the top of a double boiler set over hot but not boiling water. Stir in the almonds and amaretto. Remove from the hot water and cool to room temperature. Fold the chocolate mixture into the Tofu Whipped Cream in a large bowl. Divide evenly among 8 dessert dishes. Refrigerate until well chilled. Garnish with the grated chocolate or chopped almonds and serve.

8 SERVINGS

Calories 585 Kc • Protein 13 Gm • Fat 32 Gm • Percent of calories from fat 47% • Cholesterol 0 mg • Dietary Fiber 1 Gm • Sodium 126 mg • Calcium 134 mg

Raspberry Mousse

Agar flakes are made from sea vegetables and are used as a vegetarian gelatin. They are available in most natural food stores. Strawberries can be substituted for the raspberries, if you prefer.

3 cups apple juice
¼ cup agar flakes
¾ cup vanilla soy milk
2 tablespoons tahini (sesame paste)

1¼ cup raspberries
Whole, fresh raspberries for garnish
Mint leaves for garnish

Put the apple juice into a saucepan and sprinkle on the agar flakes. Bring to a simmer without stirring. Simmer for about 3 minutes, stirring occasionally. In a food processor or blender, combine the soy milk, tahini, and 1/4 cup of the raspberries until smooth and well blended. Remove the agar mixture from the heat, add the soy milk mixture, and fold in the remaining 1 cup raspberries. Pour the mousse into 6 individual serving dishes. Chill for at least 1 hour, or until firm. Serve garnished with whole raspberries and mint leaves.

6 SERVINGS

Calories 127 Kc • Protein 3 Gm • Fat 4 Gm • Percent of calories from fat 28% • Cholesterol 0 mg • Dietary Fiber 2 Gm • Sodium 19 mg • Calcium 38 mg

Brownies

The chocolate lovers in your house will be pleased to know how they can enjoy delicious brownies with no dairy products. This recipe calls for the commercial egg replacer product that is available in natural food stores.

Egg replacer for 2 eggs (or 2 eggs)
¾ cup sugar (or a natural sweetener)
¼ cup cocoa
¼ cup corn oil
1 teaspoon vanilla extract

½ cup soy milk
1 cup unbleached all-purpose flour
½ teaspoon baking powder
⅓ cup chopped walnuts (optional)

Preheat the oven to 325 degrees. Lightly oil an 8-inch square baking pan or coat with nonstick cooking spray and set aside. Reconstitute the egg replacer according to package directions, and place in a mixing bowl. Add the sugar, cocoa, oil, and vanilla extract and blend well. Stir in the soy milk, flour, and baking powder, blending well after each addition. Fold in the walnuts, if using. Spoon the batter into the prepared pan and bake for 20 minutes or until the top springs back when touched and a toothpick inserted in the center comes out clean. Let the brownies cool before cutting into squares.

MAKES 16 2-INCH SQUARES

Calories 106 Kc • Protein 2 Gm • Fat 4 Gm • Percent of calories from fat 33% • Cholesterol 0 mg • Dietary Fiber 0 Gm • Sodium 32 mg • Calcium 13 mg

Oatmeal Almond Butter Cookies

The almond butter, available in natural food stores, presents a subtle change from peanut butter in these moist, rich cookies.

2 cups firmly packed light brown
    sugar (or a natural sweetener)
¾ cup (1½ sticks) margarine,
    softened at room temperature
½ cup almond butter
½ cup soft silken tofu, drained (or
    2 eggs)
¼ cup soy milk

1 teaspoon vanilla
2 cups unbleached all-purpose
    flour
1 teaspoon baking soda
1 teaspoon cinnamon
1 teaspoon salt
1½ cups quick-cooking oats

Preheat the oven to 350 degrees. Lightly oil two baking sheets or coat with nonstick cooking spray. Cream the sugar with margarine and almond butter in large bowl of an electric mixer on medium speed. Beat in the tofu, soy milk and vanilla. Mix in the flour, baking soda, cinnamon, and salt. Stir in the oats. Drop the dough onto the prepared sheets by heaping tablespoons, spacing 2 inches apart. Bake until golden brown, about 15 minutes. Transfer the cookies to wire racks or wax paper to cool.

MAKES ABOUT 40 COOKIES

Calories 113 Kc • Protein 2 Gm • Fat 4 Gm • Percent of calories from fat 30% • Cholesterol 0 mg • Dietary Fiber 1 Gm • Sodium 110 mg • Calcium 27 mg

No-Bake Fruit and Nut Cookies

The perfect cookie to make during the summer—quick and easy, and no need to heat the oven.

1 cup sugar (or a natural
  sweetener)
⅓ cup margarine
Pinch of salt
⅓ cup soy milk
¾ cup creamy peanut butter
1 teaspoon vanilla extract

2 cups quick-cooking oats
¼ cup raisins or chopped dates
¼ cup chopped nuts (peanuts,
  pecans, etc.)
¼ cup shredded coconut
  (optional)

Place the sugar, margarine, and salt in a large saucepan over medium-high heat, stirring occasionally until the margarine melts. Add the soy milk and bring the mixture to a boil. Reduce the heat and simmer for 1 minute, stirring occasionally. Remove the pan from the heat, and add the peanut butter and vanilla, stirring until thoroughly incorporated. Stir in the oats, raisins, nuts, and coconut, if using, mixing well to combine. Drop by spoonfuls onto cookie sheets lined with wax paper. Refrigerate cookies for 30 minutes to set. Keep cookies refrigerated.

MAKES ABOUT 30 COOKIES

Calories 106 Kc • Protein 3 Gm • Fat 5 Gm • Percent of calories from fat 43%
• Cholesterol 0 mg • Dietary Fiber 1 Gm • Sodium 51 mg • Calcium 7 mg

Date-Nut Cookies

My husband's favorite. Just like his mother used to bake—and just as good without dairy products.

¾ cup pecan pieces
1 cup (2 sticks) margarine
¾ cup sugar (or a natural
   sweetener)
½ cup soft silken tofu, drained (or
   2 eggs)
1 teaspoon vanilla extract

1 teaspoon ground cinnamon
1 teaspoon baking soda
¼ teaspoon ground cloves
⅛ teaspoon salt
2¾ cups unbleached all-purpose
   flour
¾ cup chopped dates

Preheat the oven to 350 degrees. Place the pecans on a baking pan and toast in the oven for 6 to 8 minutes, stirring occasionally. Remove from the oven and set aside to cool. Reduce the oven temperature to 325 degrees. Place the cooled pecans in a food processor and chop them with on/off pulses. With an electric mixer, cream the margarine and sugar together until well blended. Beat in the tofu, vanilla, cinnamon, baking soda, cloves, and salt. When mixed, add the flour, toasted pecan pieces, and chopped dates. Drop by teaspoonfuls onto lightly oiled cookie sheets, spacing about 2 inches apart. Flatten the cookies with a fork to create a crisscross pattern. Bake 15 minutes, or until golden brown. Remove the cookies from the pans and cool on wire racks.

MAKES ABOUT 3 DOZEN COOKIES

Calories 101 Kc • Protein 1 Gm • Fat 4 Gm • Percent of calories from fat 37% • Cholesterol 0 mg • Dietary Fiber 1 Gm • Sodium 83 mg • Calcium 16 mg

Lemon-Almond Tea Loaf

A light and luscious tea loaf. Serve plain for breakfast or tea. Top with the Grand Marnier Sauce on page 317 for a tempting dessert.

½ cup (1 stick) margarine, softened at room temperature
1 cup sugar
½ cup soft tofu, drained (or 2 eggs)
1½ cups unbleached all-purpose flour

1½ teaspoons baking powder
½ teaspoon salt
½ cup almond milk
½ cup chopped almonds
2 tablespoons finely grated lemon zest

Preheat the oven to 350 degrees. Lightly oil and flour a loaf pan or coat with nonstick cooking spray. Cream the margarine and sugar with an electric mixer or in a food processor. Blend in the tofu. Sift together the flour, baking powder, and salt, and add to the mixture, mixing at low speed until smooth. Blend in the almond milk. Fold in the almonds and lemon zest. Pour the batter into the prepared pan. Bake until a toothpick inserted in the center comes out clean, about 40 minutes. Cool in the pan on a cooling rack for 10 minutes. Invert the loaf onto a rack and cool completely before slicing.

MAKES 1 LOAF

Calories 302 Kc • Protein 5 Gm • Fat 12 Gm • Percent of calories from fat 35% • Cholesterol 0 mg • Dietary Fiber 2 Gm • Sodium 501 mg • Calcium 64 mg

Spiced Orange-Walnut Tea Cake

Topping:
2 tablespoons margarine, softened
2 tablespoons sugar
2 tablespoons unbleached all-purpose flour
½ teaspoon cinnamon
Cake:
¾ cup orange juice
¼ cup corn oil
¼ cup soft silken tofu, well drained (or 1 egg)

2 tablespoons grated orange zest
½ cup sugar (or a natural sweetener)
2 cups unbleached all-purpose flour
2 teaspoons baking powder
1 teaspoon cinnamon
½ teaspoon allspice
¼ teaspoon salt
½ cup chopped walnuts

Preheat the oven to 350 degrees. Combine the topping ingredients in a small bowl, mixing with a fork until mixture resembles coarse crumbs. Set aside. Combine the orange juice, oil, tofu, orange zest, and sugar in a bowl until well blended and set aside. In another bowl, sift together the flour, baking powder, cinnamon, allspice, and salt. Combine the wet and dry ingredients, and mix until smooth and well combined. Fold in the walnuts, and pour the batter into a lightly oiled loaf pan. Sprinkle the reserved topping mixture on top of the batter and bake for 45 minutes. Allow to cool in the pan before slicing.

MAKES 1 LOAF

Calories 319 Kc • Protein 5 Gm • Fat 14 Gm • Percent of calories from fat 38% • Cholesterol 0 mg • Dietary Fiber 2 Gm • Sodium 404 mg • Calcium 56 mg

Blueberry Banana Bread

Use bananas that are almost too ripe to eat—they make the sweetest banana bread. Be sure to use frozen blueberries, or you may end up with a purple dessert.

2 cups unbleached all-purpose
   flour
1¾ teaspoons baking powder
¼ teaspoon salt
2 very ripe bananas
½ cup vanilla soy milk

¼ cup corn oil
½ cup sugar (or a natural
   sweetener)
½ cup soft silken tofu, drained
1 teaspoon vanilla extract
1 cup frozen blueberries

Preheat the oven to 375 degrees. Lightly oil a loaf pan and set aside. Sift the flour, baking powder, and salt into a large bowl and set aside. Place the bananas, soy milk, oil, sugar, tofu, and vanilla in a food processor and blend until smooth. Add the wet ingredients to the dry ingredients and mix well. Fold in the frozen blueberries. Fill the prepared pan with the batter, and bake for 50 minutes, or until a toothpick inserted into the center comes out clean. Allow to cool in the pan before slicing.

MAKES 1 LOAF

Calories 278 Kc • Protein 5 Gm • Fat 8 Gm • Percent of calories from fat 26%
• Cholesterol 0 mg • Dietary Fiber 2 Gm • Sodium 170 mg • Calcium 81 mg

Apple-Tahini Cake

1 cup soft silken tofu, well drained
1 cup sugar (or a natural
  sweetener)
¼ cup corn oil
¼ cup tahini (sesame paste)
¼ cup apple juice
3 cups unbleached all-purpose
  flour

1 tablespoon baking powder
1 teaspoon cinnamon
½ teaspoon ground
  cardamom
½ teaspoon ground allspice
¼ teaspoon salt
1 cup chopped peeled apple

Preheat the oven to 350 degrees. Lightly oil a 9-inch cake pan or coat with nonstick cooking spray, and set aside. Combine the tofu, sugar, oil, tahini, and apple juice in a food processor; reserve. Sift together the flour, baking powder, cinnamon, cardamom, allspice, and salt in a bowl. Add the blended wet ingredients to the dry ingredients and fold in the apple. Mix well. Pour the batter into the prepared pan and bake for 50 minutes, or until a toothpick comes out clean. Place on a rack to cool.

MAKES ONE 9-INCH CAKE

Calories 411 Kc • Protein 8 Gm • Fat 13 Gm • Percent of calories from fat 28% • Cholesterol 0 mg • Dietary Fiber 2 Gm • Sodium 226 mg • Calcium 147 mg

Spiced Coffee Cake

A dairy-free version of my mother's favorite coffee cake recipe. The commercial egg replacer (available from natural food stores) works well in this recipe.

Egg replacer for 2 eggs (or 2 eggs)

3¼ cups unbleached all-purpose flour

1½ cups firmly packed brown sugar (or a natural sweetener)

1 cup corn oil

2 teaspoons cinnamon

¾ teaspoon ground ginger

½ teaspoon salt

¼ teaspoon allspice

⅛ teaspoon cardamom

½ cup chopped walnuts

1½ cups soy milk

1 teaspoon vanilla extract

1½ teaspoon baking powder

1½ teaspoon baking soda

Preheat the oven to 350 degrees. Lightly oil a 10-inch springform pan. Reconstitute the egg replacer according to package directions and set aside. Combine the flour, sugar, oil, 1½ teaspoons of the cinnamon, the ginger, salt, allspice, and cardamom in a large bowl and mix well. Transfer ½ cup of the mixture to a small bowl; stir in the walnuts and the remaining ½ teaspoon cinnamon and set aside for the topping. Add the soy milk, egg replacer, vanilla, baking powder, and baking soda to the remaining batter mixture and blend thoroughly with an electric mixer. Be sure to scrape the sides and bottom of the bowl to achieve a smooth batter. Spread the batter evenly into the prepared pan, and sprinkle with the topping mixture. Bake 30 to 40 minutes or until a toothpick inserted in the center of the cake comes out clean. Serve warm or at room temperature.

12 SERVINGS

Calories 450 Kc • Protein 6 Gm • Fat 23 Gm • Percent of calories from fat 44% • Cholesterol 0 mg • Dietary Fiber 2 Gm • Sodium 349 mg • Calcium 103 mg

Pumpkin Tea Loaf

This tea loaf is especially good with the Brandy Cream Sauce on page 342.

1½ cups canned pumpkin
¾ cup sugar (or a natural
  sweetener)
½ cup peeled and grated apple
½ cup corn oil
¼ cup soft silken tofu (or 1 egg)
2 cups unbleached all-purpose
  flour

1 teaspoon baking soda
½ teaspoon baking powder
¼ teaspoon salt
½ teaspoon cinnamon
½ cup chopped pecans
½ cup golden raisins

Lightly oil a loaf pan and set aside. Preheat the oven to 350 degrees. In a large bowl, combine the pumpkin, sugar, apple, and oil. In a separate bowl mix the tofu, flour, baking soda, baking powder, salt, cinnamon, pecans, and raisins. Combine the wet and dry ingredients until well blended. Spoon into the prepared pan, and bake for 50 to 60 minutes. Cool in the pan.

MAKES 1 LOAF

Calories 398 Kc • Protein 5 Gm • Fat 19 Gm • Percent of calories from fat 41% • Cholesterol 0 mg • Dietary Fiber 3 Gm • Sodium 258 mg • Calcium 61 mg

Neapolitan "Ice Cream" Cake

Vanilla and strawberry "ice cream" between layers of chocolate cake makes this a dessert worthy of a special occasion.

2 cups unbleached flour
1 teaspoon baking soda
¼ teaspoon salt
½ cup cocoa
1 cup sugar (or a natural sweetener)
½ cup corn oil
1 cup soft silken tofu, well drained
½ cup water
1 tablespoon cider vinegar

2 teaspoons vanilla extract
1 pint strawberry frozen nondairy dessert
1 pint vanilla frozen nondairy dessert
1 cup fruit-sweetened strawberry preserves
8 to 12 whole strawberries for garnish

Preheat the oven to 350 degrees. Lightly oil and flour two 9-inch cake pans. Sift together the flour, baking soda, salt, and cocoa; add the sugar and set aside. In a large mixing bowl, blend the oil, tofu, water, vinegar, and vanilla with an electric mixer. Add the flour mixture, and mix until well blended. Divide the batter equally between the two pans and bake for 20 minutes, or until a toothpick inserted in the center comes out clean. Cool the cakes in their pans for about 10 minutes. Then remove the cakes from the pans and place in the freezer. Meanwhile, soften both containers of frozen dessert to a spreadable consistency, about 20 minutes at room temperature. Remove the cakes from the freezer and place one cake in the bottom of a lightly oiled 9-inch springform pan. Spread the top of the cake with the strawberry dessert. Place the next cake on top, and press gently to fill in any gaps. Spread the vanilla dessert on top of the cake. Place the cake back in the freezer for several hours or overnight.

About 5 minutes before serving time, place the preserves in a small bowl and stir to break up into a spreadable consistency. Spread the top of the cake with the strawberry preserves and garnish with fresh strawberries, spaced evenly along the outer edges of the cake.

8 TO 12 SERVINGS

Calories 420 Kc • Protein 5 Gm • Fat 14 Gm • Percent of calories from fat 31% • Cholesterol 0 mg • Dietary Fiber 1 Gm • Sodium 266 mg • Calcium 49 mg

Fresh Fruit with Ginger Sauce

The sweet-spicy bite of the crystallized ginger permeates the creamy tofu to create a lovely sauce for the fresh fruit. Vary the fruit according to availability and personal taste. Be sure to use only very ripe fruit for maximum flavor.

2 cups silken tofu, well drained
2 tablespoons sugar (or a natural sweetener)
1 tablespoon minced candied ginger
1 pineapple, peeled, cored, and cut into ½-inch-thick rings

1 cantaloupe, peeled, seeded, and cut into 1-inch cubes
3 kiwi fruit, peeled and cut into ¼-inch slices
2 cups hulled strawberries, halved

In a small bowl, whisk together the tofu, sugar, and ginger until well blended; reserve. Divide the fruit among 6 decorative plates. Spoon the sauce over the fruit and serve.

6 SERVINGS

Calories 191 Kc • Protein 7 Gm • Fat 3 Gm • Percent of calories from fat 14% • Cholesterol 0 mg • Dietary Fiber 3 Gm • Sodium 51 mg • Calcium 88 mg

Figs in Ginger Brandy Cream

½ cup plus 1 tablespoon ginger
   brandy
12 to 18 fresh ripe figs, pricked
   all over with a fork

1 cup Tofu Sour Cream (see page
   258)

Sprinkle 3 tablespoons of the brandy over the figs and allow to stand at
room temperature for 1 to 2 hours. Combine the Tofu Sour Cream with
the remaining brandy and pour over the figs. Chill before serving.

6 SERVINGS

Calories 165 Kc • Protein 3 Gm • Fat 2 Gm • Percent of calories from fat 8%
• Cholesterol 0 mg • Dietary Fiber 4 Gm • Sodium 105 mg • Calcium 56 mg

Grapes in Cream

2 cups Tofu Sour Cream (see
   page 258)
2 cups firmly packed dark brown
   sugar (or a natural sweetener)

3 pounds seedless green grapes,
   washed and dried

Combine the Tofu Sour Cream and sugar together until well blended.
Fold in the grapes, and refrigerate overnight.

6 TO 8 SERVINGS

Calories 399 Kc • Protein 4 Gm • Fat 3 Gm • Percent of calories from fat 5%
• Cholesterol 0 mg • Dietary Fiber 2 Gm • Sodium 206 mg • Calcium 101 mg

Tofu Whipped Cream

A nondairy, healthful version of a favorite topping. The optional addition of almond butter adds firmness and flavor.

1 cup extra-firm silken tofu, well drained
¼ cup honey (or a natural sweetener)
1 tablespoon safflower oil

1 tablespoon almond butter (optional)
1 teaspoon vanilla extract
Pinch of salt

Combine all of the ingredients in a blender and process until smooth. Transfer to a container, cover, and refrigerate several hours to firm up.

MAKES 1¼ CUP

Calories 54 Kc • Protein 2 Gm • Fat 2 Gm • Percent of calories from fat 30% • Cholesterol 0 mg • Dietary Fiber 0 Gm • Sodium 16 mg • Calcium 10 mg

Mocha Tofu Cream

1 cup silken tofu, well drained
¼ cup sugar (or a natural sweetener)
3 tablespoons almond butter

1 tablespoon instant coffee granules
1 teaspoon cocoa

Combine all of the ingredients in a food processor and blend until well combined. Transfer to a small bowl, cover, and refrigerate several hours before serving.

MAKES ABOUT 1 CUP

Calories 81 Kc • Protein 3 Gm • Fat 4 Gm • Percent of calories from fat 47% • Cholesterol 0 mg • Dietary Fiber 0 Gm • Sodium 3 mg • Calcium 27 mg

Brandy Cream Sauce

A simple yet sophisticated sauce which can turn a simple tea cake into a special dessert. Also good on fruit and dairy-free ice creams.

1 cup apple juice

2 tablespoons sugar (or a natural sweetener)

2 tablespoons cornstarch dissolved in 2 tablespoons water

²/₃ cup vanilla soy milk

3 tablespoons brandy

In a small saucepan, heat the apple juice and sugar almost to a boil. Slowly stir in the cornstarch mixture, stirring constantly with a wire whisk until thickened. Reduce the heat to low. Add the soy milk, heat for 1 minute, then add the brandy. Cool slightly before serving.

MAKES 2 CUPS

Calories 29 Kc • Protein 0 Gm • Fat 0 Gm • Percent of calories from fat 3% • Cholesterol 0 mg • Dietary Fiber 0 Gm • Sodium 4 mg • Calcium 2 mg

Creamy Brown Sugar Frosting

While you can make this frosting with a natural sweetener, it won't have the distinctive "brown sugar" taste. This frosting can be drizzled over cakes or brownies to make a sweet, creamy glaze.

1 cup brown sugar (or a natural sweetener)

¼ cup soy milk
¼ cup soft tofu, well drained

In a heavy saucepan, mix sugar, soy milk, and tofu and cook over medium heat, for 2 minutes, stirring constantly to dissolve the sugar. Remove from the heat and beat with an electric mixer or with a wire whisk until cool and creamy. Drizzle on your choice of dessert and let it set in a cool place.

MAKES 1¼ CUPS

Calories 90 Kc • Protein 0 Gm • Fat 0 Gm • Percent of calories from fat 3% • Cholesterol 0 mg • Dietary Fiber 0 Gm • Sodium 12 mg • Calcium 22 mg

Bourbon Sauce

½ cup (1 stick) margarine
1 cup sugar (or a natural sweetener)

¼ cup bourbon

Combine the margarine and sugar in a small saucepan over medium heat and stir until the sugar is dissolved, about 5 minutes. Cool 5 minutes, then whisk in the bourbon. Serve immediately.

MAKES ABOUT 1 CUP

Calories 163 Kc • Protein 0 Gm • Fat 6 Gm • Percent of calories from fat 32% • Cholesterol 0 mg • Dietary Fiber 0 Gm • Sodium 50 mg • Calcium 3 mg

Rum Cream Sauce

A fabulous topping for fresh fruit or bread pudding.

1¼ cups silken tofu, well
    drained
¼ cup brown sugar (or a
    natural sweetener)

2 tablespoons dark rum
1 tablespoon lemon juice
½ cup golden raisins

Combine the tofu, sugar, rum, and lemon juice in medium bowl and whisk until smooth. Blend in the raisins. Cover and refrigerate at least 2 hours before serving so the flavors can blend.

MAKES ABOUT 1³/₄ CUPS

Calories 39 Kc • Protein 1 Gm • Fat 1 Gm • Percent of calories from fat 15% • Cholesterol 0 mg • Dietary Fiber 0 Gm • Sodium 3 mg • Calcium 11 mg

Peanut Butter Icing

½ cup honey (or a natural
    sweetener)
¾ cup creamy peanut butter
½ cup extra-firm silken tofu,
    well drained

½ cup (1 stick) margarine,
    softened at room temperature
1 teaspoon vanilla extract

Combine all of the ingredients in a food processor or blender and blend until smooth and creamy. Refrigerate at least 1 hour before using to firm.

MAKES 2¹/₂ CUPS

Calories 107 Kc • Protein 3 Gm • Fat 7 Gm • Percent of calories from fat 58% • Cholesterol 0 mg • Dietary Fiber 1 Gm • Sodium 70 mg • Calcium 7 mg

Lemon Cream Topping

A light and delicious dessert topping. Spoon over fruit, puddings, cakes, or pies.

1½ cups extra-firm silken tofu, well drained

1½ tablespoons frozen lemonade concentrate

2 tablespoons tahini (sesame paste)

1 tablespoon honey (or a natural sweetener)

1 tablespoon corn oil

Combine all of the ingredients in a food processor or blender and puree until smooth and well blended. Chill at least 1 hour before serving.

MAKES ABOUT 1³/₄ CUPS

Calories 45 Kc • Protein 3 Gm • Fat 3 Gm • Percent of calories from fat 57% • Cholesterol 0 mg • Dietary Fiber 0 Gm • Sodium 17 mg • Calcium 16 mg

Mocha Frosting

1 cup tofu chocolate or carob
chips
½ cup tahini (sesame paste)
¼ cup prepared strong coffee

¼ cup corn oil
1 cup extra-firm silken tofu,
drained
1 teaspoon vanilla extract

Melt the chocolate slowly in a double boiler and reserve. Combine the tahini and coffee in a food processor or blender until smooth. With the motor running, slowly add the oil, blending to incorporate. Add the tofu, vanilla, and chocolate, and blend again until smooth. Chill for about 1 hour before using.

MAKES ABOUT 3 CUPS

Calories 102 Kc • Protein 3 Gm • Fat 8 Gm • Percent of calories from fat 73% • Cholesterol 0 mg • Dietary Fiber 0 Gm • Sodium 9 mg • Calcium 27 mg

9
Beverages

Even though we know the downside of dairy products, we may still have that occasional craving for a glass of cold milk, a creamy milk shake, or maybe some milk and cookies. If you're like me, holiday time will trigger the desire for a cup of eggnog, and, luckily, this chapter offers a dairy-free eggnog recipe that's hard to distinguish from the original.

Higher in vitamins and lower in calories than traditional milk shakes, the thick and creamy shakes in this chapter are every bit as delicious as their dairy counterparts. Made with soy milk, almond milk, or rice milk, these drinks are combined with a variety of fruits, extracts, and other flavorings to produce a wide range of delicious combinations. Enjoy such delights as Very Vanilla Shake or Peach-Almond Shake as between-meal treats, snacks, or even as a nutritious breakfast or lunch.

Try the recipes for Hot Cocoa or Holiday Nog as dairy-free alternatives to old favorites. Add a scoop of frozen nondairy dessert or silken tofu for extra-rich goodness. Many of these beverage recipes yield one to two servings, depending on the size of your glasses and if you're willing to share. All of these recipes can be easily doubled if desired by adding proportionally more of the ingredients that suit your taste.

Strawberry-Banana Shake

Keep peeled, frozen bananas on hand for when the "milk" shake mood strikes. Used instead of ice cubes for thickness, the banana adds flavor as well as potassium and other nutrients to your favorite concoction.

1 cup strawberries
1 cup soy milk

1 medium banana, peeled, cut
   into chunks, and frozen

Wash and trim the strawberries. Combine the strawberries and soy milk in a blender and blend until smooth, about 30 seconds. Add the frozen banana and blend until thick and smooth, about 30 seconds. Pour into 1 large or 2 small glasses and serve.

1 TO 2 SERVINGS

Calories 150 Kc • Protein 5 Gm • Fat 3 Gm • Percent of calories from fat 17% • Cholesterol 0 mg • Dietary Fiber 3 Gm • Sodium 59 mg • Calcium 44 mg

Peach-Almond Shake

2 fresh peaches, peeled and
   halved
1 cup almond milk

½ teaspoon almond extract
1 medium banana, peeled, cut
   into chunks, and frozen

Place the peaches, almond milk, and extract in a blender and blend until smooth. Add the frozen banana and blend until thick and smooth, about 30 seconds longer. Pour into 1 large or 2 small glasses and serve.

1 TO 2 SERVINGS

Calories 173 Kc • Protein 4 Gm • Fat 7 Gm • Percent of calories from fat 35% • Cholesterol 0 mg • Dietary Fiber 5 Gm • Sodium 5 mg • Calcium 44 mg

Pear Blueberry Shake

You may want to add a tablespoon of honey or 2 soft dates if extra sweetness is desired.

1 ripe pear, peeled and cored
½ cup rice milk

1 teaspoon vanilla extract
1 cup frozen blueberries

Quarter the pear and place in a blender with the rice milk and vanilla extract. Blend until smooth. Add the frozen blueberries and blend until thick and well combined, about 30 seconds. Pour into 1 large or 2 small glasses and serve.

1 TO 2 SERVINGS

Calories 127 Kc • Protein 1 Gm • Fat 1 Gm • Percent of calories from fat 7% • Cholesterol 0 mg • Dietary Fiber 4 Gm • Sodium 24 mg • Calcium 19 mg

Banana Split Shake

¼ cup pineapple juice
2 medium bananas, peeled
¼ cup carob soy milk
½ cup vanilla frozen nondairy
   dessert

1 or 2 whole strawberries for
   garnish

In a blender, combine the pineapple juice, bananas, and soy milk until well blended. Add the frozen dessert and blend until thick and smooth. Pour into 1 large or 2 small glasses and garnish with whole strawberries.

1 TO 2 SERVINGS

Calories 195 Kc • Protein 3 Gm • Fat 1 Gm • Percent of calories from fat 6% • Cholesterol 0 mg • Dietary Fiber 3 Gm • Sodium 57 mg • Calcium 51 mg

Orange Tahini Shake

1 cup fresh orange juice
1 tablespoon tahini (sesame
   paste)

¼ cup silken tofu, drained
¼ cup vanilla soy milk
Cinnamon for garnish

Place all of the ingredients except the cinnamon in a blender and blend until smooth and well combined. To serve, pour into a glass and sprinkle with a dash of cinnamon.

1 SERVING

Calories 278 Kc • Protein 9 Gm • Fat 12 Gm • Percent of calories from fat 39% • Cholesterol 0 mg • Dietary Fiber 0 Gm • Sodium 26 mg • Calcium 91 mg

Tropical Shake

½ cup fresh or canned mango
½ cup pineapple juice
½ cup almond milk
1 medium banana, cut into
   chunks, and frozen

Small pineapple wedges or whole
   strawberries for garnish
   (optional)

In a blender, combine the mango, pineapple juice, and almond milk, and blend until smooth. Add the frozen banana and blend until thick and creamy, about 30 seconds. To serve, pour into 1 large or 2 small glasses and garnish with fresh fruit, if desired.

1 TO 2 SERVINGS

Calories 160 Kc • Protein 2 Gm • Fat 4 Gm • Percent of calories from fat 20% • Cholesterol 0 mg • Dietary Fiber 3 Gm • Sodium 4 mg • Calcium 37 mg

Berry Delicious Shake

½ cup cranberry juice
½ cup strawberries
1 cup rice milk

1 tablespoon honey (or a natural
    sweetener)
½ cup frozen blueberries

Combine the cranberry juice, strawberries, rice milk, and honey in a blender, and blend until smooth. Add the frozen blueberries and blend for 30 seconds or until thick and creamy. Pour into 1 large or 2 small glasses to serve.

1 TO 2 SERVINGS

Calories 159 Kc • Protein 1 Gm • Fat 1 Gm • Percent of calories from fat 7% • Cholesterol 0 mg • Dietary Fiber 2 Gm • Sodium 44 mg • Calcium 20 mg

Mocha Shake

For those who like the flavor of coffee and chocolate, this shake hits the spot.

½ cup prepared strong coffee
½ cup carob soy milk

1 cup carob nondairy frozen
    dessert

Place all of the ingredients in a blender, and blend until thick and smooth, about 30 seconds. Pour into a large glass to serve.

1 SERVING

Calories 282 Kc • Protein 7 Gm • Fat 3 Gm • Percent of calories from fat 9% • Cholesterol 0 mg • Dietary Fiber 0 Gm • Sodium 222 mg • Calcium 152 mg

Very Vanilla Shake

1 cup vanilla nondairy frozen
  dessert

1 cup vanilla soy milk
1 teaspoon vanilla extract

Combine all of the ingredients in a blender and blend until smooth and creamy. Pour into a large glass to serve.

1 SERVING

Calories 365 Kc • Protein 11 Gm • Fat 5 Gm • Percent of calories from fat 14%
• Cholesterol 0 mg • Dietary Fiber 0 Gm • Sodium 295 mg • Calcium 60 mg

Breakfast Shake

Loaded with protein, calcium, and vitamins, this shake is a great way to start your day.

1 cup apple juice
½ cup silken tofu, drained
2 pitted soft dates, or 1
  tablespoon honey (or a natural
  sweetener)

1 tablespoon tahini
  (optional)
1 medium banana, peeled, cut
  into chunks, and frozen

Combine the apple juice, tofu, and dates in a blender. Add the tahini, if using, and blend until smooth, about 30 seconds. Add the banana and blend until thick and creamy, about 30 seconds. To serve, pour into a large glass.

1 SERVING

Calories 333 Kc • Protein 8 Gm • Fat 5 Gm • Percent of calories from fat 12%
• Cholesterol 0 mg • Dietary Fiber 4 Gm • Sodium 26 mg • Calcium 67 mg

Peanut Butter Shake

A positively decadent adaptation of a favorite candy bar!

1 cup carob soy milk
2 tablespoons creamy peanut
  butter

½ cup carob nondairy frozen
  dessert

Combine the soy milk and peanut butter in a blender and blend until smooth. Add the frozen dessert and blend until thick and creamy, about 30 seconds. Pour into a large glass to serve.

1 SERVING

Calories 448 Kc • Protein 16 Gm • Fat 21 Gm • Percent of calories from fat 43% • Cholesterol 0 mg • Dietary Fiber 2 Gm • Sodium 323 mg • Calcium 311 mg

Orange Dream Shake

The addition of a splash of Grand Marnier turns this shake into something extraordinary.

1 cup orange juice
½ cup almond milk
½ teaspoon vanilla extract
½ medium banana, peeled, cut
   into chunks, and frozen

½ cup vanilla frozen nondairy
   dessert
2 tablespoons Grand Marnier
   (optional)

Combine the orange juice, almond milk, vanilla, and banana in a blender and blend until smooth, about 30 seconds. Add the frozen dessert and Grand Marnier, if using. Blend until thick, about 30 seconds longer. Pour into 1 large or 2 small glasses to serve.

1 TO 2 SERVINGS

Calories 174 Kc • Protein 3 Gm • Fat 4 Gm • Percent of calories from fat 20%
• Cholesterol 0 mg • Dietary Fiber 2 Gm • Sodium 49 mg • Calcium 34 mg

Apple-Almond Milk Shake

½ cup apple juice
½ cup almond milk
½ teaspoon almond extract

1 medium banana, peeled, cut
   into chunks, and frozen

Combine the apple juice with the almond milk and extract in a blender and blend until well combined. Add the banana and blend until thick and creamy, about 30 seconds. Pour into a glass and serve.

1 SERVING

Calories 256 Kc • Protein 4 Gm • Fat 8 Gm • Percent of calories from fat 25%
• Cholesterol 0 mg • Dietary Fiber 4 Gm • Sodium 9 mg • Calcium 52 mg

Root Beer Float

This is sure to bring out the kid in all of us. Natural root beer has a robust flavor and is available in natural food stores and some supermarkets.

1 to 2 scoops vanilla frozen nondairy dessert

1 to 2 cups natural root beer

Place the frozen dessert in large "ice cream soda" glass (or glasses). Add the root beer to fill the glass. Add drinking straws and enjoy!

1 TO 2 SERVINGS

Calories 150 Kc • Protein 2 Gm • Fat 0 Gm • Percent of calories from fat 0% • Cholesterol 0 mg • Dietary Fiber 0 Gm • Sodium 106 mg • Calcium 6 mg

Banana Nog

I usually make this version of holiday cheer when I want to enjoy the whole batch myself—using frozen bananas instead of ice cream makes me feel virtuous while I indulge.

1 cup vanilla soy milk
1/8 teaspoon nutmeg
Pinch turmeric

2 bananas, peeled, cut into pieces, and frozen
Dash nutmeg for garnish

Combine the soy milk, nutmeg, and turmeric in a blender and blend until smooth. Add the frozen bananas, and blend until thick and creamy, about 30 seconds. Serve in small cups, and garnish with an extra dash of nutmeg, if desired.

1 TO 2 SERVINGS

Calories 181 Kc • Protein 5 Gm • Fat 3 Gm • Percent of calories from fat 15% • Cholesterol 0 mg • Dietary Fiber 3 Gm • Sodium 59 mg • Calcium 37 mg

Holiday Nog

True holiday cheer—no cholesterol, but loaded with flavor. Replace the rum extract with a splash of real rum for a "spirited" version.

1 cup vanilla soy milk
1 teaspoon rum extract
⅛ teaspoon nutmeg
Pinch turmeric

1½ cups vanilla frozen
   nondairy dessert
Dash nutmeg for garnish

Combine the soy milk, rum extract, nutmeg, and turmeric in a blender and blend until smooth. Add the frozen dessert, and blend until thick and creamy, about 30 seconds. Serve in small cups, and garnish with an extra dash of nutmeg, if desired.

2 TO 4 SERVINGS

Calories 154 Kc • Protein 4 Gm • Fat 2 Gm • Percent of calories from fat 11% • Cholesterol 0 mg • Dietary Fiber 0 Gm • Sodium 128 mg • Calcium 20 mg

Note: This recipe makes 2½ cups. It you are making this for a crowd, you might want to make several batches and place in a serving bowl with a ladle and small cups. If so, taste each batch and add more or less rum extract (or rum) to taste.

Hot Cocoa

Vanilla or carob soy milk can be used for an even richer flavor.

1½ cups soy milk
1½ tablespoons cocoa or carob
  powder

1 tablespoon sugar (or a natural
  sweetener)
½ teaspoon vanilla extract

Combine all of the ingredients in a small saucepan over medium-high heat, stirring with a wire whisk for 1 to 2 minutes, or until hot and well combined. Do not boil. Pour into 2 cups or 1 large mug to serve.

1 TO 2 SERVINGS

Calories 157 Kc • Protein 6 Gm • Fat 4 Gm • Percent of calories from fat 21% • Cholesterol 0 mg • Dietary Fiber 1 Gm • Sodium 89 mg • Calcium 74 mg

Index